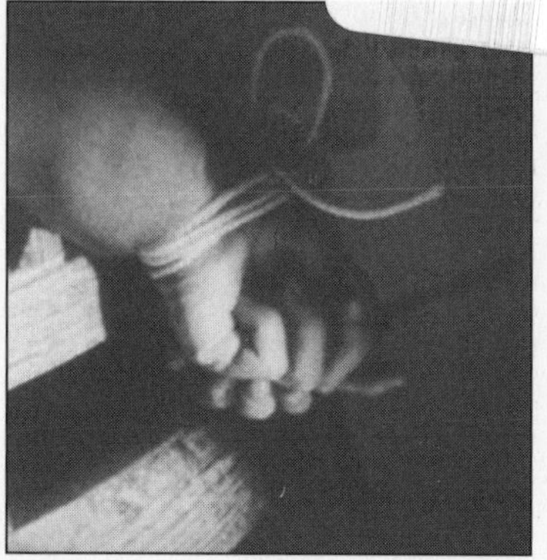

Hostage

NANCY MANKINS

To Betty & Gene Cash,
God Bless –
Nancy Mankins Hamm

Isa 41:10
5/11/2010

W PUBLISHING GROUP™

www.wpublishinggroup.com

A Division of Thomas Nelson, Inc.
www.ThomasNelson.com

HOSTAGE

Published by W Publishing Group, a division of Thomas Nelson, Inc., P.O. Box 141000, Nashville, Tennessee 37214.

Scripture references not otherwise marked are from the King James Version of the Bible.

Scripture references marked NIV are from The Holy Bible, New International Version, copyright © 1973, 1978, 1984, International Bible Society. Used by permission of Zondervan Bible Publishers.

Library of Congress Cataloging-in-Publication Data

Mankins, Nancy, 1950–
Hostage / Nancy Mankins.
p. cm.
ISBN 0-8499-4354-X
1. Mankins, Nancy, 1950– 2. Cuna Indians—Missions. 3. Missionaries—Panama—Biography. 4. Hostages—Colombia—Biography. I. Title.

F1565.2.C8 M35 2002
266'.0092—dc21
[B] 2002016717

Printed in the United States of America

02 03 04 05 06 PHX 9 8 7 6 5 4 3

To the children
and grandchildren
of
Dave, Mark, and Rick

How Firm a Foundation

How firm a foundation, ye saints of the Lord,
Is laid for your faith in His excellent Word!
What more can He say than to you He hath said,
To you who for refuge to Jesus have fled?

Fear not, I am with thee; O be not dismayed,
For I am thy God, and will still give thee aid;
I'll strengthen thee, help thee, and cause thee to stand,
Upheld by My righteous, omnipotent hand.

When through the deep waters I call thee to go,
The rivers of woe shall not thee overflow;
For I will be with thee thy troubles to bless,
And sanctify to thee thy deepest distress.

When through fiery trials thy pathways shall lie,
My grace, all-sufficient, shall be thy supply;
The flame shall not hurt thee; I only design
Thy dross to consume, and thy gold to refine.

The soul that on Jesus still leans for repose,
I will not, I will not desert to his foes;
That soul, though all hell should endeavor to shake,
I'll never, no, never, no, never forsake!

From Rippon's *A Selection of Hymns*, 1787

Contents

In loving appreciation to

My father, who encouraged me to write this book, believed that I would succeed, and spent many hours editing and proofreading.

My mother, who prayed faithfully for me and protected my time.

My sister, who proofread and encouraged me along the way.

My children, who prayed for me, gave up time with me, and loved me through the process.

Patti and Tania, who put up with me and my many phone calls with questions about the book. For their input and corrections, and most of all for their love and friendship through the trials we've faced together these seemingly never-ending years.

Nancy Everson, who spent countless hours editing for and praying for me. For the many laughs and tears, and for the bond of friendship that grew even stronger during those hours of working together.

The Crisis Management Committee, who worked sacrificially on our behalf and prayed so diligently for us during these long years.

Circle Community Church, for their many prayers for the writing of this book.

The countless people who have given to us and prayed for us.

Our Almighty God. May this book encourage those who are hurting. May it help those who are seeking to find the one true God. May it challenge many to take the gospel to people groups all around the world—people who have no other opportunity to hear in their own language about God's provision of salvation for them through Jesus Christ.

Thank you.

Foreword

Jesus said, "In this world you will have trouble. But take heart! I have overcome the world" (John 16:33 NIV). This book tells the true story of God's children who overcame the world.

How would you or I react or respond to such personal trauma? We never know until the unthinkable happens, do we? These sweet women, loved of God and trusted with unbelievable trials, give us a glimpse of what is possible for all Jesus lovers.

First, these are ordinary women under such duress, and that's encouraging! They love their husbands and their little ones; they cry; they are frightened. They hurt so much they can hardly breathe. And yet they possess a power equal to the test! They are ordinary women, but with a great big, extraordinary God living inside them. The power we read on these pages is so evidently of God and not of themselves. They want us to know that!

Second, they are courageous women. Courage is not the absence of fear. Courage is doing the right thing when you are frightened out of your mind! They did the right thing going to Púcuro, they did the right thing taking their families along, and they did the right thing establishing a presence there, gaining credibility among the people in order to "speak Christ" into those dark hearts and minds. They did the right thing because God, who came in Christ to reconcile the world to himself, told them to go into all the world, preach the gospel, and make disciples.

"How could it be the right thing when such wrong things happened?" you may well ask. Because they believed—and rightly—that the people had not rejected Christ; they had simply not had a chance to receive him. They believed that the Great Commission did not say, "Go into all the world and preach the gospel to every creature—if they look like they would listen, or if it's safe, or if it makes you happy, or if you can afford to give God a couple of years out of your busy schedule." No "if's" in their glad-hearted responses and surrender to life service, the call of discipleship.

Third, they are compassionate and forgiving women. Does anyone wonder if the forgiveness of heinous crimes and their perpetrators is possible? Read this book! Love, as 1 Corinthians 13 says, doesn't hold grudges, seek vengeance, or keep a running record of somebody else's wrongdoings. But then you can't love like this, without the God who *is* love living in your heart.

Fourth, they are American women. Women who were born in the land of the free and the home of the brave. A place where human life is precious and human liberty a treasure to be guarded. A society where freedom of religion has meant the freedom to believe in Christ and to be respected for it. A land where democracy prevails, but above all, a country that believes all of the above is worth fighting for whenever the battle is joined.

Fifth, they are soldiers of the cross. They have endured hardship as good soldiers of Jesus Christ. These soldiers have joined the army of redemption marching right into the enemy's camps across the globe. They knew there were no wars without casualties, but they went anyway. Are we stirred to believe like this? To believe this much? Will we allow the example of these men and women to reduce us to size and send us out to sign up for active duty ourselves?

Finally, they are women who belong to the family of faith. God's great "forever family" spans God's great world, a world Christ died for. This is his world, and he wants it back. Because they are our "family," we must feel their pain and loss, and we must "close ranks" in powerful prayer on their behalf. They are our sisters, they are our mothers, and they are our daughters and granddaughters!

And so, with joy and tears and a huge sense of challenge, we will read their story and encourage others to read it, too. We will identify and learn the lessons they seek to teach us. They are writing their hearts, their message of love and challenge to us all. Their greatest joy would be to know we catch their vision and their passion for Christ and his kingdom and join in the battle until he whom they love and serve comes! Read this book with your heart, mind, soul, and will. Let it provoke you to love and good works and to win your world for Christ.

Jill Briscoe

Preface

My husband, Dave, and I, along with the Tenenoff family and the Rich family, lived in the village of Púcuro, which is located in the Darién province of Panama, about ten miles from the border of Colombia. In relating our lives as missionaries to the Kuna people in the small village of Púcuro, I have re-created events and stories to the best of my recollection. Patti Tenenoff and Tania Rich assisted in providing details. I did, however, combine incidents from our first three short visits to Púcuro into the one first visit relayed in this book. The dialogue has been re-created to assist the reader with the narrative.

I have endeavored to precisely record the events of the capture of Dave Mankins, Mark Rich, and Rick Tenenoff. I have not embellished the facts of their abduction.

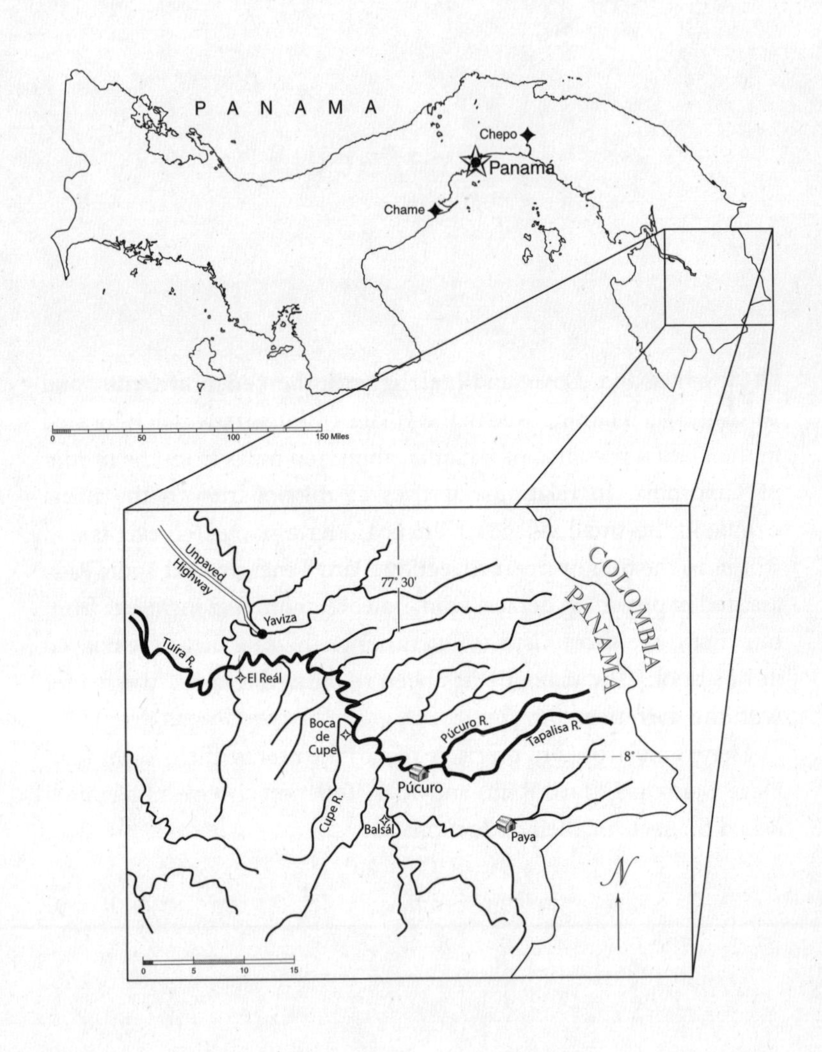

PANAMA
Chepo
Panamá
Chame
0
50
100
150 Miles
Unpaved Highway
Yaviza
77° 30'
Tuíra R.
El Reál
Boca de Cupe
Púcuro R.
Tapalisa R.
COLOMBIA
PANAMA
8°
Púcuro
Cupe R.
Balsál
Paya
N
0
5
10
15

1

Night of Terror

January 31, 1993

On January 31, 1993, millions of Americans were watching the Dallas Cowboys and Buffalo Bills compete in Super Bowl XXVII. At that same time, in the middle of the dense rain forests of eastern Panama, the lives of three missionary families were being torn apart, moment by terrifying moment.

For seven years, my husband, Dave, and I had served as missionaries in this remote Kuna Indian village. We were living in the small house that we had built just six months earlier. Our two children had graduated from high school and were no longer staying with us, so we didn't need the larger house we had been occupying. We gave that house to our newest missionary partners, the Riches, and built a one-room house with a loft bedroom and a small back-porch area, where we had a shower, a dresser, and a small workshop. The downstairs walls were made of screen from floor to ceiling, allowing the air to move through and make it seem a little bit cooler in the sweltering Panama heat.

The last remnants of sunlight quickly faded away, signaling the end of another day in the village. We were lying in our hammocks on either side of the front door. Dave was listening to the news on his shortwave radio. Thinking he heard a noise outside, he turned his attention to me. "Nancy, is someone coming?"

I stopped reading my book and leaned close to the screen. "I don't think so, honey. I don't see a light," I said.

I had no sooner gotten the words out of my mouth than we heard the sound of running feet. As both our heads jerked up and our questioning eyes met, the screen door flew open. Three men in camouflage uniforms rushed in and aimed their machine guns at Dave. They yelled something at him in Spanish, and he stood up out of his hammock. They yelled at him again, so he sat back down. A third time, they yelled at him. When he stood up again, they hit him with the butts of their large automatic weapons.

In horror, I watched the scene play out before me. By God's grace, however, my mind instantly returned to a one-hour course on terrorism we had attended four years earlier. Like a recording playing in my brain, I thought, *Stay calm. The first few minutes are the most dangerous.*

I said to them in Spanish, "We cannot understand what you are saying. Please show him what you want him to do. He will do whatever you say."

They led Dave to the half-wall that separated our living area from our office and made him kneel, facing the wall. Then they tied his hands behind his back. One man stood with a machine gun aimed at Dave's head, while another man propped open the screen door and fired a deafening shot outside. Dave's body jerked and all of the blood drained out of his face.

My ears were still ringing as I prayed, *Please, Lord, maybe they don't know that there are two other American families in the village. Please, let it only be us.*

But, even as I was praying, I heard another gunshot from the direction of the Riches' house, and a third report echoed from the direction of the Tenenoffs' house. I knew then that these must be signals and that all three houses had been captured at the same time.

I felt like I was moving in slow motion as one of the armed men signaled for me to follow him around our house. *How incongruous*, I thought. *This intruder is nice looking and clean cut.* He stood about five-foot-eight. His light-colored eyes, fresh haircut, and neat appearance made him look totally out of character in his camouflage uniform. Never mind his orderly outward appearance—his evil motives were all too apparent. Systematically, he began collecting tape recorders, radios, batteries, and our laptop computer—things he obviously was stealing from us. He swept his arm across the desk—sending books and papers sailing to the floor.

"Pack a suitcase for your husband," he demanded in Spanish.

I walked up the wooden stairs to our small loft bedroom. Dave's satchel was still sitting on our bed. Just that afternoon I had looked in it for our vaccination records because I'd heard that a cholera epidemic had broken out across the border in Colombia. Along with the vaccination records, I'd found our birth certificates, marriage license, and other important papers. So when I grabbed the satchel, I remembered the papers, took them out, and quietly slid the packet underneath my pillow. Carrying his bag down the stairs, I asked, "What should I pack?"

"Three sets of clothing. He will need warm clothes. Does he have boots for hiking?" the man barked.

"Yes, he has boots," I said numbly, as I walked toward the back porch. My mind was still running in slow motion as I tried to process his words. *Why would he need warm clothes? Even on the coolest nights it never seems to get below seventy-five degrees in this part of the country,* I thought to myself, so I grabbed two pairs of long pants and a pair of shorts. The thought of Dave being too hot all of the time seemed unbearable to me. He didn't have any long-sleeved shirts or jackets. *Three sets of clothes—they must be keeping him for three days.* I found myself trying desperately to make sense out of their words and commands. I grabbed Dave's good leather hiking boots and took the packed suitcase and boots back into the main room of our house.

There sat my beloved husband, hands still bound, the machine gun still pointed squarely at his head. But unlike the intruder, who had asked me to pack the physical necessities, Dave called out in Spanish, "I want my Bible."

I looked toward the guerrilla and he nodded his permission. Walking over to Dave's desk, I searched for a small Bible containing both the Old and New Testaments. I wanted to give him something that wouldn't be too heavy to carry. Out of the clutter I retrieved a Bible, but Dave said, "No, not that one."

My hands trembled as I frantically searched through the mess to find the one I knew he wanted. Frustrated, and afraid to take any more time, I just picked up the closest Bible, a Spanish/English New Testament, and I stuck it in the suitcase.

The man holding the gun at Dave's head saw Dave's eyeglasses sitting on a shelf. He asked, "Are those his glasses?"

"Oh, yes, his glasses," I said gratefully, as I put them in his suitcase. *This has to be a strange nightmare! I need to wake up,* I thought. *How could a man holding a machine gun at my husband's head point out that he would need his reading glasses?*

"Señora," called the guerrilla who had told me to pack the suitcase. "Is your husband taking any medication?"

"No, he is not," I said.

"Are you sure he does not take any medicine?" he asked again.

"No," I repeated.

"Well, what is all of this?" he asked. He stood beside a pantry shelf filled with medicine bottles.

"That is medicine."

"What is this one?" he asked as he pointed to a bottle.

"Those are cold pills; this is aspirin; that one is an antibiotic," I explained as he pointed to different ones.

He took the bottles that interested him and then said, "You are sure your husband is not on any medications? If we give him a sedative, he won't react to it, right?"

A sedative? My mind tried to digest the ominous word. "I do not know," I mumbled. My brain was on overload. It couldn't keep up. Nothing made sense to me anymore. *Why would they give him a sedative?*

Suddenly, a fourth man rushed noisily in the door. With bushy black hair and wild, dark brown eyes, he stood much taller than the man who had been talking to me. He began shouting orders at me but I could barely understand his Spanish.

"*¡Teléfono! ¡Teléfono!*" were the only two words I finally understood.

Oh, he wants my phone number. Could he really mean phone number? How could anyone think that we would have a phone in this remote village? Help me, Lord. I don't understand. Then, it all clicked in my mind. *These men are kidnapping my husband and they want a way to contact me. Should I give them our mission's phone number? Would that be wise?*

Agitated and waving his arms wildly around, the man again yelled, "Give me a telephone number!"

"All right," I said. Somehow I located a pen and a scrap of paper and forced my foggy brain to remember our mission's Panama office number. I wrote it down, folded up the paper, put it into a small plastic bag, and handed it to him. If they were going to use the phone to contact me about my husband, I wanted that number to stay safe.

With his wild eyes boring into my own, he said, "Money! Give me all of your money!"

I willed my legs to move toward the staircase. My purse was upstairs under my nightstand. With that wild man following me, I was afraid to go back up the stairs. *God, help me,* I prayed, as my feet finally began to move toward the staircase. Both men followed close behind me. As I reached the top landing, I leaned over and grabbed my purse. I spun around and found myself looking the meaner man right in the eyes.

"Go up the stairs," he said.

"No," I said firmly, remembering from our little course that after the first few minutes you can demand a few basic rights. *Look them in the eye. Don't be* easily *killed or abused.*

"Go up the stairs!" shouted the wild-eyed guerrilla.

"No," I said quietly but firmly. Then, reaching around him, I handed my purse to the second man, who stood behind him on the stairway. He grabbed it and ran down the stairs. Then the meaner guerrilla ran down after the man with my purse, and they began to quarrel over its contents.

I walked down the stairs and over to Dave, who was still kneeling on the floor. I wondered if my own face looked as sickly white as his. He looked at me and I looked at him. We were both so relieved and thankful that I hadn't been harmed by those men. *How helpless Dave must feel, being tied up and unable to defend me. Yet he is calling out to our mighty God, who is able*, I thought as I looked into Dave's loving eyes.

A shot rang out from somewhere in the night, causing us to jump and to question each other with our eyes. All four men became more intense, and the first man (who had walked me around the house) demanded, "Give me your watch and your flashlight."

"What?" I asked, not really comprehending what he wanted.

"Watch! Your watch!" he shouted as he pointed to my wrist.

As I took off my watch, he grabbed it and my flashlight.

"Say your farewells," he barked.

I walked over to Dave, who was now standing near the door. I kissed him softly on the lips. "I love you," I said.

Our moment was interrupted by that same man, saying, "Have faith, this will all be over soon."

Dave looked the man in the eye. The last words that I heard Dave say as they led him out the door were, "We do have faith, but our faith is in the Lord Jesus Christ."

They were gone. I was alone, standing in the front part of our little house. The hammocks were still. The house was deathly quiet. Shadows played on the table as a gentle breeze flickered the flame in the kerosene lamp. My thoughts drifted back to the first time I came to this village.

2

First Impressions

1984–1986

I was amazed that it was so bright and clear above the clouds. Flying in a Cessna 185 was going to take a little getting used to. I had never been in a small plane before.

Oh, dear Lord, I prayed silently, *keep us safe and bring us back to our children.*

We were brand-new missionaries. Our children, Chad and Sarah, were in the tenth and seventh grades at the mission school in the town of Chame, Panama. We were all living there while Dave and I were taking the Spanish language course. Once that was completed, Dave and I would move into the village of Púcuro to work with the Kuna Indians. We would then begin learning the Kuna language—the native tongue of these remote people, few of whom speak fluent Spanish. We were very thankful for this weekend, which would allow us to visit the village, even though it would be at least a year before we would be ready to move in and begin our life among the Kuna.

Underneath the plane, the clouds were so thick I couldn't see the trees or the river. At last our pilot found a hole to break through, and he banked the plane sharply to dip down through the cloud cover. When we emerged below the clouds, the view was spectacular. I couldn't stop looking at the seemingly never-ending blanket of green. Occasionally, a giant treetop stuck up far above the rest. Here and there, I could see the thatched roof of a hut.

The brown switchbacks of a river snaked along, mile after mile. The pilot was following that river toward our destination. I heard him tell Dave, "See the town down there? That is Boca de Cupe. It won't be long now."

Dave looked back at me with a broad smile on his face. One look told me what he could not say over the din of the plane's motor: *We are here; we are really here.* He could hardly contain his joy.

Dave was thirty-five years old. Khaki cargo shorts and a striped T-shirt clothed his lean, tanned, five-foot-ten-inch frame. His brown hair was thinning on top. Like so many men, he kept a wisp of hair parted and combed across his head, and it was constantly falling down into his face. His gentle brown eyes almost always conveyed his quiet, peaceful spirit. He was taking in everything, making sure he would have more stories to add to his repertoire. To him, life's experiences were always an adventure that, one day, could be retold to his family and friends.

I was thirty-four years old and Dave's opposite in many ways. At five-foot-two, I had to diet constantly to keep myself at an acceptable weight. I had thick brown hair and hazel eyes, and I had anything but a peaceful and quiet spirit. My imagination raced through every conceivable outcome to this trip.

Dave was pointing out the window and looking back at me. Below a narrow, treeless green strip of land had appeared with a river on the right, separating the airstrip from the village. We could see the thatched roofs of about thirty or more huts. I thought, *This is just like flying into the pages of* National Geographic.

My heart began to beat faster. The plane was low, but it sure seemed to be going awfully fast. As the pilot buzzed the airstrip, I learned that he tries never to land the first time. This way he can see if there are any people, animals, or large objects in his path. The strip was clear, so he banked the plane sharply to the left and we made a complete turn to approach the strip for a landing.

Some of the people from the village began to swarm across the river to greet the plane. Soon we would be meeting the Kuna people for the first time. Now we could begin matching faces with names. You see, over the past four years, we had been praying for them. Back at New Tribes Mission's Bible school we had been given prayer partners—Brian and Candy Simmons, who had just become missionaries to the Kuna people in Púcuro. Now we were looking forward to becoming missionary partners with the Simmonses.

The plane touched down and bumped along the uneven strip until it came to a stop. Then the pilot turned the small Cessna around and taxied back to the middle of the airstrip. As soon as the propeller stopped, the plane was besieged by dozens of people with beautiful large brown eyes and thick black hair. They were very curious to see who was aboard the plane.

As we stepped down out of the plane, each of us was surrounded by people. The women wore wraparound skirts made from either green or yellow prints on navy blue cotton fabric. Their blouses were intricately handsewn *molas*, a type of reverse appliqué. The yoke and puffy sleeves of their blouses were made with a bright polyester print. The Kuna people love primary colors and consider vibrant, contrasting colors to be beautiful. Some of the small children wore underwear, but most wore nothing at all.

One young lady, carrying a naked baby, asked me in Spanish, "What is your name?"

"Nancy," I replied.

"Ah, Nahn-cee, ah," she said.

"Nahn-cee, Nahn-cee," rippled through the crowd.

"Is he your husband?" asked the same lady.

"Yes," I informed her. "His name is David."

"Ah, Dah-veed, ah," was passed along again from person to person.

"How many children do you have?"

"Two children," I told them.

"How old are they? Where are they? Only two children? Will you have any more?"

At this point, I felt very overwhelmed. How personal they were becoming! I guessed this was what was meant by the term "cultural stress." I looked over at Dave, wishing for some help. But, like me, he was totally inundated. So I took a deep breath and prayed for wisdom. Then I tried to answer each of their questions.

"Oh, look, you have a watch! How much money was it?" the inquisitive spokesperson asked.

Oh dear, my mind whirled. *Our economy is so different from theirs. I can't tell them how much Dave paid for my watch. For all I know, it could be like a year's wages to them.* I said, "It was a gift from David."

"Oh, a gift," said the lady with the baby. The question of how much it cost was dropped. I put that useful tidbit of cultural information in the back of my brain. *Apparently you need not divulge the price of a gift.*

I was already exhausted. I desperately wanted to hide from their questions and from all of the eyes that had not left me since we landed. We had become their source of entertainment. The Kuna people all watched us as we watch a television program in the United States.

Now it was time to cross the river to the village. The steep bank was more than a little muddy because of all the wet feet that had scurried up and down. Dave held my hand as I cautiously edged and slid my way toward the bottom. As I struggled along, I heard snickers and outright laughs. By the time we arrived at the edge of the river, most of the people were wading across, in water up to their waists. Some were swimming.

Then I saw a man coming toward us with his canoe. From that day on, Estánislau, whom we nicknamed Stan, always met us with his canoe to ferry us across the river. Estánislau was already our brother in the Lord and would become a very dear friend. We soon discovered that Stan loved to help people. It was clearly part of Stan's new life in Christ.

Cautiously, I stepped into the slippery, wet canoe and fought to keep my balance and sit down. Dave planted his feet firmly and sat down near the middle. Stan stood up at the front end and plunged a long pole into the river, pulling us across. When we arrived at the other side, Dave helped me out of the canoe and we began to walk on the trail toward the village. My plastic sandals were wet and slippery. It was so hot and humid—sweat poured down my face. The trail led into the trees. After several yards we could see a hut up ahead. As

Kuna couple sitting outside their house. Woman sewing a mola *and man with a gourd full of warm banana drink.*

we entered the village, we saw houses made with split-palm walls and thatched roofs.

At the first house, an older lady was standing at her door. She had a large gold ring in her nose. *"Toge, toge,"* she said in Kuna.

I looked to the young lady who had asked me all of the questions at the airstrip. She quickly became my translator and said in Spanish, "'Come in,' she told you."

As we stepped into the dark house, we were assailed with the smell of wood smoke. When our eyes adjusted to the light, we saw that this was their cooking house. In the middle of the dirt floor was a fire made from three logs, the ends meeting in the middle, where the fire was built with kindling. The ends of the logs burned slowly. A large cooking pot rested on the ends of the logs, which were moved inward as they burned. This large pot was filled with a hot banana drink. We learned that *plátanos* (cooking bananas) are the Kuna's staple food. The lady took a rag and brushed off a wooden bench for me. I sat down and she handed me a cup filled with warm, thick, lumpy liquid. *Lord, help me to drink this,* I prayed. They watched me as I tried politely to sip the strange beverage. Later I learned that you should drink it down quickly—that is the proper way in Kuna culture.

A young girl pushed her small brother toward me, and he began to cry. The other people in the house laughed at him. The mother said something to him that I couldn't understand, and he began to cry harder. She tried to shove him toward me, but he escaped and ran out the door.

I looked around and saw a pile of cooking bananas in the corner.

On a wooden table sat several bowls, some spoons, a half-gallon container of oil, and a hollowed-out gourd that was used as a bowl to hold uncooked rice. On the floor sat a yellow two-and-a-half-gallon plastic container filled with water. Several stained glasses and cups rested on a tilted shelf. I saw a large log that was being used as a stool. There were also several other benches for people to sit on. The dirt floor was swept as clean as a dirt floor can be. Everything smelled like the smoke from the cooking fire. Not knowing what else to do or say, we left.

As we walked from house to house, greeting people and talking with them, we noticed how clean the whole village appeared. All of the ground between the houses, every path throughout the village, was bare of weeds and grass. There wasn't any litter lying around, anywhere.

Most people had two houses, a sleeping house and a cooking house. A few of the sleeping houses were built up off the ground. Some had palm-bark floors, the same material used for their walls. Only two houses had wooden floors. One house had a tin roof. On the sides of some of the roofs, we were surprised to see various items of clothing. I couldn't imagine why, but later I learned that is one way the Kuna women dry their clothes. They throw them on the roof, and when they are dry, they fish them off with a long stick.

Stan took us to the Simmonses' house. Brian and Candy had been ministering in the village for four years, and now they were on furlough. This weekend we were visiting the village alone. Their house had stood empty for quite some time, so it was very dirty. For our short visit, the Simmonses told us we would be welcome to stay in their small, one-room guesthouse behind their home.

The guesthouse had wooden sides and several screened windows—no window glass here in the jungle! I found a broom and dustcloth and cautiously went in to start cleaning. I wasn't quite sure what I might find in there. I saw a few dead spiders, lots of cobwebs, and evidence of cockroaches. Thankfully, I didn't find any scorpions or snakes. While it was still daylight, I made the bed. Dave had filled a kerosene lamp for me, and I put it on the small wooden table near the bed. Then I carefully put a box of matches near the lantern, in preparation for the night that would come soon enough.

This is almost like camping out, I tried to convince myself. *Almost.*

I decided to go over to Mika's house. Luís and Mika were the Simmonses' closest neighbors, and they had offered to feed us while we were there. Mika knew some Spanish, so we could talk to each other a little bit.

"Mika," I called out before I reached the door. I announced my presence in the same way my interpreter had when we visited several houses on our way from the airstrip.

"Come in," Mika said, again in Spanish.

Mika was brushing off a bench for me, so I went in and sat down. She began to prepare some root vegetables, peeling them with a machete. She also peeled a few cooking bananas and cut them into one-inch chunks. She told me she was making soup.

I hadn't been there very long when her husband, Luís, came in, rifle in hand, and threw a dead animal in the corner. It was about the size of a very large cat. This strange creature had a long, hairless tail and large, ratlike teeth.

Could there really be a rat that big? I thought. *Could that really be our lunch?* I excused myself and went back to our house. I needed to pray some more before lunch. *Could God really give me the grace to eat that thing? Perhaps once it was made into soup*, I thought. *I could pretend that I hadn't seen it.* I was already trying to convince myself that maybe I would get a bowlful without any meat in it!

Dave had gone visiting. The morning seemed like it would never end. I wanted to have something to do, so I found the broom again and started sweeping the main house. The wooden floors were uneven, made from hand-hewn lumber out of the jungle. The inside walls were fashioned from old, green, parachute material that someone had given to the missionaries. The drab army green color added to the depressing atmosphere of the dusty, abandoned room. The house had a large front room with built-in benches all around the outside walls. Hooks were positioned so that two hammocks could be hung, one on either side of the front door. The whole living area was enclosed with screen.

Two freestanding cabinets with countertops separated the kitchen from the front room. Between the cabinets was enough space to walk through. I opened one cupboard and found some canned goods. As I continued to look around, I found a tin coffeepot, a teakettle, and some coffee mugs. I decided to make some coffee. But first I would need water to clean the stove and wash the dishes. Candy had told me that Mika's daughter liked to earn money by hauling water and sweeping, so I went back over to Mika's house to ask whether Alegría would have time to haul some water for me. Mika said that the girl would be over soon. I glanced toward the corner where the animal had been, but the spot was empty.

I heard Alegría at the back door, filling a large washtub with river water. The Simmonses had a filter in the kitchen, so I found a small bucket and poured some of the water into the filter. Then I filled the dishpan with water and added a few drops of bleach so I could wash the dishes. I wouldn't be able to make coffee until the filter produced enough water to fill the pot.

About that time, Dave came in the front door. He was carrying a small notebook. While he was out visiting, he had written down Kuna words and phrases. He was hot, hungry, and very happy. "Do you know what time we'll be eating?" he asked.

"Soon, I think," I told him. "I think we are having rat soup."

"Oh, come on. They don't eat rat," he said with a smile still on his face.

"Well, I saw it. Luís brought it in. It was the size of a very large cat and—"

"There aren't any rats that big," he interrupted.

"Dave, I'm telling you, it had ratlike teeth and a long, hairless tail. It has to at least be a cousin to a rat. That still makes it a rat." My voice was going up an octave.

"Oh, Nancy, don't get worked up. If they eat it, then it has to be edible. I'm sure it isn't a rat."

"Nahn-cee, Dah-veed, are you there?" Mika called out from her house.

"Yes, we are here," Dave called back.

"We are going to eat," Mika said.

We walked over to Mika's house, where she had the small table set with two bowls, two small plates, two glasses, and two tablespoons. We looked around and saw that the rest of the family was sitting around in various spots, watching us. Mika filled our bowls with soup and heaped our plates with rice. The glasses were already filled with water—river water, no doubt. Mika and Luís were believers, so Luís asked Dave to pray before we ate.

"Heavenly Father," Dave prayed in Spanish, "thank you for Luís and Mika. Thank you for this food that you have provided and for the hands that have prepared it for us. Thank you for allowing us to come to this village to tell people more about you. We love you, Lord. Amen."

"This rice is delicious," I told Mika. "It tastes different."

"It is coconut rice," she said proudly.

I decided I needed to try the soup. It was very good. Then I saw it. I didn't get little chunks of meat in my soup—I had a whole leg bone! I looked around the room. Luís, who had also been served soup and rice, was picking up a bone and chewing the meat off of it. He spooned the meat and vegetables onto his rice and then ate them together. So I breathed a short prayer and spooned the rat leg onto my rice. I picked it up and ate the meat off of the bone. It had a strong, wild flavor that I didn't care for, but I had done it. Mika was smiling at me. I ate more rice. And I ate the rest of the soup, which, thankfully, didn't have any more meat in it. "The rice and soup are very good," I said. "Thank you Mika."

Dave asked, "Luís, what kind of meat is this?"

"It is *oos*," Luís said.

"What is *oos?*" Dave asked again.

"It is called *ñeke* in Spanish," Luís replied.

"Oh, okay," said Dave.

We finished our meal, still not understanding what kind of

strange animal we had eaten. It wouldn't be the last time, however, that we would eat *oos*.

• • •

Nearly a year later, having finished our Spanish study, we moved to Púcuro to begin our ministry with the Kuna.

Dave and Nancy's move to Púcuro in February 1986.

Dave helped me sweep the small guesthouse, making sure that no snakes or scorpions had taken up residence since our last visit. We put sheets on the bed and then walked back into the Simmonses' main house.

The string hammock in the front room of the Simmonses' house invited Dave for an afternoon rest. I walked into the kitchen to check on our water supply in the filter. I had learned last year to start filtering the water as soon as possible. Even so, I was barely able to fill the old tin coffeepot. Setting it on the stove, I realized that I would need matches to light the gas burner. Matches . . . I cautiously opened each drawer that had been abandoned for a year. Fear leaped into my chest as a cockroach scurried between silverware. Nothing in our mission's training course had truly prepared me for the realization that cockroaches and scorpions could be lurking behind every closed drawer or cupboard door. Carefully I picked up a knife and clanged it against the other silverware, announcing my presence to any other creatures that might be near. Then I grabbed the utensils from the drawer and put them into my dishwater. *Where did we find matches last year?* I wondered.

"Nancy," Dave called from the hammock.

"Yes?" I answered from the kitchen.

"Will you wash the globes to the lanterns while I fill them with kerosene? It seems like the sun is beginning to set very quickly."

"Sure," I told him. "I need some help finding matches when you're done. I want to make some coffee."

"Coffee sure sounds good. We'll most likely have company, so make a lot," he said as he passed through the kitchen, carrying the lantern bases to the back porch.

"Okay, bugs, here I come. So get out of the way!" I actually spoke out loud as I opened the cupboard door as noisily as possible to retrieve a roll of paper towels and a bottle of Windex that I had seen earlier. Spotting a Tupperware container, I opened the lid and found matches inside.

The two lantern globes began to shine as I wiped the soot and dirt from them. Dave returned with the bases and lit the wick of one lantern. He placed the clean globe on it. The flame promptly flared up and covered the glass with black soot. We exchanged scowls as Dave blew out the fire. As darkness enveloped the house, Dave went to get the flashlight from the guesthouse, while I washed the globe again. A beam of light preceded him back into the room.

"Have you found scissors in any of the drawers?" he asked.

"Yes, but the problem is, there are bugs in there, too. I think I saw some scissors in that drawer over there," I said, pointing. "I don't remember the bugs being this bad last time we were here."

Dave opened the drawer and shone the light in before retrieving the scissors. I held the flashlight while he trimmed the lantern wick. He lit it again and adjusted the flaming wick down low before replacing the globe. A gentle light brightened the area around the kitchen table, casting unique shadows on the parachute wall. The air was cooling off and unfamiliar sounds of frogs or birds or monkeys were surrounding the house.

"This is exhausting," I complained. "I sure hope it gets much easier than this."

Before Dave could answer, we heard Mika and Luís call out as they entered the front door.

In Spanish, Luís asked, "Where are you sleeping tonight?"

"In the small house out back," Dave replied in Spanish. "That's where we stayed when we visited last year."

"No. You need to sleep in here tonight," Luís told us.

"Why?" Dave asked. Both of us were puzzled at our guest's bold statement.

In a very low voice, Luís practically whispered, "There are two bad men here in the village. We sent someone to the border to get the *guardia* (police). They'll be back in the morning. For now you need to spend the night in here and lock your doors. Do you understand?"

"Yes," Dave agreed. "We'll stay in here tonight. Thanks, Luís."

"Good-bye," they both said as they disappeared from the front door.

"It doesn't look like we'll have any visitors tonight," Dave said.

"Dave, what bad men? I'm scared. I don't have the bedroom in here ready. Who knows where the sheets are or what bugs could be in them?" I could hear the panic that I felt inside creeping into my voice.

"It's okay," Dave said in his characteristic steady and reassuring manner.

"Well, let's go look for sheets in the bedroom," I said, not wanting to do it alone. Picking up the lantern, Dave followed me into the room and set the lantern on the dresser. He handed me the flashlight so I could search the shelves in the closet. I found several sets of sheets and laid one set on the bed. I took each piece and shook it out carefully, wishing desperately that I had cleaned this room. Dave helped me put the sheets on the bed.

"Are the doors all locked, Dave?" I asked as we finished putting the pillowcases on the musty pillows.

"Yes, they're locked," he answered with a yawn.

We crawled into bed exhausted, hot, and dirty. This was not at all how I had planned the end of our first day, moving here to this village that we would call home. Tomorrow we would clean out the shower and make sure the towels were ready, so nightfall wouldn't catch us again before we prepared to go to bed.

Dave was still excited to be in the village, and he held me close.

We talked about our day. I was very afraid of the night, the sounds, the bad men in the village, and the bugs that might be lurking in the dark. Dave didn't seem to be worried about all of my "what if's."

"Let's pray together and commit it to the Lord," he said. "Heavenly Father, thank you for bringing us to Púcuro. Thank you for this day and this work that you've given us to do. Give us the strength and your power and might to be what we need to be and do what you'd have us to do. We love you, Lord. Amen."

Within just a few minutes I could hear his breathing grow heavy and rhythmic. *It isn't fair*, I thought as I lay awake hearing every sound. *Who could these "bad men" be?* I wondered. *We are only ten miles or so from the Colombian border. They could be drug runners or guerrillas. I wonder if they have guns. These walls wouldn't protect us from bullets. Lord, I don't like this. We don't have any radio communication, we are in the middle of a jungle, and it will be another week before the plane comes to bring in our partners. I feel very trapped. You didn't tell me that being a missionary could involve bad men who might have guns. I came here to work with the Kuna people. Lord, I don't know how to give this to you. I am afraid.*

I heard a sound outside. I was trying desperately to listen for another noise, but it was impossible to hear above the sound of my own racing heart. I couldn't even cry. *Please, Lord, just let me go to sleep. Please Lord, take this fear away from me. Please, Lord . . .*

The sunbeam shining across my face woke me up gently. The smell of coffee preceded Dave as he walked into the room with a steaming mugful of the fresh brew. I propped the pillows behind me, grabbed my Bible, and reached for the cup—which was all part of our little morning ritual.

"Where did you find the coffee filters?" I asked, quite impressed that Dave made the coffee without knowing where everything was.

"In a white bucket with a lid on it," he told me matter-of-factly.

"Dah-veed, Dah-veed!" came a male voice from the front of the house.

"Brian said to expect early morning visitors. See ya," Dave said as he hurried from the room.

I started to read my Bible. My mind drifted off to the enormity of the past day's events. Our first day living in Púcuro seemed to me to be anything but typical. I was soon to realize that nothing would ever be "typical" again.

• • •

A week later, the Simmonses moved back into their home. We sure were glad to see them. Candy got the house in shape in no time. She cooked delicious meals—almost like the meals she would be able to cook if she were out in the city. She made it all look very easy, which gave me hope.

Brian immediately began teaching the Kuna language to Dave and me. They wanted us to learn Kuna as quickly as possible, so Brian taught us, and Candy did all of the cooking. Even though they had just returned from furlough, Brian and Candy believed that God wanted them to go back to the States for a different ministry there. We were praying that somehow the Lord would burden them to stay in Púcuro. Regardless, we all sensed an urgency for Dave and me to learn the language.

Staying in the guesthouse seemed to be the best way to protect our time for language study, but after a week or so, we were anxious to move into our own house across the village. We appreciated our partners so much. Their generosity and hospitality were remarkable, affording us many extra hours for language study. But we needed to move on from being visitors to establishing our own place in the village. I wanted to cook and keep up my own house. We needed our own routines and privacy.

Today was the day we would see the inside of the house that would soon become our very own home. Being midmorning, most of the people were out in their gardens. We were able to walk quickly across the village without stopping to greet people.

Our house was the last one at the opposite end of the village. Fourteen years earlier, the first missionary team who had come to Púcuro had built this house, as well as the one the Simmonses were now living in. One side of the house faced the village.

As we approached the house, we could see that the palm-bark siding looked sadly in need of repair. When we stepped up onto the front porch, the weight of our feet caused the decaying boards to creak ominously. We moved cautiously toward the wooden front door, wondering what condition the inside of the house would be in. Dave fit the old key into the lock and turned it. The door squeaked as it opened.

We stepped into the living room, which spanned the full length of the front of the house. The gray-painted floor, like that of the other house, was made from hand-hewn lumber cut from the surrounding jungle. But unlike the Simmonses' house, which was built at the same time, the boards were even and level. The paint was still in fairly good condition. A smile brightened Dave's face and we hugged each other. Being a draftsman who also liked working with wood, Dave loved to be surrounded by good workmanship.

"Just look at these boards," Dave whispered almost reverently as he squatted down and rubbed his hand along the floorboards. "A lot of hard work went into this, and it was done right. I love it."

A wooden couch sat against the inside wall. It, too, was well made. Built-in benches lined the front walls. There were four big windows in the living room with shutters that could be opened from the inside. We knew that opening all the shutters would attract people, so we opened only the window that faced the river. A slight breeze brushed past our faces. We leaned on the window sill and listened to the comforting sound of the water rushing down the river.

"Riverview property," I said.

"Yeah, this is really going to be a rough life," Dave answered with a twinkle in his eye.

We walked between the two freestanding cupboards that separated the kitchen area from the living room. Dave opened a second set of shutters, revealing another view of the inviting river. We surveyed the ten-foot-long cupboard that fit along that wall. It was complete with a double sink and a faucet fed by water piped in from the rain barrels. To the right sat a small gas stove. It looked well over twenty years old, yet it appeared to be in good repair. Beside the stove, another door beckoned toward the river. As Dave cracked open the door, light beams cut through a dancing haze of dust. We were disrupting years of solitude in this empty structure.

My eyes were drawn to the now-familiar parachute walls. *Someday, maybe we will be able to replace this parachute with boards that can be painted white,* I thought. *In the meantime, how can I make brown and army green look less depressing and more inviting?*

From the kitchen, two doorways led toward the back of the house, and one doorway faced the village. The doorways leading outside were fitted with a wooden door and a screen door. The inside doorways, however, were each covered with a red curtain—dusty, dirty, and faded with age. As we pulled back the curtain to the room facing the village, we found it totally empty, except for two blue plastic thirty-five-gallon barrels with lids. On the left side of the room was a closet without any curtains or doors. Half a dozen rusty hangers dangled forlornly on the rod. For years, dust had been collecting, undisturbed—in the corners, on the parachute walls, and on the open rafters that held up the tin roof. The midmorning sun was beating on the tin, and I began to feel the familiar trickle of sweat run down my face and neck. The air felt thick and hot as I breathed it into my lungs.

Next, we entered the bedroom that faced the river. It was another small room with an empty closet, but it was furnished with a set of homemade wooden bunk beds and a metal chest of drawers. I opened the shuttered window in that small bedroom before moving on to the largest bedroom, where Dave had already preceded me.

Dave, however, wasn't stopping to explore this room. He had discovered a back door that opened out onto a screened porch that spanned the width of the house. I followed him and watched. An expression of delight illuminated his face as he encountered the treasures that would soon be his. The missionary who had first lived in this house was definitely a man after Dave's own heart. A six-foot-long workbench lined the inside wall. This sturdy homemade bench was equipped with a vise on one end. Some old tools remained under the workbench, and several old shovels and rakes stood in one corner. Boxes of odds and ends completed the décor of this craftsman's workshop.

I spotted a shower along the outside wall and a door that led outside. We went out and discovered that the river was very close to our house. The bank leading down to the river was about ten feet high. Our backyard was only ten feet from the bank. Obviously, the years had eaten away at the once-larger yard that had separated our house from the encroaching river.

Dave's eyes surveyed the river and then took in the yard. To the right stood a small outhouse. The palm-bark sides and tin roof of this four-foot-square structure didn't look at all inviting to me, but I followed him cautiously to its door. Dave swung open the piece of tin that served as a door and we peered into the darkened privy.

"This might need some work," he said.

That is an understatement, I thought.

Turning around, we walked inside the porch and back to the front door again. This time we took out our notebooks, and we each started lists of things that we would need to buy or do in order to make our home more livable. Both of us were very anxious to move in. We enjoyed each other, married life, and all the routines of living in a house of our own.

"I'm glad I brought this broom and these rags," I said as I began sweeping furiously.

"What about a refrigerator?" Dave asked from the kitchen. "Can you do without one?"

"Without a refrigerator?" I could hear the harshness creeping into my voice, so I forced my next words to be more reasonable than I felt. "Like, for how long are you thinking?" I asked a little too sweetly.

"Well, I don't know. Couldn't we keep cold stuff at the Simmonses' house and make a run there three times a day?" Dave asked.

"I'm sure we could, until we can get our own. It would be nice to have cold water, though, and how much extra room will they have in their refrigerator? I wonder how much money a new one will cost?" I questioned out loud.

"I wonder what happened to the refrigerator that was in here. I'm sure no one moved it back out to the city, especially if it is anywhere near the size of the Simmonses' refrigerator. Those old ones sure were monsters. I can't imagine how on earth they even got it in here in the first place," Dave said. "We'll ask Brian what happened to it."

"I need to clean the gutters and the rain barrels," Dave said as he wrote notes in his little book. "Really, everything is in surprisingly good shape. The palm-bark siding on the walls needs to be replaced; the screens have had it—we'll need new ones. What would you think of having four-foot-high walls and the rest screened all the way up to the roof? It sure would be cooler. We'll take out the two front shutters and upper walls."

"That sounds good to me," I answered, my mind really on which bedroom should be our son, Chad's, and which one should be for our daughter, Sarah.

Chad and Sarah were out at the mission school in Chame (which is about an hour's drive from Panama City, but more than an hour by plane from Púcuro). They would spend every available vacation with us in the village. Chad was already a junior in high school and Sarah was in the eighth grade. Just thinking about them brought an unfamiliar pain into my heart. One of the greatest costs, so far, to our missionary work was leaving our children in the boarding school.

"Dave," I called out, "which bedroom should be for Chad and which one for Sarah, and what about our office?"

Walking into the middle-sized room Dave said, "This bedroom that faces the river would be quieter and cooler for an office, don't you think? It's larger than the one that faces the village, so it would still fit a bunk bed for Chad when he's here. We could put a desk along the window side or two desks so we would each have our own space. Maybe there are some extra tables for now, until I can build us each a desk." Dave wrote down "tables" in his notes.

Moving on to our bedroom, we looked at the wooden double-bed frame. We would need to buy foam for a mattress. That bed could go in Sarah's room. It would also serve as a guest room. We would set up our waterbed in our room.

"Dave, look at this nice dresser. I wonder where they got this," I said as I opened each drawer of the metal dresser.

"Probably the same place as the parachute. It looks like army surplus to me," Dave said.

"Oh my!" I exclaimed as I looked at my watch. "It's way past noon. I'm sure they're waiting on us for dinner. The time has just flown by."

"Yeah, we'd better go," Dave said. "We need to get back to language study after we eat. It'll be hard to keep our minds on it now, though."

As if on cue we heard the voice of a young child calling out, "Dah-veed, Nahn-cee!" A small girl about four years old smiled up at us with her huge brown eyes. She was wearing a yellow shift-style dress with an eight-inch black border around the bottom. Stains, dirt, and mildew spots covered her dress. Her feet were bare. Handing me a piece of paper, she stood and watched us with great curiosity. I read the note in Candy's handwriting. Lunch was ready.

"What is your name?" I asked the little girl in my faltering Kuna.

"Sandra," she replied in a quiet little voice.

We moved back through the house, locking the back doors and closing the shutters. Then we locked the front door and began our trek across the village. Our new little friend silently walked between us. She didn't know any Spanish and we felt we had already exhausted our repertoire of Kuna. Sandra seemed to be quite comfortable with the situation. I, on the other hand, couldn't wait to be able to communicate with her.

People began to call out to us from their houses. We answered, using the few greeting words that we had been learning in their language, and we kept on walking. We didn't stop to visit, because we didn't want to be too late for lunch.

"Candy, is there anything I can help you with? Or is it all ready?" I asked as we washed our hands at the sink.

"It's all ready, thanks. Brian is washing up at the basin on the porch. Sit down," Candy replied.

"It smells delicious. What is it?" Dave asked.

"*Nubi*," Candy replied in Kuna. "Rabbit. Luís went hunting today and brought us some of the meat."

Brian walked in briskly with a wide smile on his face. "I have some good news for you," he said. "I talked to some of the men today and I asked about the refrigerator that used to be in your house. The village took it and put it in the chief's house. They hardly ever use it because they don't have the money for propane. They said you can have it. As a matter of fact, they are going to haul it over there later today. We just need to pray that it will still work."

"That's great," Dave said.

"I'm so thankful. What a blessing that will be to us!" I said, thrilled at the news.

Brian pushed back his now-empty plate and said, "The village men will go out and collect palm bark for your walls at the next full moon."

Dave and I exchanged looks before Dave asked, "Why wait for a full moon?"

"I guess the sap rises in the plant and the bark doesn't rot as quickly. They only collect it when there's a full moon. Candy, what do we have for dessert?" Brian asked hopefully.

I wonder when the next full moon is, I thought. *This is a whole new world for me.*

3

Night of Darkness

January 31, 1993

Pleasant thoughts of times past receded silently back into my mind. I stared numbly at the room, unable to find a sane connection between past joys and present terror.

"Nancy," Tania's voice broke into my reverie.

"Tania?" I asked, surprised to hear her voice. She stepped into the doorway and I took her trembling hand. As she entered the lighted room, I could see that terror had replaced the sparkle of joy that usually reflected from her beautiful large blue eyes. She stood five-foot-three-inches tall, with long blonde hair cascading softly below her shoulders. Only six months earlier, Tania and her husband, Mark, both only twenty-three years old, had moved into the village with their two young daughters. Now Mark was gone.

The events that had happened that night in Mark and Tania's house were very similar to what Dave and I had just experienced.

Mark had been lying in his hammock on the right-hand side of their front door, talking to several Kuna men who were sitting nearby on benches. Two-and-a-half-year-old Tamra sucked on her pacifier as she was being lulled gently to sleep by the soft heartbeat of her father and the gentle sway of the hammock.

Eleven-month-old Jessica had already lost her battle for wakefulness. On the opposite side of the room, she swung peacefully in the arms of her mother. Tania was thinking about the supper dishes stacked on the counter near the sink, waiting to be washed. The flickering light from the lantern on the kitchen table cast dancing shadows on the stack of folded clothes next to it. A laundry basket perched on a bench nearby bulged with more clean laundry, still needing to be folded and put away.

Tania, a third-generation missionary, had grown up on the mission field, so life without modern conveniences seemed normal to her. Getting out of the hammock, she shifted Jessica in her arms and carried her through the kitchen and into her bedroom. Jessica barely moved as Tania gently laid her into her crib for the night.

Walking back into the kitchen, Tania looked at the clothes and the stack of dishes. Then she wondered whether she should put Tamra into bed before finishing the household tasks. Looking over at Tamra, peacefully asleep in her daddy's arms, she thought, *I'll just let Mark put her into bed, like he usually does.* Turning around toward the sink, the thought impressed her, *I really should go put Tamra into bed.* Shrugging her shoulders slightly, she walked across the wooden floor toward Mark and his Kuna visitors. Smiling at her good-looking, blond-haired husband of three-and-a-half years, Tania lifted their little girl out of his arms.

Mark answered his visitor's question in Kuna. Tania couldn't help feeling a little put out. *I have dishes to wash, laundry to fold and put away, and Tamra to put into bed. Mark's work is to relax in this hammock and visit with friends.*

Mark's eyes sparkled with love as he watched his wife carry their precious little girl across the room. Mark, also a third-generation missionary, was very much at home here in the village. Having grown up in Peru, he spoke Spanish as fluently as he spoke English. In six short months he had learned more of the Kuna language than the rest of us had been able to grasp in more than a year. Mark was on fire to serve the Lord. He desired to learn the language quickly so he could teach God's truths to these very remote Kuna.

Mark hadn't always felt that way, however. At one time Mark had wanted to be a dentist. Instead, he followed his high-school sweetheart, Tania, to New Tribes Mission's Bible school. After a few weeks, however, Mark realized that he was not at Bible school for the right reasons. He went away alone—just he and the Lord—for a couple of days. Mark needed to settle in his own mind what God wanted for his life.

When he came back, Tania could sense the change in him before he said a word. From that time on, Mark was single-minded, knowing that God wanted him to be a missionary. People were dying, going to the grave eternally separated from Christ, without ever knowing God's plan of salvation. Mark wanted to dedicate his life to bringing God's Word to remote people who didn't have a Bible in their own language. He wanted them to have the opportunity to hear that Jesus Christ died for the sins of all people, everywhere. He wanted them to know that Christ rose from the grave to give eternal life to all who believe in him. He wanted people to hear that message in their own language so that they could have the opportunity to put their faith in Jesus Christ as their personal Savior. Tania, who had planned to be a missionary since she was in the seventh grade, was overjoyed. Now she felt free to marry the man she loved. Mark never looked back, and Tania found herself hanging on for dear life as he moved forward with a fervency she had never seen in him before.

Tania came out of the bedroom and turned once again toward the dishes. This time she was interrupted by the sound of loud voices coming from outside.

"It is probably drunken Latinos from downriver," one of the Kuna men said in Spanish, speaking from a dark corner of the living room.

Gilbertita, a thirteen-year-old Kuna girl, had come into the kitchen to see what Tania was doing. Having declared herself Tania's official helper, Gilbertita was usually in their house. Her mother had died two years earlier, shortly after giving birth to twins. The twins had been separated. The baby girl was living with a Latino family downriver, and the baby boy was still in Gilbertita's home, in the care of her grandmother. The father was seldom in the village anymore. Even though five children were still at home, Gilbertita was very lonely. She loved being a part of Mark and Tania's family whenever she could get away from her own house.

Always full of energy, Gilbertita said, "I will go see what is going on." She rushed toward the front door. Her feet ground to an abrupt halt as the door swung open before her, and three men with guns rushed in. Gilbertita spun around and ran back to Tania, grabbing her by the arm and pulling her into the girls' bedroom.

"¡Siéntate en el piso! ¡Manos arriba! (Sit down on the floor! Put your hands up!)" thundered the ominous voices from the front room.

Tania sank down onto Tamra's bed, pulling Gilbertita down with her as they clung together. "Heavenly Father, Almighty God, help us," Tania began to pray aloud in Spanish.

The scuffling of boots on the wooden floor and sounds of Mark struggling against their strong arms assailed her ears as she cried out to God on his behalf.

In Kuna, Mark called out to their neighbors, "Go tell Dave! Get Dave! Let him know what's happening!"

"Stop talking in English!" shouted one of the attackers in Spanish as he wrestled Mark to the floor.

"I'm not talking in English," Mark replied as they tied his hands behind his back.

A shot rang out from the front room. More shots reported from different parts of the village. Temporarily deafened, Tania and Gilbertita huddled, motionless, on the bed. *They've killed Mark!* Tania thought, her heartbeat pounding in her ears. *They've killed my husband. And now they'll just leave.*

The sound of water squishing in rubber boots announced the presence of a man. He walked purposefully toward their room. Tania sat paralyzed with fear.

"Señora, señora!" he called out.

Tania sat frozen—unable to speak, unable to move.

The curtain parted, a beam of light slipped into the dark room. A man with a gun entered. He shone the light around the floor of the room and demanded, *"Dáme el dinero.* (Give me your money.)"

I don't want him to see my children, Tania thought, so she quickly stood up from the bed.

Startled, the man aimed his machine gun at her. "Where are you going?" he barked.

"To get the money you asked for," Tania answered in Spanish.

He motioned toward the door with his gun, so Tania walked through the doorway and went toward her bedroom to get her purse.

Mark's voice rang out in Spanish, "Don't hurt my wife! Don't you touch my wife!"

Mark is alive! Tania realized. With relief flooding her heart, Tania's eyes took in her husband's form, lying facedown, flat on the floor. Over him stood a man in a camouflage uniform, holding the end of a rope that tied Mark's hands behind his back. The man was aiming a gun at Mark's head. A second man stood near Mark's feet, aiming a gun at his back. The Kuna visitors were nowhere to be seen.

"Honey, it's okay," Tania said in English, much more calmly than she felt. "He hasn't touched me; I'm fine. I just need to follow his orders."

Mark's tense body relaxed somewhat as Tania went into their bedroom, followed by the guerrilla.

"Here's your money," Tania said, emptying her purse onto the bed.

"Pack your husband's clothes," ordered the armed intruder.

Silently, Tania walked through the bedroom and out the back door to the porch, where the clothes were. She picked up a gym bag and opened up the middle drawer of the dresser. It was too dark to see very well, so she grabbed whatever was in the drawer and shoved it into the bag. She entered the bedroom again with the man still shadowing her. Chills ran up and down her spine.

Several large Rubbermaid containers lined the wall of their room. The guerrilla began opening the lids and searching through the contents. He pulled out a couple of bags of coffee and set them on the bed.

"Do you have any sugar?" he asked in Spanish.

"Yes," Tania said as she went to the pantry just outside the bedroom door. She picked up a five-pound bag of sugar and then spotted some grocery bags on the shelf. Grabbing one on her way out, she handed it, along with the sugar, to the man, saying, "Here, would you like a bag to put your stuff in?" Immediately she thought, *Did I really say that? Was I nice to this man who is stealing from me and who has my husband tied up in the next room?* Tania's God-given gift of hospitality was shining through, despite the situation.

The guerrilla's face registered his surprise. Cocking his head slightly to one side, he seemed to be looking at Tania as though she were very strange . . . different from any of his other victims.

He motioned toward the door, and Tania took that as her cue to go back into the living room, where the others were. Placing Mark's bag on the countertop, she turned toward the group of men.

"Go get his shoes," ordered one of the guards.

Tania moved back through the darkened bedroom to the darker porch and located his dirty, everyday tennis shoes. She hurried back in and walked over to Mark, who was now sitting up on the floor. She placed the tennis shoes by his feet as she knelt down to put them on him.

Seeing his nearly worn-out shoes, Mark asked, "Oh, would you get my good tennis shoes for me?"

"Honey, I can't," she replied, looking around nervously at the men and the guns. "I can't."

Being accustomed to putting little shoes on tiny feet, Tania was struggling to get man-sized tennis shoes onto Mark's feet. It was not easy. Hastily tying them, she could sense Mark's constrained annoyance at the way she was doing the job. She knew he wasn't really upset with her; he was just a very meticulous person who liked his shoes tied a certain way. But this was just going to have to do.

Tania stood and backed up against the counter that held Mark's bag. While tying his shoes, the thought had occurred to her that a luggage tag was attached to the bag. She didn't want them to have the address that was written there. Grabbing the tag, she yanked it. It snapped off with a sharp noise, startling the men. Their heads jerked toward her suspiciously. The tag had already fallen to the floor.

A gunshot, coming from somewhere in the distance, distracted the group. One of the men called out, "Come on; let's go. You're coming with us!"

Tania stared incredulously at Mark, who was still sitting in the middle of the floor. She thought to herself, *Mark, get up. They have guns; why are you just sitting there?* And then it dawned on her that Mark didn't have any leverage to stand up. His hands were still tied behind his back. Tania walked over and grabbed Mark's upper arms, struggling to get him up off the floor. Once he was up on his feet, she stepped back into the shadows again.

"Come on!" the man yelled again, looking directly at her. "Let's go. You're coming, too!"

Tania's expressive eyes filled with worry as she and Mark exchanged meaningful looks. *Gilbertita,* she thought. Looking around for her, she saw that the girl still stood valiantly, nearby.

"Gilbertita," Tania said, looking into her eyes, "take care of my girls for me. They will be better off with you. I don't know what is going to happen to me, but take good care of my girls."

"Okay," Gilbertita said solemnly as she watched the group move toward the door.

Outside, the night was still and humid. The village was deathly quiet.

"We are going up to your partners' house," said one of the men from behind them. As the group herded them toward a thicket of banana trees, Mark said to the men, "There is a trail to your right that leads up to the Mankinses' house."

The group paused, looking at Mark in the same quizzical way as the man had looked at Tania when she gave him the grocery bag to carry the things that he had taken from their house. *These people are different,* seemed to hang in the air, unsaid.

Using the trail made the walk much easier. After five minutes or so, Mark and Tania could see the light radiating from the inside of our house.

"Can I call out to the Mankinses?" Mark asked. "We always call out from right about here."

"No," growled one of the men in a low tone. "Just be quiet."

They got close enough that they could see inside. One man was ransacking our house, throwing things all over the floor. Another man was pacing back and forth, yelling.

I don't want to believe it is happening to them, too, Tania thought dismally. *They can't see us, so they probably don't know that we are out here watching all of this.*

Mark's athletic, five-foot-nine-inch body began to shiver. He was wearing only a pair of shorts and his tennis shoes. Though the night air was still warm and humid, the night's events were taking their toll. Mark was in shock. Tania wanted to find a shirt for him, so she caught the eye of the man she had given the grocery bag to.

"I need to get a shirt for my husband," she said, looking toward Mark's gym bag.

The man ignored her, looking the other way.

"Please, he needs to get a shirt on. Just let me get him a shirt," she pleaded.

The man nodded slightly, and with his foot he shoved the bag closer to Tania.

Dear Lord, please let me just grab a shirt, right away. They aren't going to have the patience for me to search around for it, Tania prayed silently.

She reached her hand into the bag and pulled out the first thing she touched. It was a shirt. *Thank you, Lord,* she breathed.

Pulling the shirt over Mark's head, Tania soon realized that his hands would have to be untied. The shirt remained in a heap around his neck.

Mark's eyebrows raised. Despite the gravity of the situation, his teasing grin appeared. His look said, *That really worked well, honey. What are we going to do now?*

Tania caught the guerrilla's eye again and, with a pleading look, said, "Please untie him so I can get his shirt on."

With a disgusted sigh, the man untied Mark's hands long enough for Tania to get Mark's arms into the shirt sleeves and to pull the long rope through the sleeve.

A mean, nervous man stomped out of our house and approached

Mark and Tania and the group with them. With every step, he was yelling at them.

"Give me a phone number!" he thundered as he paced to and fro.

"There aren't any phones out here," Mark said.

"That lady in there gave me a phone number," he countered.

"Well, we do have a phone in the city," Mark said, telling him our mission's phone number.

"Is that the same number she gave me?" he asked, as though they could know what number he was given.

"I don't know," Tania said as he stormed off again.

Pacing back over to the group, the man stopped in front of Tania. She could feel his eyes look her over, from her long blond hair that draped below her shoulders to her sandal-clad feet. Her throat tightened, and she wondered whether she would be able to take another breath. The man she had given the bag to stepped between them, blocking his line of vision. As though coming out of a trance, the wilder man stomped away again.

Commotion inside the house caught their attention. Dave was herded outside, at gunpoint, followed by the guerrillas.

"Can I go inside now?" Tania asked nervously.

"Go," a gruff voice affirmed.

Walking toward the house, she was startled by a man who was still standing in the shadows near the door.

"Stop," he said, signaling for her to go back where she had been.

As she returned to Mark's side, one of the men said to her, "What are you doing back here? Go on in the house."

"The man at the door told me not to," Tania said, "so I came back."

The two men argued back and forth several times. Finally the one closest to her said, "Go on."

Reaching the door of our house again, Tania ascended the two steps.

"Nancy," Tania said.

"Tania?" I asked, surprised to hear her voice.

She moved into the light. I couldn't believe my eyes. *Tania is here!* I grabbed her trembling hand and pulled her inside. Her face was chalky white. She began shaking all over.

"Oh, Nancy," she trembled.

"Tania, I know," I said. I could feel the protective instinct in me take over. I needed to get Tania and her girls, and Patti and her children, through this. I needed to help them, to be strong for them. I needed God's strength and power to do what I was not capable of doing on my own.

What should we do? I questioned myself. *Call 911,* would have been my first thought when I lived in the United States. However, for seven years here in the village, *we* had been "911."

4

Village Life

February 1986–December 1986

Dave awoke with the first rays of dawn. For the past two weeks we had been studying in the mornings and working very hard until dusk, getting our house ready to move into. We were tired enough that we slept well, even though the foam mattress was a little too thin against the hard wooden frame of the bed.

Dave sat up, lit the kerosene lantern, and put on his flip-flops. He could see a light already shining from the Simmonses' kitchen, so he picked up his glasses and Bible and slipped out the door.

I awoke to the sound of the door opening and the smell of coffee. I propped up my pillows behind me as Dave came and sat on the edge of the bed. Handing me one of the mugs, he smiled. "Today is the day. We're moving into our own house." Behind his usual calm I could see that he was full of enthusiasm and energy.

"And in two more days Chad and Sarah will be coming!" I said excitedly. "I can't wait to see them again and to catch up on how things have gone for them, living in the dorm."

"Me, too. We have a lot to do. Maybe I'll go on to our house now. I'll ask Stan to get some guys and go to the shack on the airstrip to get our waterbed frame and take it to our house. I'll set that up and then you can come and help me fill it. I sure will be glad to have our waterbed to sleep on again. I just don't have enough padding on me for this bed," Dave said as he tried to stretch the kinks out of his back.

"Sounds good," I replied. "Love you."

"Love you, too, sweetheart," Dave said. He smiled as he rose and walked three feet across the room to the front door of our small abode.

I finished my coffee and then slid my feet into plastic sandals at the side of the bed. I put on my Kuna blouse and struggled with the wraparound skirt. *They make this look so easy,* I thought. *I may never get used to these clothes—they are hot and tight. I'm sorry, Lord, I'm starting out my day by complaining. These inconveniences are a small price to pay for getting your gospel to these people. Help me to adjust to these clothes. And to learn how to put on this skirt . . . and how to keep it on!*

"How did you greet the dawn?" I called out to Mika in Kuna as I passed her hut on the way to my new house.

"Good, and you?" Mika called back.

"Good, too," I said.

After the fifth greeting, and having six children shadowing behind me, I was smiling at the thought of the Pied Piper. I was also wondering how we would ever get our work done if half the village ended up in our house. Then one of the little girls tugged at the pail in my hand. I looked down at her. She smiled up at me and I realized she wanted to help me by carrying the pail. I relinquished it gladly. Another child took my broom, and yet another looked at me with pleading eyes. *How different these children are*, I thought, *vying for the opportunity to help, to work*. I divvied up all the things that I was carrying: a rag to the smallest, a dustpan to one, a bottle of ammonia to another.

I felt a little guilty walking along without anything in my hands, but the proud smiles on their faces made me realize that they wanted to be a big help to me. *What precious children, Lord. I want them to come to know you as their Savior someday. Bless these little ones, Father.*

Several more greetings and a few children later, I approached the front of my house. The shutters had all been opened. In fact, several young boys were leaning out of the window! I wasn't the only one collecting children.

I walked through the house to our bedroom. Dave was kneeling on the floor by the waterbed frame. A young man was holding boards at one end, and a boy who was about eleven years old was smiling from the other side.

"Almost done," Dave said. "I hope there will be enough water in the rain barrels to fill it. The barrels aren't very full. The neighbors may be using water from here occasionally. I'm thankful that the dry season is just about over. We can clean out the gutters, and with one good rain, the barrels will be full again."

"I'll clean up the kitchen. Call me when you're ready," I said, going back out the doorway.

Our supplies and household goods were sitting around in boxes. Some had come in on the plane with us; others had come in on the Simmonses' flight. I entered the walk-in pantry that was situated between the doorway to Sarah's room and the doorway to our room. Floor to ceiling, on both sides and in back, the four-foot-wide, six-foot-long pantry was lined with shelves. I began dusting them. Three heads, with six pairs of dark brown eyes, peered in at me as I worked. They giggled when my rag caught on the rough boards. I tried sweeping with the grain of the wood instead of against it. The newly dislodged cloud of dust filled the air and I began to cough and sneeze. The heads disappeared as their giggles began again. I could hear the front screen door slam shut. *Maybe some of them got tired and went home,* I thought. I kept on trying to dust the rough wooden shelves. *I would love to paint these so they'd be easier to keep clean*, I thought.

The front door slammed again and I could hear the sound of bare feet on the wooden floor. Then two girls came in with small handmade brooms, similar to whisk brooms. One girl handed a broom to me, and then she demonstrated by sweeping off the lower shelves that she could reach. That worked much better. "Thank you. Good," I said in Kuna, smiling my approval.

Finished with the pantry, I went to the kitchen sink and turned on the faucet. Brownish water sputtered then flowed out. I let a little of it drain into a dishpan and then turned it off. As I glared unhappily at the foul-looking stuff, a little girl at my side rattled off a question in Kuna that I couldn't understand. She went and got my bucket and repeated her question, pointing toward the river. "Water?" I said in Spanish.

"Water," she said in Kuna.

"Yes, water," I repeated in Kuna. I watched her go out the back door and down the bank to the river. Soon she walked back up with the heavy bucket on top of her head. She stopped in front of me, so I lifted the bucket and set it down on the floor. "Thank you," I said. "What is your name?"

"Gladys," said the smiling girl, who looked to be about ten years old.

I then turned to the rest of the girls. "What is your name?" I asked the one who looked familiar to me, from the first time I saw this house. I think she brought me the note from Candy.

"Sandra," she said in her quiet little voice. "She is Candi, my sister." She pointed to the littlest one, about two years old, who had carried a rag for me.

"And you?" I asked the next girl.

"My name is Alejandrita," she said with a broad smile, a homemade broom still in her hand. "I am their sister," she said, pointing to Sandra and Candi.

"And you?" I asked another young girl.

"I'm Hilda," she said, giggling. "My sister, Sunilda," she said, pointing to a girl who looked about two years older than she.

I'm overwhelmed; I'll never remember all of their names, I thought. *I can't even pronounce half of them, much less remember them.* "Okay," I said. Then pointing to each, I tried to repeat their names. The giggles turned into uproarious laughter as I confused girls and mispronounced names. But they were patient to repeat their names until I finally said them correctly—and every time I got them wrong again—for the rest of the day.

"Nancy," Dave called from the bedroom.

"Yes, honey," I responded as I came into the room. I could see that he had the waterbed bladder on the frame and a hose into its spout.

"Hold onto this hose. I'm going out to the rain barrel to turn on the spigot. I'll be right back," Dave said as he strode out the back door.

"But, Dave," I said, raising my voice so he could still hear me, "that water is very dirty. Do we want it in the waterbed?"

"I ran some out on the ground first. It isn't very clean, but we'll put some bleach in it. It doesn't have to be clean. We don't have much choice anyway."

Coming back in, Dave took the hose out of my hand. I went back to the kitchen. The boys stayed with Dave and the girls followed me. I poured water into the dishpan, added ammonia, and began to scrub the countertops. Then I scrubbed the sink and emptied the dishpan. I filled it with a little more water and scrubbed it. After rinsing it, I filled it with more water. I put a few drops of bleach into it and let it sit while I filled a second dishpan with water and a few drops of bleach. Growing up in the suburbs of Chicago had not prepared me for a life without conveniences, but New Tribes Mission's training program had equipped me to adapt to it.

Then I turned to the boxes we had brought in. I began opening each box until I found our dishes, silverware, and glasses. I took them out and set them on the counter to wash. Finally, I located my dishwashing liquid and added that to one of the pans, swishing it with my hands to make suds. *I'm not sure if I'll ever get used to washing dishes in cold water,* I thought. I washed and rinsed a couple of glasses and placed them in the drainer.

One of the older girls, who knew a little Spanish, said, "We want to do it. Can we do it?"

"Okay," I said, a little tentatively. *I'm not sure how wise this is,* I thought. "Okay," I repeated. "Here, wash your hands first," I said in Spanish, because I couldn't say it in Kuna. Lifting the dishpan out of the sink, I ran water over one girl's hands. I put dish soap on them and had her rub them together. Then I rinsed them. When I turned my eyes to the rest of the girls, all of them broke out in wide smiles. Soon five other pairs of hands were crowded into the sink, from every conceivable angle around me, as I ran water over them, put soap on them, and rinsed them off. I showed the girl who had asked first how to wash dishes. Then I showed the next-oldest-looking one how to rinse. I gave towels to the others, except for the two-year-old, who was shyly peeking in and out from behind Sandra's wrap-around skirt.

Soon the talking, giggling girls had the whole countertop filled with clean dishes. I had a cupboard ready, and I began to stack them where I wanted them to go.

A rumble in my stomach made me realize that it was getting close to noon. I looked at my watch. It was eleven o'clock. I rummaged through another box and found a bag of hard candy. Our partners had told me that the kids in the village were often given treats for running errands, so I opened up the bag and gave each girl a piece. I also took some in to the boys.

"How's it going?" I asked Dave.

"I think we're about out of water. It isn't even half-filled. I have an idea, though. Go get your washtub, will you?" Dave said.

"Okay," I said, going to the back porch where the new shiny blue plastic washtub was leaning against the screen. I picked it up and returned to Dave's side. "Here."

"Set it down. Hold this hose again while I turn off the water," Dave said. He quickly walked outside and turned off the spigot on the rain barrel.

Striding back in, Dave took the hose out and turned the plug so water wouldn't come back out of the bladder. He then went into the kitchen and moved the table over near the doorway. He set the washtub up on the table. "I don't think this is high enough. Let's move the cupboard over here. That will be better."

"Here, let me move the table out of the way," I said, pushing the table to the side.

We each took a side of the freestanding cupboard and moved it near the doorway. All the kids were looking at us very curiously. Dave set the washtub on top of the cupboard. Then he looked at the girls and said in Spanish, "We need some water."

I held out the bucket and said, "Water," in Kuna.

The older girls all smiled. They scurried out of the house, each in a different direction. I looked at the empty pail, which was still in my outstretched hand, and shrugged at Dave. He returned my bewildered look. Before we could decide what to do, one of the girls ran back in with a large bucket that had at one time been a five-gallon oil container. She had changed into older clothes. Soon, all four of the older girls returned. They, too, had changed into their work clothes. There they stood in front of us, armed with buckets. *Our proud bucket brigade,* I thought. We smiled at them and Dave said, "Good. We need lots of water." Whether they fully understood or not, they went out the back door and down the bank to the river. Each one came back in, dripping wet, with a bucket of water on her head. Dave took each bucket in turn and dumped it into the tub. The hose was then put into the tub and into the waterbed, and it began to siphon.

"We need more," Dave said to his little group. Not needing any more encouragement, they ran happily toward the river. Again they stood in a line before Dave, who lifted off each bucket and emptied it into the tub. This time each girl ran back to the river without being asked. They seemed to take in everything and learn very quickly what these strange foreigners wanted.

I was a little dismayed as I surveyed the mud puddle that ran the length of my once-clean kitchen. *Oh, well,* I determined, *I'll think about the comfortable, soft, cool bed that we'll sleep in tonight.*

After the next round of water, Dave said, "Let's go eat lunch and let these gals rest. Man, they are workers! I don't want them to do too much. Brian said they work like this at home and are used to it. They sure seem to want to do it. Are you keeping track so we can pay them?"

"I'll write down their names and how many bucketfuls they have carried. We can ask Brian and Candy what the going rate is so we can pay them," I said as I went to look for a notebook and pen.

Then I turned to the four girls and said, "Thank you." I looked at one and asked her name, again.

She laughed and said, "Alejandrita."

I wrote down her name and marked "three buckets." I repeated that with each girl.

We all filed into the bedroom and stared at the bed. It obviously still needed water. "We are going now," I said in Kuna. "We are going to eat lunch and then come back and work again," I said in Spanish. "Later, water, again," I said in Kuna.

All the faces brightened and the girls giggled at each other. Dave began closing the doors and shutters. I stood surveying my mud puddle one last time. Then we all moved toward the living room and out the front door.

Outside, the sun beat down on our heads. The air was heavy with humidity. My stomach rumbled again, making me remember how hungry I was. I realized for the first time how seldom, if ever, I had felt truly hungry back home in the United States. However, the tiredness from hard work and the hunger felt good. A sense of accomplishment and contentment filled us both as we walked back to the Simmonses' house. Then I looked down at the two little girls who still walked by our sides. Two pairs of dark eyes met my own. *These little ones must be hungry, too,* I thought. *Does their mom have food for them at home?* I wondered. *If they follow us all the way to the Simmonses' house, maybe we'll have some food left over from lunch that we can offer them.*

Lunch was delicious. We asked Brian and Candy all of our questions about paying the kids and whether they were working too hard for us. We were told that, in exchange for work, the children would love to have paper and pencils for school, which would be starting soon. We were also assured that the work was not too hard. The girls were very accustomed to carrying water, as well as carrying wood and rice in large baskets.

When we finished eating, I asked whether we could give some food to the two little girls who had followed us home and were still sitting quietly in the front room.

"Sure," Candy said. "We give them food quite often. Those are two of Stan's girls. Candi was named after me. Their mom's name is Mambo. She has epilepsy. At times she finds it very difficult to keep food in the house and cook for her family."

"I think their sister was at our house, too, but she didn't follow us here," I said.

"Actually, they have three other sisters and two brothers," Candy informed me. "These two are the youngest."

I filled a bowl with food and took a spoon out of the drawer. I held it out to Sandra, who took it and began feeding her little sister. Sandra ate the rest and brought the bowl as far as the counter, holding it up for one of us to take. She then turned around and sat back down on the bench by her sister.

Candy told me she would be glad to do the dishes so we could go and finish up at the house. I looked at Sandra, still sitting on the bench. Little Candi was curled up with her head in Sandra's lap, fast asleep. I walked over and picked up Candi to carry her home. Sandra walked by my side.

"Stan's house is behind the meeting house," Dave said.

We walked past the meeting house and toward Stan's hut. It looked more run-down than the rest of the houses. Dave called out, "Estánislau, are you there?"

Sandra went into the cooking house. We followed. A few seconds passed, and my eyes adjusted to the darkness of the room. Finally, I could see a woman sitting on a bench. She stood up and greeted us, motioning for us to sit down. I laid Candi in a hammock and then took a seat on a bench.

The room was filthy. It needed to be swept out. Old banana peels, dirty dishes, dirty clothes, and rubbish were scattered all around. This was the only Kuna house that I had seen in such poor shape. There wasn't any hot banana drink cooking on the fire—there wasn't even a fire. *I'm so glad we fed them,* I thought. My heart ached for these precious little girls. Yet they did have a family; they weren't orphans. My mind went back to the various foster children that Dave and I had taken in before joining the mission. The neglect and abuse that we had seen some children endure was heartbreaking. *Show me, Lord, how to find ways to help this woman so she can provide a better home for her family. She is ill, but that doesn't mean that she doesn't care or that she doesn't love her children with all of her heart.*

"What is your name?" I asked the woman, not knowing what else to say in the Kuna language.

"Mambo," she replied.

"Your girls helped us today," I said in Spanish.

Mambo lowered her eyes. She didn't know any Spanish.

"We are going to our house," I said in Kuna. "I'm gone," I said—a typical Kuna farewell.

"I'm gone," Dave said as he ducked through the doorway.

We silently walked to our house with Sandra close at our heels.

By the time we had opened the doors, our bucket brigade was back. Dave set up the hose again and was ready when the first dripping girl arrived with her bucketful of water. Soon we realized that our brigade had grown. They must have elicited help from other girls in the village. I had six new names to write down in my notebook. With ten girls working, the job was soon finished. The waterbed was filled.

"I'll make the bed," I told Dave as I rummaged through more boxes, looking for sheets.

Kids try out the waterbed.

"No, why not wait?" he said. "Let them try it out. They must be curious. This is the first waterbed these people have ever seen, you know."

"Okay," I agreed.

Dave picked up one small boy and set him on the bed. That was all it took. Four more piled on, and Dave made a "wave" with the weight of his hands. They laughed, begging for more. Soon, Chipu, the young man who had been helping Dave earlier, sat tentatively on the bed. Dave motioned for the boys to get off. Chipu then lay down. "It's cold," he said in Spanish. "It's too cold to sleep on." He got up off the bed. The girls were looking at us, hoping it was their turn.

"Come on," Dave said, waving his arm toward the bed. The giggling group descended on the bed, then screamed and got off as quickly as they could. The older ones laughed, almost embarrassed at their fear, it seemed. Then they tried it again, more cautiously.

Most of the kids left the house after getting their turn. Dave and I started working in different areas of the house. Soon, however, people started arriving. The word had spread, and everyone wanted to see the waterbed.

Well into the evening, we were still greeting people and ushering them into our room. We let them lie down on the bed. The men enjoyed it, but some of the women wouldn't even try it. The babies all screamed.

People visiting the newest missionaries.

It was an exhausting day, but we could feel a bond with the people beginning to form. They seemed so happy to be a part of our strange lives.

The soft lantern light flickered on the faces of people sitting on the benches. I was in the kitchen, making the first pot of coffee in our new house. I counted the people and set out cups. I filled each cup with coffee and put sugar and creamer in each one, the way the Kuna people like it. I had my Kuna phrase ready as I approached each person. "Do you want to drink coffee?" I asked.

"Yes," was the reply as each person took a cup from my hand.

I handed Dave his own special mug. Dave and I both drank our coffee black, which didn't go unnoticed by the crowd.

As the night grew darker and the conversation lagged, people began to leave. Each person handed me an empty cup, pointed a finger at me, and said, "I'm gone." They then pointed at Dave and said, "I'm gone. Until tomorrow."

We turned the lantern down low and locked the doors. We looked out the window that faced the village. Night sounds filled the air—the rushing river, bugs, frogs, and birds joined to make a symphony that was still unfamiliar to our ears. The sounds were soothing. Even the village was quiet. We looked at each other and remembered the waterbed.

The clean sheets and the cool bed felt wonderful. Our bodies were exhausted, but our hearts were full.

• • •

Two days later I found myself straining at every sound, hoping to hear our airplane arrive with Chad, Sarah, and the Simmonses' two girls. Two Kuna ladies were sitting at the kitchen table. In the front room several small children were looking at books. I was making a cake. The cookbook was open in front of me, and I had flour, sugar, salt, and baking soda out on the counter. I measured one cup of flour and put it into the bowl. I measured the second cup of flour.

"Nahn-cee, Nahn-cee," I heard from the door.

"Come in," I replied. "How did you greet the dawn?"

"Good," Mambo said. "And you?"

"Good, too," I replied. "Sit."

Oh dear, was that two cups of flour I already put in? I wondered as I was interrupted again. *It looks like two.*

I continued making the cake, trying to concentrate between questions. All of a sudden everyone got excited and started talking fast. One of the ladies said to me, "The plane is coming; the plane is coming." They all rushed out of the house.

I want to go across the river and meet them, I thought. *What about the cake? I have to close up the house. Now I hear the plane; it sounds like it's ready to land.*

"Nahn-cee, Nahn-cee," came a small voice at the door.

"Come in," I said as I put the cake into the oven and set the timer.

Sandra walked toward me with a note. I handed her a piece of candy as I read the words: "I'm going on over to meet the plane. Love you, sweetheart—Dave."

I put the lids on the canisters of sugar and flour and returned them to the pantry. I wiped off the countertop and put the dishes into the dishwater. Sandra walked over and pointed to a towel. She looked up at me and said something in Kuna.

Certain that she'd asked if she could help me, I said, "Yes." I couldn't keep from smiling at this gentle little girl who seemed far too young and too small to dry dishes. However, as I started washing and rinsing the few bowls and utensils, she dried them and put each one where it belonged.

Soon Chad and Sarah burst in the door, along with a dozen or more kids of all ages. We hugged and then I said, "Do you want to see your rooms?"

"Oh, yes!" they both exclaimed. "Which one is mine?" came both voices again.

"Chad, yours is straight ahead, Sarah, first room to the right."

We all walked into Chad's room first. He put his gym bag full of clothes on the floor. "Oh, wow! Bunk beds. Does that mean I can invite a friend sometime when I come?"

"We'll see," came the standard answer as we walked out of Chad's room and into Sarah's.

"Oh, I get a double bed. Neat," she said, flopping down on the new four-inch foam mattress that was covered with fresh-smelling sheets that had been washed and line-dried the previous day.

"I want to go out visiting, Mom," Chad said, walking out of the room. "A guy named Chipu will go with me. What time is supper?"

"Sure, you can go around the village with Chipu. Supper will be at five-thirty. But I have a cake in the oven. It will be done soon if you want to wait."

"Cake sounds great, Mom. What kind is it? I'll change my clothes," Chad replied.

"It's a chocolate crazy cake," I replied. "Actually, it may be a crazier cake than usual. It will be a miracle if it turns out," I said with a chuckle.

"Why's that?" asked Sarah.

"I have no idea whether I put in the right amounts of each ingredient. People kept coming in and talking to me. I couldn't concentrate at all," I replied.

"Oh, Mom," Sarah said sweetly. "I've never seen you bake a bad cake." Then with a mischievous grin she said, "Well, except for the time you accidentally put ammonia in the cake instead of vinegar."

"Not that story again!" I said. "I'll never live that one down. At least I am sure this one has vinegar in it, anyway."

The timer buzzed. I left Sarah's room and took the chocolate cake out of the oven. I saw that at least eight children were still in the living room. The smell of the cake surely wasn't going to make them want to leave. I cut a large piece and put it on a plate.

"Chad, have you changed already?" I asked.

"Yeah," he called from his room.

"Well, stay in there and I'll bring you some cake. That way you won't have to eat in front of all these kids."

"Okay," he said. "This is great, Mom. I sure miss your cooking."

Sarah came out and sat at the kitchen table. Immediately six girls came and sat around her. One girl was rubbing the hair on Sarah's arm and talking in Kuna.

"What's she saying, Mom?" Sarah asked, obviously uncomfortable with the situation.

"I don't know. Try talking to her in Spanish. The school-aged kids know some Spanish. Her name is Hilda," I informed Sarah. The girls were touching Sarah's long blonde hair that fell halfway down her back. Everything about thirteen-year-old Sarah's appearance was the opposite of these girls. Their brown eyes were the darkest I'd seen. Sarah's were the lightest blue. They were short and stocky, and she was tall by comparison and very slender. Their hair was black and coarse, hers was blonde and fine. Their bodies were used to hard work and exposure to the elements, but she was delicate and her skin was pampered.

Chad walked into the room and set his empty plate on the counter. At sixteen, he was about five-foot-seven. Here, he was tall, even in comparison to the adult Kuna men. His light blond hair, green eyes, and fair skin also stood out in stark contrast to Chipu and the other guys who had just entered the house to wait for him. But Chad's muscular physique matched that of any hardworking man in the village. His outgoing personality drew these people to him. "I'm gone," Chad said, already using the Kuna phrases that he had learned.

I should have known, I thought. *By the end of this week in the village with us, he'll probably speak better Kuna than we do. How did we get such a smart child?* By God's design, Chad was a gifted linguist.

Sarah looked pleadingly over at me and said, "Mom, can I go in my room?" Sarah never liked being the center of attention. Life in this village was going to be hard on her.

"Sarah, why not come and help me make supper. Then in a while you can slip into your room if you want to," I said.

"Okay," she replied, getting up. "What are you making? I never got any cake."

"Oh, that's right. I have an idea. Why don't you set the table? That way the kids will know that they need to move away from the kitchen because we'll be eating soon. They usually go home when we're eating."

"Can we help?" Hilda asked.

"Wash your hands," I answered.

Sarah stood, amazed, as the girls washed their hands and then went right to the cupboards and took out the dishes. They laughed when they realized they only took out two of everything. They went back for more. Sarah slipped silently into her bedroom and shut the curtain.

When the girls realized she was gone, they went over to the curtain and pulled it back to peer in. I decided that I needed to draw the line there. I went over and said, "No. That is Sarah's room. Come out here. Do you want a piece of cake?" I cut small pieces of cake for each girl and one for Sarah. I took hers in to her. The girls said, "Thank you," and then they left the house.

I realized that adjustments to life in this village would be difficult, not only for Sarah, but also for Dave and me. It would be hard for us to have time with our children when they were here with us.

The house was empty, so I went in and sat down on Sarah's bed. "Tell me about school and the dorm, fast—before another visitor comes in," I said in mock exaggeration.

Sarah laughed and then launched into her account of what school and dorm life had been like in the weeks we had been apart.

The next day, Brian, Dave, and Darío took all of our kids on a hike. Darío, a young Kuna man, guided them several miles into the jungle. A beautiful clearing emerged. Dense forest had given way to huge white boulders shouldering the sides of the rushing river. For an hour or more the kids took turns sliding down smooth rocks that had formed a natural waterslide in the river.

In the evening, Chad, Sarah, and the Simmonses' girls played board games at the Simmonses' house. Candy put their little boy to bed and then joined Brian, Dave, and me for a visit. Soon a dozen or more villagers joined our happy group.

The day after that, Chad went hunting with Dave and some of the Kuna men. Returning to the village, Chad carried the deer on his back. We were given a couple of pounds of the meat in exchange for the bullets Dave had provided for the hunting expedition.

At night, after the people left, Dave would read a book out loud to us. Sometimes we just talked, and we laughed—a lot.

One night, Dave asked the kids, "Do you want to hear about the trip I made into the jungle to help collect palm bark for the siding on our house?"

"Yes," they both replied enthusiastically.

"We love your stories, Dad," Chad told him. "Living here in Púcuro, you've probably added lots more stories to your repertoire."

"Well, this one," Dave said, "has a moral to it.

"As you know, the siding on our house was rotten. The Kuna people held a town meeting and set a date to replace the siding. They all work together to repair all of the huts here in the village. Every family is told how many bundles of palm bark they have to bring by a certain date, and then they schedule a work party. It's all very ingenious. Sometimes they collect thatch to repair a roof. Other times they'll build a whole house. All of the men are required to participate.

"They only collect palm bark when there is a full moon," Dave continued.

"A full moon?" Chad asked. "Why would that matter?"

"Good question," Dave said with a grin. "They say it has something to do with the sap rising in the plant. It's not supposed to rot quickly if it is cut when the sap is higher in the plant."

"That is interesting," Chad said.

"It doesn't make any sense to me," I said.

"Anyway," Dave continued, "I went out in the jungle with Estánislau, Esteban, and Rodrigo. We each had to bring in one bundle of palm bark. We waded across the Púcuro River and then hiked up to the Tapalisa River and crossed there. We found another trail—well, they found another trail—that went way back into the jungle. We walked along that trail for more than forty-five minutes. The Kuna people, you see, are having to go farther and farther away for materials to make their houses. The palm bark and thatch aren't growing back as fast as they are using it."

"Was it hard to keep up with them, Dad?" Chad asked.

"I wore myself out trying to keep up with them," Dave said with a chuckle. "And to be honest, I think they were walking slower just for me! These people are hardy.

"Well, we finally got to the grove of trees. I watched as each man would swing his machete and cut a frond from the tree. Then he would lay the frond on the ground and cut off each branch individually until there was just a stalk left. At that point he would cut the stalk in half. To me it seemed like the hard way of doing it. So I watched some more and then decided to shorten the process on the one that I had cut off. I went over and chopped that frond in the middle, first. Then the thing sprang up off the ground and smacked me right in the middle of the forehead!" Dave doubled over in laughter and wiped the tears from his eyes as he howled.

We were all laughing so hard our sides hurt.

"But, Dad," Chad said. "Why would the frond do that?"

"I don't know for sure," Dave said. "But I learned that these people are very smart. I thought I could figure things out better than they could, but look where my pride got me! It made me realize that I have a lot to learn from them, too."

"Tell us another story, Dad," Sarah pleaded. "Please?"

Dave looked at his watch. "Well, I do have one more story I can tell you.

"I went with all of the guys to clear the trail. That's another project that the village men do a couple times a year. We hiked up to the Tapalisa and began to work our way back. With machetes, we cut the weeds down to the bare earth. I was hacking away, not paying much attention to the others. After a while, I realized it was too quiet. I looked around and I was the only one working. I heard someone say something in Kuna, but I couldn't understand what he said. I kept working. Then, all of a sudden, Nestor, the medic, rushed out from behind a tree, waving his arms. He said in Spanish, 'Stop! Quiet! There are wasps!' Then he got stung three times trying to shoo the wasps away from me.

"The danger soon passed, and all the men came out from where they were hiding. Then a fight broke out between two men. They were actually swinging their machetes and yelling at each other. It turns out that one guy was mad because the man who tried to warn me said it in Kuna, instead of Spanish. That's why I didn't understand him. Thankfully, neither one got hurt.

"I felt really bad that Nestor got stung," Dave finished.

"Did the stings really hurt him a lot?" Sarah asked.

"Yeah," Dave said. "He had to leave and go back to the village. Those wasp stings are very bad. The reason they wanted me to be quiet is that the wasps react to noise. It makes them attack."

"How about another story, Dad?" Chad asked.

"No, I'm sorry," Dave said with a yawn. "I get up before the sun. I've got to go to bed. But I sure love you guys. And it is great having you home. Good night, kiddos. Love you both."

Yes, it was great to have them home! But it was going to be hard to have time together as a family. One afternoon the four of us hiked up a trail and then floated down the river together on two inflatable rafts. That was our only daytime activity all week with no one else around.

During the other daytime hours our children were able to see firsthand why we were here in Púcuro. They helped us when people were cut and needed stitches. They went to church meetings with us. They began to bond with these people whom God loves. Chad and Sarah could see the difference between those who had already accepted the Lord as their Savior and those who were still lost and living in spiritual darkness. Hope radiated from the faces of the believers—a softness that was not evident in the faces of the others.

During some of our late-night talks we told Chad and Sarah how much they were helping us. When they were in the village, we considered them a part of our team. We appreciated any input they had in the people's lives. We let them know that going away to a mission school was also part of the effort of reaching these people with the gospel of Christ. It was a sacrifice on all of our parts. They were truly members of the team—even when they were away at school.

The week ended all too soon. The house was full of people. I could feel resentment rise up in me. I wanted this last day alone with my kids. It seemed to me that these people were being very rude, intruding on our last hours together. All too soon I could sense the excitement level rise. "The airplane, the airplane," I heard various voices say.

Chad and Sarah brought their suitcases out of their rooms. Kids took the suitcases from them, wanting to carry them to the airstrip. We locked the doors. Chad and Dave hurried on ahead of us. When Sarah and I reached the river, we had to wait for the canoe to come back across to get us. Several of the Kuna girls hung on Sarah's arms.

"Sah-dah," Hilda said, handing her a beaded necklace that she had made. "I want to be your good friend."

"Thank you," Sarah said in Spanish.

"Bring me a gift when you come back," Hilda told Sarah.

We had been warned about the Kuna friendship system. It looked like Sarah had made her first "good friend" in the village. This relationship, however, definitely would come with strings attached.

Stan arrived with the canoe and we piled in. He said something stern to the dozen kids, and some of them jumped out and started wading across the river in front of us. Stan stood at the front of the canoe with a long pole in his hands. He plunged the pole into the

Sarah holding a Kuna child who was one of her "good friends."

water and applied all of his weight to it. The canoe lurched forward as we headed across the current toward the other bank.

My feet slipped on the mud as I climbed the bank. I stopped and took off my flip-flops. One of the girls grabbed my hand to help me balance as I sought a dry foothold. I finally reached the top and dropped my shoes to the ground so I could slip my muddy feet into them again.

Tears stung my eyes as I watched the pilot loading the kids' suitcases into the belly pod of the plane. I fought for control. I knew that I wasn't fooling anyone, least of all Chad and Sarah. The pilot looked over at us. He was ready to go. We walked toward the plane. Girls were telling Sarah good-bye; boys were laughing and talking with Chad. Dave came over and gave Chad and Sarah each a big hug. I hugged and kissed them, unable to say anything. Chad stepped up into the front passenger seat. The pilot directed the Simmonses' girls to climb into the middle seats, while Sarah was told to crawl into the backseat. We moved away from the plane. We watched as the pilot bowed his head to pray. Then we heard him say, "Clear prop" out the window, and we saw the propeller begin to turn.

The plane taxied to the far end of the strip, turned around, revved its engine, and sped back for a takeoff. As the little Cessna passed us and lifted off the ground, my heart ached for the precious cargo it held. *Please, dear Lord, deliver them safely to school.* All eyes seemed to be on me as the tears trickled down my cheeks. I wanted everybody to go away and leave me alone for at least a brief interlude of private grief. At that moment, they all seemed rude and uncaring to me. I turned and headed toward the bank, the river, and home.

I finally arrived at the house, but not before having to endure the words "They're gone," in Kuna, from every person we passed along the way. I was angry, and in that state I couldn't think about the Kuna culture and the fact that they didn't do things the same way we do. They were different, but not necessarily wrong. When the house filled up behind me with people, I couldn't help but think how thoughtless they were. I even felt that they were making fun of me. It wasn't until years later that I learned that, according to their culture, they were showing me love and concern. To them a quiet house is a sad house. To be alone is to be very sad and lonely. They were attempting to make our house a happy one.

• • •

Several months passed. Language learning, although a long, slow process, was progressing well. For the most part, the Kuna people accepted the fact that we needed to study each morning from eight o'clock until noon. We would eat lunch and then rest in our hammocks until one-thirty. Dave would start studying again while I cleaned up the table and did the dishes. We would try to go visit people in their homes during the afternoons. We called this the "contact time" of our language study—interacting with the people, using the words and phrases that we had been learning. It was very difficult to get out of our house for our contact time, however, because usually at least one person would come to see us before we could get away. We were still able to use the language, but, in many ways, it wasn't as profitable as being with them in their homes. There we could observe their ways and hear their language being used in a natural setting—often by hearing the conversations between family members. Also, visiting them was a way of showing friendship.

One day, as I stood at the sink doing the dishes from our noonday meal, I heard a lady at the front door call out my name, "Nahn-cee, Nahn-cee."

"Come in," I called back in Kuna.

Carmen and her three-year-old boy, Darío, came in and sat down on one of the wooden benches. We exchanged a few lines of greetings and then she just sat there, as was customary. After a few minutes of silence, I told her in Kuna that I was going to go wash the dishes. She sat there silently.

After a while Carmen said, "My daughter Nereda is having her baby."

"Oh?" I said. "Nereda is having her baby?" I repeated in Spanish to make sure I was hearing the Kuna correctly.

"Yes," she replied. "Will you come?"

"Come? Me? You want me to come?" I asked again.

"Yes," she replied.

"Okay," I said. "Wait just a minute."

Walking back toward the room where Dave was studying, I could feel my heart begin to race. "Dave, Carmen is here. Her daughter Nereda is in labor and Carmen wants me to go see her."

Dave looked up at me, peering over his eyeglasses, which he wore way down on his nose. "That should be interesting. Isn't that unusual? I mean I've never heard Candy talk about helping to deliver a baby here. Have you?"

"I don't think so. I wonder why they would ask me to. Send a note to Brian and Candy, and pray for me," I said. I kissed him good-bye.

I tightened my wraparound skirt as I walked back toward Carmen and Darío, who were waiting by the front door. The bright sun blinded me as I stepped off the front porch and followed Carmen down a path toward their hut. Several naked children scurried when they saw me coming. This family was different. When I had gone to visit them in the past, they had said things to the children—things that I couldn't understand—pushing the children toward me and laughing when the children cried and ran and hid from me.

Carmen was not married, but she had three children that I knew of. Nereda was sixteen years old, Gladys was ten, and Darío was three. Nereda and her husband, along with Gladys and Darío, lived with Carmen and her parents. Also living with them were Carmen's sister and brother-in-law and their children. The whole family had moved here from one of the villages in Colombia. Brian and Candy told us that these Colombian Kuna families did not show any interest in learning about God. They wanted the people in Púcuro to return to the "old Kuna way." The chiefs in Colombia still chanted their religious beliefs to the people. Witch-doctor-type medicine was still practiced there. However, during the past twenty years, most of the people in Púcuro had gradually abandoned the "old Kuna way."

Carmen nodded toward the door with her chin and said, "Enter."

I passed through the open doorway and stood still for a moment, temporarily blinded by the darkness. Finally, I could see sheets hanging up to partition off a small place for Nereda. I was ushered inside the makeshift room by her grandmother and told to sit on a small bench near the girl. Nereda was kneeling on the hard earthen floor, with her forearms resting on another small bench.

"How are you doing?" I greeted Nereda.

"Good," said the tremulous voice of the pretty sixteen-year-old who was soon to become a mother. A contraction made her grab the bench as she leaned hard on it. I looked at my watch.

"How long have you been . . . feeling pain?" I asked, searching for words I knew—in Kuna or Spanish. I really hadn't studied any medical terms in either language. *This is going to be interesting,* I thought.

"Since dawn," she told me once the contraction eased up.

"That is a long time," Carmen informed me from outside the room.

Why is Carmen staying out there? I wondered to myself.

"This is her first baby," I tried to say with reassurance in my voice. "First babies can take a long time."

Nereda clenched her fists again and moaned as another contraction assaulted her. I looked at my watch. Five minutes had passed.

I looked around the little room. Off to one side, banana leaves lay on the floor. Somewhere in the house, I could hear Nereda's husband and grandfather talking to each other.

Nereda had her wraparound skirt tied high around her, like a dress. Her long black hair was knotted at the back of her head so it wouldn't hang in her face. She looked very young and very scared.

Another contraction racked her body and she called out something in Kuna and moaned loudly. I looked at my watch and saw that another five minutes had gone by. Nereda's grandmother came in with a gourd. As she held it up to Nereda's lips, I saw a small amount of black liquid disappear into her mouth. Nereda shuddered as she swallowed the foul substance.

"What was that?" I asked the small but stern woman.

"Medicine," she replied a bit gruffly. Her glare seemed to defy me to question her or the medicine any further, and she left the little room.

I felt the chill of fear enter me. *Lord, what do you want me to do? Am I in the middle of witch doctor's territory? Perhaps some of the believers in the village are encouraging others not to cave in to these old practices again. Will my being here appear to condone something evil? What do you want me to do?* I prayed.

As the strange drink began to affect her, Nereda relaxed. I looked at my watch. Eight minutes had passed. The contractions no longer were at regular five-minute intervals. I decided to leave.

I stood up and exited Nereda's chamber. I said, "I'm going home."

"When are you coming back?" asked Carmen.

"I don't know." I was frustrated that I didn't have the words to tell them that the contractions were no longer regular and that the medicine may have done more harm than good to this precious girl.

Oh, Lord, I prayed as I walked along the trail back to our house. *I am so afraid. I am afraid of doing something wrong in their culture. I am afraid because I don't have the words I need to communicate properly. I am afraid because I have never delivered a baby before. I need you, Lord. I need wisdom like I've never needed it before. Help me, Lord.*

I stepped up onto the front porch of our house. Before I opened the screen door, I could hear our partner talking inside. Entering the house, I saw Dave, stretched out in his hammock, talking with Brian. Several Kuna men were sitting around on benches.

"How'd it go?" Dave asked. "Has she already had the baby?"

"No," I answered. "They gave her some kind of medicine that slowed down her contractions. I don't know what to do, because I don't know if that is witch-doctor-type medicine. I don't have enough of the language. It is really frustrating.

"Brian, why didn't they ask for Candy instead of me? Should we go get her? Or what about Nestor, the medic?" I asked.

"The Kuna have a lot of taboos about childbirth," he explained. "We think that one of the taboos involves their beliefs about who should be a midwife. They don't want anyone who may be pregnant herself. They believe that if a pregnant midwife is carrying a female child, and the woman who is giving birth delivers a male child, then the male child will die. They also believe that the opposite is true. But if the women are each carrying a child of the same sex, they believe that both children will survive."

Nestor, the medic, standing inside the village clinic.

"Now I know why I have been asked so many times whether I am going to have any more children," I said.

"Regarding Nestor," Brian continued, "because he is a man, they don't want him to deliver a baby. The people from Púcuro have departed from some of the taboos, especially in extreme cases. But I doubt whether that family will. Nestor is not here in the village right now, anyway. I know Candy will come and translate for you if they'll let her, even though medicine is not her forte."

"Thanks," I said.

"Well, we'll keep praying," Dave said.

"We're praying, too," Brian assured us as he took his leave from the house.

I'll look in my medical books, and I'll get some supplies ready to tie off and cut the cord, in case they call me back there again, I thought. I walked toward the pantry where I kept those things. I carried the books and supplies out to the kitchen table and sat down to read all about delivering babies.

Suddenly I realized the sun was setting. I had been totally absorbed in the medical books. I got up and went to the refrigerator to look for leftovers. *I would love to have a loaf of bread and some lunchmeat for a quick meal,* I thought. But this was Púcuro. Our jungle refrigerator was stocked only when the plane came in, which was normally every ten weeks. I took out some homemade soup and leftover biscuits. Emptying the bowl of soup into a pan, I lit the burner with a match. I started a pot of coffee and then set the table for two. I lit the lantern that was sitting in the middle of the table, just as the soup began boiling on the stove. But before I could tell Dave that supper was ready, I heard Carmen call from the front door as it swung open.

"Nahn-cee, Nahn-cee!"

"Come in," I replied, even though she was already inside.

"Come quickly," Carmen said with a worried look on her face.

"Okay. Carmen, do you want Candy to come, too?" I asked as I picked up my books, supplies, and flashlight.

"I do not know," Carmen answered.

"Dave, soup is on the stove for your supper. I've got to go."

I hurried out the door with Carmen. Back down the path we went. In the dark, it seemed to be a much longer walk. The thought of snakes came into my mind. I jumped as a dog barked, and I realized how tense I was. Then I saw the soft beams of light streaming out from the gaps in the palm-bark siding of the hut.

We entered the door and, once again, I went inside the little room. This time Nereda was lying in a hammock and she appeared to be incoherent. I had brought a stethoscope to listen to the baby's heart. Now, however, my immediate concern was Nereda. I checked her heartbeat. It was irregular and very fast. Then I placed my hand on her abdomen, waiting to feel a contraction. I didn't have to wait long. A contraction started and she began to moan. Her grandmother entered the room and tied a piece of yellow cloth around her, above her swollen belly. When the contraction pushed the baby down lower, she tied the cloth tighter.

"Why are you doing that?" I asked the woman.

I couldn't understand the tirade of words that followed.

Another contraction hit Nereda. Again, I looked at my watch and wrote down the time on a sheet of paper that I had brought with me. Nereda's eyes seemed to roll back in her head. The grandmother moved the yellow fabric down and tied it tighter.

I could see that she was determined to do things her own way. Again I wondered why they wanted me here. I wasn't sure how I could help them. Another contraction. They seemed to be getting more regular again, and they were lasting longer and were much stronger and harder for Nereda to bear. She cried out in pain. Her grandmother called out to someone—again in words that I couldn't understand.

Soon a gourd was pushed inside the curtain and handed to the grandmother. Nereda was again encouraged to swallow the ominous black liquid.

Dear Lord, I began to cry out in my heart, *I have no idea what to do here. I am frustrated and afraid. I don't have the knowledge or means to help them. Even if I did, I can't communicate well enough to let them know what needs to be done. I don't want to be condoning activities that may be evil. I fear for this girl's life, for her baby's life. I have no idea how to take a stand against these evil practices and yet to help these people. God, I had no idea how hard all of this was going to be. I am so inadequate for this job. Only you, God, can get me through this. Only you can give me the wisdom and strength I need right now. Help me, Lord. Help me.*

Nereda moaned in her sleeplike state. I felt her swollen abdomen, which was again contracting. Looking back at my paper I realized that the contractions were again becoming more irregular since she had taken yet another dose of their "medicine."

I walked out of the little room and looked around for Carmen. The solemn, stern faces of Nereda's grandmother and grandfather eyed me suspiciously. Then I glanced at Nereda's handsome young husband. I was drawn to his fearful brown eyes as they pierced my own, seeming to plead with me to do something for his wife and baby.

"Where is Carmen?" I questioned, reverting to Spanish. My mind was on emotional overload, and I couldn't even begin to recall the few Kuna phrases that I knew.

"She is outside," Nereda's husband answered, also in Spanish.

Glad to escape, I hurried out the door and inhaled a deep breath of fresh night air.

"Carmen?" I said, looking around for her.

"I am here," Carmen answered from the left side of the doorway. She was sitting on a log, leaning against the wall of the house.

The river rushing by us sounded so peaceful. I wanted to get lost in the sound and not come back to the reality and the trauma. I felt so helpless. But I turned and walked toward Carmen.

"Carmen," I began. *How can I tell her?* I thought. *I don't understand the medicine that you are giving Nereda. I think the medicine is slowing down the birth. It's hurting her, and maybe the baby, too. I don't know how to help. If your mom and dad want to use your medicine and your ways, why do you call me?*

Again, however, the only words I knew to say to her were, "I do not know how to help. I will go home and pray for all of you. I will pray."

I turned on my flashlight and located the trail that would lead me back home. I walked along with a heavy heart, groping for answers, searching for the way that God would have me cope with this situation. *Lord,* I began to pray again silently as I walked, *I desperately want to learn this language and to understand how these people think. I want to understand their culture and their ways. Lord, I want to help them. The darkness is oppressive—not just their physical needs, but their spiritual needs. Oh, how they need you and the new life in you that they can have here on earth and for eternity. Right now, all they can think of is their precious girl and her baby. But, even though they love them, they are caught in a stranglehold of taboos and rituals. Please spare their lives, Lord.*

Dim lantern light greeted me as I approached my house. As I stepped up onto our porch, a dog barked from the shadows near the door. I jumped at the unexpected sound. "Quiet," I snapped in Kuna as I reached for the door. *Now, I suppose, we've inherited a neighbor's dog,* I thought as I shook my head in exasperation.

The house was quiet. Dave looked up from the hammock. "How'd it go? Is there a baby yet? I've been praying for you."

I sank down onto the bench next to him and recounted the details of the visit.

"All we can do is continue to pray, Nancy. It's in God's hands," Dave said. "Why don't we go to bed? If they need you again, they'll come back. It sounds like it could be a long night, and even an hour's sleep will help. Come on," he said gently, rising from his hammock and taking my hand to pull me up from the bench.

As I walked to the bedroom, I felt drained of energy. We left the lantern burning dimly on the table. We were expecting more activity that night.

I lay down on top of the covers, without changing my clothes. Soon after we prayed together, I could hear Dave's rhythmic breathing announcing that sleep had claimed him. As exhausted as I felt, however, my eyes would not close. My mind refused to turn off and allow sleep to come. All I could do was replay in my mind the scenes of Nereda swallowing the black liquid and the eerie, sleeplike stupor that had claimed her. I could see her dark brown eyes rolling back in her head with each contraction, almost as if she were having a seizure. My mind began to search desperately for Kuna and Spanish words and phrases that I could use to communicate with them. If I had to go back in the night, I wanted to be prepared.

I couldn't tell how much time had gone by before I heard someone calling out my name. At the front of the house, a man's hushed yet urgent voice pleaded, "Nahn-cee, Nahn-cee!"

Quickly I sat up and got out of bed. I picked up my flashlight and turned it on, straightening my clothes as I rushed out the bedroom door. I grabbed my books and supplies from the kitchen table as I headed outside.

"Hurry, hurry!" Nereda's husband urged frantically. "She is not breathing."

"Not breathing?" I questioned by repeating the strange words. *I must not be understanding him,* I thought as I ran to keep up with him on the trail.

I rushed into the hut. The familiar partition was gone. Nereda was lying on a flat bed made of palm bark covered with a sheet. Her face was a strange pasty-white color. I bent over her and held her face in my hands. I felt for a pulse. Her heart was still beating. I felt for breath under her nose. Nothing. Tipping her head back, I pried her mouth open with my finger. Her tongue was dry and it had stuck to the roof of her mouth. I swept my finger over her tongue to loosen it. Tilting her chin up, I held her nostrils closed with my other hand. I looked at the faces surrounding her bed. *What will they think of this?* was my last thought as I bent over and breathed into her mouth. Then I tilted her head to the side as she took in a breath on her own. She vomited on the ground. After emptying her stomach she became more alert. Her contractions were strong and very close together.

Soon a baby boy made his appearance into the world. He was a good-sized baby, but his color didn't seem right to me. He wasn't crying. I picked up his slippery body and wrapped him in the cloth that they had placed nearby. Turning him on his stomach, I placed him across my arm. Opening his tiny mouth, I swept my finger across the top of his tongue. Nervously, I patted and massaged his back until he finally began to cry.

Soon the placenta was delivered. I set the baby down on the hard bed so that I could tie the umbilical cord. Then I held up the scissors, as if to ask who wanted to do the honors. Everyone seemed to want me to cut it. I hesitated—I had never cut an umbilical cord before, and I wasn't sure about their culture in this matter. I shook my head no. Nereda's grandmother, looking a little disappointed, took the scissors from my outstretched hand and cut the cord herself.

A brand-new life had come into the world. I looked around at the relieved faces. The ordeal was over. Tears stung my eyes—what a miracle I had just witnessed, the miracle of birth. *Thank you, Lord, thank you.* I breathed a prayer of thanksgiving and relief.

Nereda's husband walked me back home again. In silence I followed him along the path between our houses. I stepped up onto the porch, this time looking for the neighbor's dog in the shadows, but nothing was there. Reaching for the door handle, I said, "See you tomorrow."

"Thank you," came the reply as Nereda's husband turned and disappeared down the dark jungle path.

Again I climbed into bed. I told Dave that a baby boy had been born, and then I closed my exhausted eyes to allow sleep to claim me. But many minutes passed before I quit replaying in my mind the scenes of the birth. The wonder and miracle of it all consumed me.

• • •

Weeks and months of language study blurred together. Life in Púcuro took on somewhat of a routine. All too soon we realized that the Simmonses were leaving the mission and that we would be left alone in the village. We would all sorely miss the Simmonses. They had such a good command of the language, and the Kuna people loved them. Brian had been holding church meetings every night of the week and teaching them in Kuna.

How could we ever get along without Brian and Candy? How could we meet the needs of a growing church when we were still struggling to learn the language? It was with very sad and heavy hearts that we bid our partners farewell.

Dave began preparing lessons in Spanish to teach every night in church. He just wasn't far enough along in the language to teach in Kuna. Spending more time in Spanish slowed down his Kuna language study even more.

Life was more stressful when all the decisions rested on just the two of us. Without Brian to encourage and help us along, language study became routine and boring. We began to get discouraged.

One night, as the last visitor departed, Dave blew out the flame in the kerosene lantern. He walked back and looked out the window that faced the village. I joined him and we stood hand in hand, staring out at the scene before us. Moonlight bathed the path with a romantic glow that didn't match our discouraged hearts. We began talking about the feelings that weighed so heavily on us, wondering whether we would have more of a ministry if we went back to the States. There, we at least spoke the language and could witness to people right away. We felt like we would never understand Kuna well enough to minister effectively to these people.

The thatched roofs of the huts made a beautiful picture in the serene night—until we heard a strange sound, one that we had never heard before. It came to our ears like a wave and then receded again into the shadows of the night. We looked into each other's eyes, wondering what the sound meant. It grew stronger and louder again. We began to hear the voices of people calling a message from hut to hut. Finally our neighbor called out to us, "Tito's son has died."

The sound was wailing, the mourning of a death. We shuddered involuntarily.

Earlier that day we had walked to Tito's house to see the boy. However, some chiefs from another Kuna village in Colombia were visiting Tito. They wanted to use their "medicine," not ours. They had placed a white medicine rock under the boy's hammock and were chanting over him. They had refused Nestor's help, and now this teenage boy was dead.

The eerie, heartbreaking sound of wailing wrenched our hearts. It reminded us of the hopelessness that many of these Kuna people still lived in, because they didn't know Jesus Christ as their personal Savior. How could we give up on these people? Back home, people could buy a Bible in their own language. They had churches to attend and Christian radio stations they could listen to. But the Kuna didn't have any of those opportunities. The new Christians in the village needed to be encouraged and taught from God's Word. A functioning church needed to be established, with Kuna leaders.

The people needed to be taught how to read the Word of God in their own language. Our hearts were burdened again with the needs right in Púcuro. We knew that God was the One who had placed us here in this village, and his plan for us hadn't changed.

Dave and I prayed together, dedicating our lives again to the job that God had called us to. After praying, we turned from the window and walked with renewed strength back to our bedroom. We eventually fell asleep to the mournful sound of wailing that continued throughout the night.

5

The Nighttime Meeting

January 31, 1993

"Nahn-cee, Nahn-cee," a male voice called out at the door as three Kuna men stepped inside. "Look at this mess! Did they take things? What about the village's money that we gave Dave earlier to buy stock for our store? Did they take our money, too?"

I shook my head a little, as though I could clear my brain or wake up from a bad dream. *Why are they concerned about their money when our husbands have been abducted?* I thought disgustedly.

Then I replied, "I think they took everything they could find, but I'll look for you."

I walked over to Dave's desk and looked in the cubbyhole where he kept his notebook and the money people gave him to pay for the items they wanted us to buy for them when we went out to Panama City. The cubbyhole was empty and the notebook was on the floor.

"Your money is gone. What about Rick and Patti?" I asked. "Did the men take Rick away?"

"Yes, Rick is gone, too, but Patti thinks that you and Tania were taken with your husbands. She thinks she is the only one left here, with all of the children," Encelmo, one of the Kuna men, informed me.

"We need to go to Patti's house," I replied as I felt my determination and energy surge. "I'll go get my suitcase," I said as I ran up the stairs. My small overnight bag was already packed in anticipation of the trip to Panama City that we had scheduled to make in three days. I grabbed the bag and ran back down the stairs.

"They took our flashlights," I informed the Kuna men. Then I asked, "Are they gone?"

"Yes, they are gone," Encelmo assured me. "Let's go."

I forced myself not to look around the house again as I followed everyone out and locked the door behind me. I took hold of Tania's arm and we walked side by side, following the three men down the packed-earth trail toward Rick and Patti's house. I could feel Tania's body shaking and my own teeth chattering, even though the night air was at least eighty degrees. It was hard walking side by side on the narrow path, but neither of us wanted to let go of the other one's arm. The man in front had a flashlight, but it barely illumined the path in front of him. We stayed very close to the heels of the man in front of us, because we couldn't see.

Soon I heard one of the men say in hushed tones, "Look, over there!"

Then I heard another one of their voices. "Look, up in the trees!"

I whispered back to them, saying, "What are we looking at? I don't see anything!"

Encelmo pointed with his chin. "In the shadows over there, and up in the trees, are the bad men of the jungle." His chin jutted again to point in the Kuna manner. "There are more than one hundred bad men with guns. The village is surrounded," came the ominous words.

"What do you mean?" I snapped back at them. "You told me they were gone!"

"We meant your husbands were gone," came the innocent reply.

"Who are these bad men of the jungle?" I asked.

"*Guerrilleros* from Colombia."

Colombian guerrillas. The words ricocheted like a gunshot inside my head. Time seemed to stop. I already knew, somewhere deep down, but hearing the words confirmed my deepest fears.

Silence pounded in my ears. *Just put one foot in front of the other. Don't look to the left or to the right. Just put one foot in front of the other.*

The trail led us toward the soccer field and away from the trees where the guerrillas were. We trudged on. The path followed the length of the village soccer field and then turned toward the Tenenoffs' house. We walked along the width of the field, and a Kuna house came into view. We knew we were close to our destination.

The sound of a gun cocking sent a chill down my spine and I froze in my tracks. At the same instant, Tania broke loose from my arm and ran toward the Kuna house.

"Tania, don't run!" I called out. Whether it was yelled or no more than a whisper, or simply a raging thought in my brain, I couldn't tell.

I feared that Tania would be shot by the machine gun protruding from a man's hands—the man who stood in the shadow of a tree, close to my left.

I faced him and said in Spanish, "We are just going to the other missionary's house. We all want to be together."

The three Kuna men who had escorted us this far moved between me and the man holding the gun and started to talk to him. I turned away from them and walked slowly but deliberately toward the Kuna house where Tania had run. I found her between the cooking house and the sleeping house. Terrified, she stood motionless. I felt very vulnerable, as though we could be trapped there. We couldn't see whether anyone was coming toward us.

I opened the door to the sleeping house and whispered as I went in, "Is anyone here? I'm Nancy. I'm coming in." But no one answered me. I pulled Tania in behind me. We squatted down. The dank smell of the earthen floor assaulted our nostrils, adding to the eeriness of hiding in this empty hut. We looked out through the spaces in the palm-bark siding. We could see inside the Tenenoffs' house. Two men in camouflage uniforms were walking toward the front door, carrying some things. Patti was following them. She had her small son, Lee, in her arms and her daughter Connie by her side, holding on to Patti's skirt. The men left her house.

Soon we heard Trigo, the Kuna man whose house we were in, calling my name. "Nahn-cee, Nahn-cee, where did you go?"

"We are inside your house," I replied as we stood up and walked toward the door.

Trigo opened the door before we could reach it, and we exited.

"You can go on to Patti's house now," he told us.

We walked back to the path. More than a dozen Kuna men were standing outside of Patti's house, talking excitedly. I noticed Stan and went over to him.

"Estánislau," I said quietly. "Can you go and get the canoe and take us downriver?" I asked.

"No, not tonight. It is too dangerous. They told us not to leave the village. I am afraid they will hurt you—or kill you," he said.

"Okay," I replied reluctantly. I turned to look at Tania, but she was nowhere to be seen. I was frantic! "Where is Tania?" I asked the crowd of men that was still milling around.

"She went back to get her girls," one of the men replied. "She went with Pablo."

Somewhat relieved, I went into Patti's house.

"Nancy! You're here! You weren't taken! But where is Tania?" Patti asked.

"Tania went back to her house to get Tamra and Jessica. She and Mark were taken up to our house—the kids weren't with them. They took Dave and Mark away. Are you okay, Patti?"

"Well, that depends on what you mean by okay," she said. Patti, a petite brunette, looked pretty, as usual, even though the tension and fear made her creamy complexion a ghostly white. "Are you and Tania going to spend the night here?" she asked.

"Yes. I brought some things, and Tania will come back with what she and the girls need for the night, I'm sure. I'll feel much better when she gets back here. I'm surprised she just took off without telling me, but I guess she is with Pablo," I said anxiously.

"Nancy, I think I'll go and put Connie and Lee to bed. I'll put them in my room with me. Tania and her girls can have my children's bedroom. Do you think that will be all right with Tania?"

"I'm sure it will," I answered absent-mindedly.

"There are some sheets in the dresser drawer in the front bedroom. Do you mind getting them and putting them on the bed in there for you? Or would you rather be in a room with someone else?"

I looked at her two small, blond-haired children. Connie was three years old and Lee was eighteen months. Their eyes were wide with bewilderment, but neither child said a word as their mom took them down the hall to the bedroom.

"That's fine," I called after her. "I need something to do, anyway." I went in search of the sheets. The room was dark, and again I missed my flashlight. I called out to Patti, "Do you have an extra flashlight? They took all of ours."

"I need to look for one," Patti called back. "But there should be a lantern in every room. The matches are on the kitchen counter."

"Okay, thanks," I replied and headed for the kitchen.

I heard footsteps approaching. The front door creaked as someone took hold of the handle. Again, I froze in my tracks, and then I heard Tania's voice. She entered the house with Jessica in her arms. Pablo followed her, carrying Tamra. Gilbertita trailed in behind them.

"Patti said you three can sleep in the kids' bedroom. She's putting Connie and Lee in her room," I said, softly, so I wouldn't wake her sleeping children.

"Thanks," she said as she led the procession back through the house.

I returned to the guest room and lit the lantern. The bottom drawer of the dresser creaked as I opened it. Several sets of sheets lay folded neatly. I grabbed one set and closed the drawer with my leg. I put the sheets on the bottom bunk and was putting the pillowcase on the pillow when I heard my name called softly.

I left the room and saw Stan at the front door, so I walked over and unlocked the screen. Stan entered and followed me to the kitchen.

He stood at the counter and then began to talk to me in low tones. "Dave had a signal over at the airstrip. Dave showed me how to signal the pilot, if ever the plane should not land. Do you want me to go over to the airstrip now and do what Dave told me?"

That's right, I thought. *It is standard procedure to have a signal on any remote airstrip to warn the pilot not to land if there is any danger. But whoever would have guessed that we would need to use it?*

"Estánislau," I said, "if it is too dangerous for us to go downriver tonight, then it is too dangerous for you to go to the airstrip and arrange to signal our pilot."

"I will still do it if you want me to," Estánislau said solemnly.

His dedication to us touched me so much that I could barely get my next words out. "Estánislau, thank you, but no. I don't want you to risk your life. Tomorrow, in the daylight, if it is safer in the morning, then yes, do whatever Dave showed you. But don't do it tonight."

"Okay. Do you want me to stay here in the front room tonight? I will guard the house for you. Trigo can stay, too. The two of us will guard the house," Estánislau said, wanting desperately to help us.

"Yes, that would be good. We would like that. I will bring you some sheets. There are two hammocks," I said. "You can sleep there."

"We would like the sheets, but I won't sleep," he replied.

I walked back to the guest room and pulled two more sheets from the drawer. I located two small pillows on the top bunk and took them out to the two men who would be our guards for the night. I felt comforted knowing that they would be there—not that two unarmed men could be any match for guerrillas with machine guns. But just knowing that someone was listening and watching and could warn us was somehow a big help to me. *What a difference,* I thought, *between Stan, our dear brother in Christ who cares about us, and the three Kuna men, unbelievers who showed more concern about the village money than about our welfare.*

Patti and Tania emerged from the bedrooms. All of the children were asleep. We sat down at the kitchen table.

"Tania," I said. "You scared me to death by just disappearing, without telling me where you were going!"

"I'm sorry, but when we left Trigo's house, all that I could think about were my girls. I just had to get back to my girls!" she replied with feeling. "I saw Pablo and asked him to go with me to get Tamra and Jessica. We walked over to the main path and headed toward our house. I began to look around the village and I could see men in camouflage uniforms, sitting on top of the houses, holding machine guns! There were groups of men in the shadows around houses and more men standing under trees. With every step I took, I became more frightened. I grabbed Pablo's arm and he walked with me."

"You walked arm-in-arm down the center of the village with Pablo?" I asked incredulously. A Kuna man would not even walk arm-in-arm with his own wife in public. We all laughed at the thought. The sound of our laughter startled our own ears. It seemed so hollow and strange to laugh in the middle of the trauma we were living at that moment. "You'll certainly be the topic of conversation for some time to come, Tania," I said with a smile.

"Well, I was scared," she defended herself, her large, innocent eyes wide with sincerity. "Anyway, we got to Ambrosio's house and some of the ladies started calling out to me, 'Your girls are at Nanzhel's house; they are at Nanzhel's.' So we went there. I should have realized that Gilbertita would be afraid to stay alone at my house. Nanzhel, the matriarch of the village and the closest neighbor—it makes sense that Gilbertita would take them there. When I walked in I expected to see them crying for me, but they were both sound asleep in a hammock with Gilbertita. God kept them asleep! I picked up Jessica carefully so she wouldn't wake up. Pablo lifted Tamra out of the hammock and slung her over his shoulder. Amazingly, she didn't wake up, even though I watched her head bounce off of his back all the way here."

"How many armed men do you think are out there?" Patti asked.

"Encelmo told us he thought there were more than one hundred men surrounding the village," I informed her.

"Let's pray together," Patti said.

We bowed our heads. Tania prayed that God would prompt Christians around the world to wake up and pray for us. Patti prayed for our husbands. I prayed for a plan of action and for God's wisdom and direction for us.

Voices at the door cut short our prayers. Stan opened the door for Tito Henry, the village chief. He strode up to the counter that separated the front room from the kitchen. The Henrys were another family that had come from one of the Kuna villages in Colombia, possibly ten or more years ago. Tito was fairly tall for a Kuna man. His face reflected a hardness that was different from most of the Kuna from Púcuro. Unlike them, he wasn't fun-loving and didn't smile readily.

"Nahn-cee," he began, "the guerrillas want to talk to you tonight at nine o'clock."

"Good," I said, hoping they would give us some information. "But they will have to come here. I don't want to leave the house to meet them anywhere," I said with a boldness that surprised even me.

"Okay, I will tell them," Tito said. He looked at us for a moment as if he wanted to say more.

"Nahn-cee," he said, "the Kuna in Colombia have become friends with the guerrillas. We need to become their friends, too." He turned around and strode back outside into the night.

I could feel the blood drain out of my face. *I don't know who we can trust anymore,* I thought. *He spoke so fast—I'm sure Patti and Tania didn't understand that conversation. I'll just keep it to myself for now. We need to rely on the believers and not trust anyone else. How much worse can all of this get, Lord?*

Facing Patti and Tania again, I told them, "Tito said the guerrillas want to meet with us at nine o'clock. I told him they should come here so we won't have to go outside again."

Patti, Tania, and I bowed our heads again and prayed about the meeting with the guerrillas—the meeting that we believed would take place in a short time. We prayed that they would tell us who they were and why they took our husbands from us.

Time dragged on. Nine o'clock came and went. Finally, we again heard a voice at the door. Tito returned, but he was alone.

"The guerrillas said they don't want to meet with you. They want to talk to me, across the river, at midnight," he informed us matter-of-factly.

"Okay," I said. "Come back and let us know what they tell you."

"Okay," he affirmed and quickly left the house again.

Silence filled the room. A clock ticked on the kitchen wall. We were each lost in our own confused thoughts. How could we wait until midnight? Waiting is such a haunting and lonely thing to do.

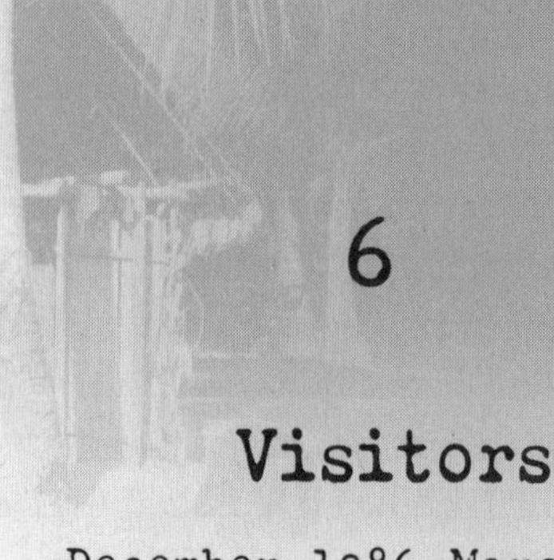

6

Visitors

December 1986–March 1987

Cecilia sat across from me at the kitchen table. By doing our laundry, she had earned some money, and now she was telling me what she wanted me to buy for her in Panama City.

My spiral notebook had dozens of lists in it, swatches of fabric to match colors, and patterns traced around feet to match with shoe sizes. I couldn't convince the ladies that their money would not buy even half of the things on their lists. When the time came, I would have to make my own decisions about what to buy and what not to buy.

I also had dozens of *molas*, beautiful handsewn creations, to sell for them. Most of the items on the lists were in hopeful anticipation of the sale of a *mola*.

My patience was wearing thin. I had to finish defrosting the freezer, and I knew that the plane could be here any minute. *I hope the plane comes today,* I thought. *We are completely out of food. This would not be a good time for the plane not to show up.*

Cecilia told me the last item for her list. "I want yellow diaper pins."

The Kuna women were beginning to use diapers for their babies. Each mother tried to own at least three, which she saved for very special occasions. The diaper pins, when not in use, would be attached to their necklaces and worn with pride.

"Why do you want yellow? Everyone today has asked for yellow diaper pins. What if I can find only white or blue?" I asked her, a bit exasperated.

"Anita got yellow diaper pins and they didn't break. Yellow ones are better," she informed me.

How do I explain that different brands, not color, are what make the difference in quality? I thought. *I won't try. I'll buy a better brand for everyone, in a variety of colors, and no yellow ones. That should work.*

"When are you coming back?" Cecilia asked me.

"In two weeks," I answered.

"Greet Sah-dah and Chandi," she said, using the nickname that the Kuna had given Chad.

• • •

As always, our first day back in the village was even more hectic than the day we left. Stoic, yet excited in their own way, ladies milled around the front room, waiting to find out whether their *molas* had sold—and if so, what items I had brought back for them.

The sweat dripped off my face as I leaned over the bed. It was heaped with panties of all sizes, diaper pins in all colors (except yellow!), yards of fabric, and dozens of spools of thread—just to mention a few. *From now on,* I reprimanded myself, *I will come back prepared—with everything in separate bags and each bag labeled with a name. Don't tell me I'm short a spool of red thread!*

Hours later the house was empty, except for children playing in the front room. I stood at the counter with a fresh loaf of store-bought bread and happily made two sandwiches. *This is the only "easy" thing that has happened all day,* I thought.

"Dave," I called out, "it's time to eat."

"Coming," came the reply from the back porch.

Dave prayed, and then we ate our sandwiches with gusto. We had worked up an appetite.

"I'm ready for my hammock," Dave said, getting out of his chair and heading for the front room.

I heard a giggle, then a thud, as a girl vacated Dave's hammock. She didn't need to be asked. I stacked the dishes on the counter and sat down in my hammock, across the room from Dave.

Dave in his hammock.

He began the conversation. "Rick, Patti, and Dora are planning to come to Púcuro to visit us. How old is Dora now?"

"Dora is about two and a half," I informed him. "The kids here will love her. They will love her blonde, curly hair, and she is outgoing and friendly."

"It will be fun to see how Rick will relate to the folks here. He loves to visit with people. Even in Chame, when he goes to the store he might not return home for half a day. He will fit right in with the people here. Having Rick and Patti come and visit us will be great. It will also be a good experience for them—seeing firsthand what life is like living in this village."

"We make our next trip out in ten weeks. Will they come back with us when we return?"

"Yes. I think they plan to stay for a week," Dave informed me. "Chad and Sarah will fly in here for Christmas break, and the Tenenoffs will leave here on the return flight. It will be nice for all of us to be able to share the cost of those airplane trips. That would be just one of the benefits of having partners."

"This will be their first trip to the interior—their first exposure to any of the mission stations. They hope to visit all of the stations before deciding where to work," Dave said.

"Wouldn't it be interesting to end up being partners with people we went through the training with?" I said.

"Yeah, we weren't even heading for the same country, much less the same tribe, when we and the Tenenoffs went through the mission's training course together," Dave said.

"If they decide that God wants them here, I wish they could move in right away," I said. "What time frame would we be looking at?"

"It sounds like they are making good progress in Spanish language study. But now the field has decided that the language students need 'immersion' time. To solidify what they have learned, Rick and Patti will move to the town of Chepo, where they will be immersed in the Spanish-speaking culture, away from other missionaries. I kind of wish we had been able to do that. By coming straight here and starting to learn the Kuna language, we lost a lot of our Spanish language ability."

"I know. At the time, we felt the urgency of moving in," I remembered. "It would have been hard to see the long-term benefits of waiting."

"We are getting way ahead of ourselves," Dave said. "This is just a visit. We don't know what God has for Rick and Patti, but we sure can pray."

• • •

"Dave," I said as we drove along the highway from Panama City to Chame, "I finally figured it out. Being out of the village isn't really a break; it's just a change!"

Dave laughed. "The lists of things to buy for the villagers keep getting longer, but I'd say we make a pretty good team. I'm proud of you, you know."

"Proud of me? Why?" I asked.

"You aren't afraid to take off by yourself and shop in the areas that have the inexpensive merchandise the Kuna people want. Dividing up the lists and combining our efforts is a huge timesaver. You even go down to the docks with me. Few women would want to go there, much less take off and shop on their own. I buy files, machetes, and fishhooks, while you buy the fabric they want for their skirts and *molas*."

"Thanks, honey. We do make a good team."

"I talked to the pilot today," Dave continued, along another line. "He told me that the plane won't be repaired in time for our trip back to Púcuro. We'll have to ask Rick and Patti whether they still want to go. A ten-hour bus ride and then an eight-to-ten-hour canoe trip the next day won't be easy for them with a two-and-a-half-year-old."

"Will the plane be ready in time to take our kids in to Púcuro—and to fly Rick and Patti out?" I asked.

"It should be," Dave answered. "The parts they need are supposed to arrive soon."

"That's good," I said as I yawned and closed my eyes. I slept for the rest of the trip to Chame.

• • •

One week later, Dave and I were staying at the guesthouse in Panama City. Our groceries had been packed in boxes and left in the hangar. Decisions had been made about which items we should take in by land and which items should be flown in with our children. Dave had weighed every box carefully and then marked it with the weight and our name. We were exhausted, and tomorrow would be another long day.

Rick, Patti, and Dora arrived, looking very tired. Obviously it had been a very exhausting day for them, too. Rick, at five-foot-eight-inches tall, had his short, light brown hair trimmed neatly. He carried their suitcases to the back bedroom. Patti, as always looking neat and pretty in a tailored outfit, walked directly into the kitchen to get Dora a drink of water. Dora, the only one with any energy, headed for the toy box, chattering away to the guesthouse hostess.

"What time do we need to leave for the bus station?" Patti asked me.

"The bus that goes to Yaviza leaves very early. I think we need to be there by six o'clock," I told her. "Do you have everything you need?"

"I hope so," Patti said. "But I've never done this before, you know. I really don't like the thought of traveling on the river, especially with Dora. I really have a fear of water. But I'm sure the Lord will undertake for me."

"He will," I assured her. "I'm sorry your first trip to the interior will be by bus and boat. Unfortunately, you are being broken in the hard way."

"Dave," Rick called out from their room, "I have a few questions for you before you go to bed. I need to take my contacts out first, then I'll join you in the living room. Okay?"

"Sure," Dave said. "I'm headed there anyway to watch the news."

I walked through the guesthouse toward our room. The bed was still cluttered with all of the things that I had bought for the people in Púcuro. I began to sort out the lists and put each person's items into individual bags. With a felt marker I wrote the person's name, the amount of money the items had cost, plus the amount of change I owed them, if any. It was a bookkeeping nightmare. As much work as it was, though, I rather enjoyed it.

"See you in the morning," I said to Patti as she walked past our room, with Dora in tow.

"Good night, Nance," Patti said, using the nickname that only she ever called me.

The obnoxious sound of the alarm clock jolted me at five o'clock the next morning.

"Hurry," Dave said. "You'll get to see your first sunrise."

He snickered as he walked out of the room to get my morning coffee.

Nothing is funny at five o'clock in the morning, I thought, grumpily.

Thirty minutes later, the five of us stood on the street corner, hailing a taxicab. Our long journey had begun.

Five hours later, we were still in the old bus, bumping along the unpaved road. Hot air and dust blew through the open windows. Blaring salsa music had given me a headache. The man sitting behind me kept time with the music by tapping his ring against the metal bar across the back of my seat.

"Won't they make any stops?" Patti asked from across the aisle.

"They should stop soon at a restaurant where we can eat lunch," I said, rubbing my throbbing temples. "I sure wish that I had a set of earplugs."

Rick and Patti did a great job of entertaining Dora for the first few hours of the trip. Since then she had been sleeping across their laps. The Panamanians were all very attracted to Dora, giving Rick many enjoyable opportunities to converse with them.

Finally, the bus pulled in at a restaurant. All of the fifty or more passengers filed off wearily. The five of us headed for the bathroom—or rather, the outhouse—and stood in the long line to await our turns.

Most of the restaurant's tables and chairs stood outside on a patio. The few inside tables were already filled with people. It didn't really matter; the inside wasn't air-conditioned. We found a place to sit, and a waitress quickly appeared at our side to take our orders.

"Where are the menus?" Patti asked me.

"I think the choices are written on that blackboard in there," I told her as I pointed. "There appears to be a very limited selection, and I don't think we have very much time."

We each ordered soup. It came with a plate of rice and tasted very delicious. Finishing our food as quickly as we could, we paid for the meal and boarded the bus again.

We had bumped along in blessed silence for nearly half an hour when a voice from the back called out, *"¡Música!"*

The four of us glanced at one another in dismay as the salsa music commenced—as loudly as it had before. I looked down at a plastic bag near my feet. Tearing off part of it, I fashioned an earplug, of sorts, and stuck it in my ear. I made another one for the other ear. *Not bad*, I thought. *It cuts down on the sound enough to make it bearable, at least.*

My three comrades looked at me as if I'd lost my mind, but I just cocked my head at them with a look that let them know that my comfort was more important to me than my pride. An hour later Dave was sheepishly fashioning his own earplugs. I couldn't resist the temptation to give him an "I-told-you-so" look.

"Dave," Rick said, "how do you know for sure that someone from the village will be waiting for us in Yaviza with a canoe?"

"We sent a message through the public radio station," Dave answered. "It's our only way of communication. But I guess we can't know for sure."

"How does that work?" Rick asked.

"The radio station has a special program every day at three o'clock. It's filled with messages for people who live in the Darién. People can send a message to relatives and friends, telling them when they will arrive by bus or asking them to send vegetables or rice out to them. Some messages tell about the condition of a person who is in the hospital. A few people in Púcuro have relatives who live in the city, and they listen for messages from them. When we are away from the village, they listen specifically to find out whether we might need the canoe to pick us up, and when. It works quite well, actually."

"Do a lot of people in Púcuro have radios?" Rick asked.

"I think there are probably four or five radios in the village. They only cost about five dollars, and they are run by batteries," Dave said.

How different these two men are, I thought. *Rick is a planner. He thinks about everything in detail and feels the need to be in control. He is very protective of Patti and Dora. Dave, on the other hand, is more relaxed. He is a thinker and a planner, too, but he never seems to worry about anything that is out of his control.*

"I'm thankful that we can stay with the Jordans tonight," Patti said. "What would we do if we didn't have missionary friends in Yaviza? Are there hotels or anything there to stay in?"

"That's a good question," Dave said. "If there are, I'm not sure what they would be like. Yaviza almost reminds me of an old Western town, back in the late 1800s."

The bus lurched in a rut and we all clung to the seats in front of us. We were arriving at our destination.

"This is it?" Rick said incredulously, staring out of his window.

"Yep," Dave said, gathering our satchels and boxes. "Actually, the bus lets us off here. We have to cross the river to get to the town itself."

We climbed stiffly down the bus steps. Estánislau's smiling face greeted us from the river's edge. Three other Kuna men, in a small canoe, were waiting in the water.

"Faithful Stan," Dave beamed.

Barb Jordan waived enthusiastically at us from the porch of their house as we trooped toward her from the riverbank. She was such a welcome sight. She and Gene served us all a delicious supper and found places for us to sleep.

Dawn came all too soon. Gene, Barb, and their girls waved good-bye as we trudged back to the waiting canoe to begin the last leg of our trip to Púcuro.

We hadn't gone very far in the small canoe when Estánislau turned off the motor and greeted a man in another canoe. The man was from the Emberá tribe. After they talked, Estánislau turned back to us and explained the conversation that we hadn't been able to hear. The Emberá man lived on the Púcuro River and had offered to exchange canoes with us because we were so crowded. They would switch back their canoes later. What a thoughtful man. We were all thrilled.

We switched canoes and motors and settled in again for the long ride. The drone of the motor was relaxing, but the sun beat down fiercely on us. I filled plastic glasses with water from our water cooler and passed them to everyone in the canoe. My back began to ache, and there was no comfortable position on the hard seat, which didn't even have a backrest. I looked at Rick, Patti, and Dora, who seemed to be doing fine. Dora ran her fingers in the water as Rick held on to her tightly. Patti seemed to be absorbed in thought.

Four hours later we stopped at the town of Boca de Cupe. The bottom of the canoe was wet and slippery. I sat very still and watched as one of the men helped Patti to step out. Rick handed Dora to Patti and then stood up and maneuvered himself out of the tipsy boat. Dave was next, and then I stood up and took hold of Dave's hand to steady myself as I stepped over to the dock.

With aching bodies, we all stretched before walking up the cement stairs to the little town. Our first stop would be another "bathroom." Then we went to a small store to buy something to eat.

"Aren't there any restaurants here?" Patti asked.

"I don't think so," I answered. "We usually buy bread. Sometimes you can get a meat-filled pastry. They do have cold sodas, though."

"A Pepsi sounds wonderful," Patti said.

"I'm hungry, Mommy," Dora said.

"I know, sweetie," Patti said sympathetically. "We will see what we can get for you to eat. You have been such a good girl for Mommy and Daddy."

"She really has been," I confirmed.

The break seemed too short to all of us, but we wanted to finish our trip before dark, so we all piled back into the canoe. A few minutes later we left the Tuíra River and headed up the Púcuro River, toward home.

Patti looked anxiously at me as the canoe struggled upstream. Soon, Estánislau shut off the motor, and all of the Kuna men stood up with long poles in their hands. They plunged their poles into the shallow but rushing water and applied all of their weight in order to propel the canoe forward. The men labored on for half an hour, and then we heard the motor drone again. All of the men, except the one in the front, sat back down. He stood with his pole in hand, watching for rocks that the propeller could collide with. Periodically this man would smack a rock with his pole, signaling to Stan where to steer to avoid the obstacle. All too soon the river became too shallow again, and all of the men stood up to propel the boat with their poles. Dave located an extra pole and began to help. I grabbed a gourd and bailed out water that was splashing into the canoe.

Rick, always eager to help, called back, "Is there another pole? I've never done this before, but I'll try."

"There aren't any more," Dave said. "Would you bail water at your end though?"

I found a second gourd and tossed it to Rick. Patti sat erectly, her eyes wide with apprehension. I couldn't blame her. The lurching sensation of the canoe was discomforting indeed—even for a person who doesn't have a fear of water!

Dave lost his footing. I winced as he struck his shin on the seat in front of him. Instinctively I reached out. Recovering on his own, he stood again and plunged his pole back into the water.

Darkness was descending upon us, and still the men labored on. Finally they guided the canoe to shore, near a path. Estánislau explained to us that it would be much better if we could hike the rest of the way. It would be too dangerous to continue in the dark with such a heavy load in the canoe.

We disembarked and stood for a moment to get the feeling back into our legs.

"Have you ever done this before?" Patti asked me. "I mean, have you had to hike from here in the dark?"

"No," I said. "I don't like it either. But it isn't too far, probably only fifteen minutes. I'm sorry your first trip in has been so hard."

Rick picked up Dora and we trudged along in single file behind our guide.

Lord, I prayed, *please don't let us see any snakes.*

We hiked up a hill and around a bend, right past a pigsty belonging to one of the Kuna families who was raising a pig to eat. Darkness enveloped us. Soon we came to a log bridge. Our guide crossed first and then stood illuminating the log for us with the beam from his flashlight. We each crossed safely. As we neared the first Kuna hut, we could hear voices. Children called out excitedly to announce our arrival.

Pausing at each hut to greet the people, we introduced Rick, Patti, and Dora to them. All of us desperately wanted to get to our house and collapse, but we couldn't be rude.

Exhausted, we finally reached our house. Dave unlocked the door, but as much as we wanted to, we couldn't go straight to bed. The demands of getting our house opened up again after we'd been away for two weeks still awaited us. Dave lit a lantern. We escorted

Rick and Patti to the bedroom that would be theirs. I lit another lantern in their room.

I still remembered well how eerie it felt the first night Dave and I spent in Brian and Candy's house—the feeling that unknown insects might be lurking in the shadows, the sound of unfamiliar noises that were so unsettling. However, I couldn't think of any way to make it easier for Rick and Patti. Arriving in the daylight hours would certainly have helped. But it was just one of those things that takes time, in order to feel the comfort of familiarity.

Dave hooked up the gas tanks to our stove and refrigerator. It would take hours before the refrigerator would be cold. The food we brought in would remain in the ice chest until morning.

Dave filled the top container of the water filter so we would have clean water to drink in the morning. I dusted off the countertops before scrubbing them. The floors could wait until tomorrow.

So our guests could shower before going to bed, Dave lit a lantern on the back porch, in the shower and dressing room area. I set out towels and washcloths.

Soon, we were all ready for a good night's sleep. I prayed again that Rick and Patti would sleep well.

I awoke to the sound of the first Kuna man coming for his morning cup of coffee and talk with Dave. Then I heard Rick's enthusiastic voice join in. More men than usual came that morning, all anxious to get to know the newly arrived American.

"Rick, do you want a cup of coffee?" Dave asked teasingly.

"You know I don't drink that stuff," Rick replied with mock indignation.

"Then you might not be able to work here," Dave teased again. "You have to drink coffee in order to fit in. All of the Kuna people love coffee."

"I'll just teach them to drink hot chocolate," Rick said with confidence. "Besides, we're just visiting, remember?"

"Well, now, hot chocolate would work," Dave said. "But you'd go broke."

Then I heard Dave talking in Kuna to his visitors. "Do you know that Ricardo keeps his brains in his pocket?" Dave said.

Silence followed. The men looked skeptically at Dave. *Hard telling what these Americans can do . . .*

Dave repeated himself. "Ricardo keeps his brains in his pocket. Ask him when the plane is coming."

A Kuna man asked Rick in Spanish, "Ricardo, when is the plane coming in for you?"

I knew then what Dave had done, and I could picture Rick taking the Day-Timer out of his pocket. I heard him flip some pages, and then he answered in Spanish, giving the date and approximate time that the plane was scheduled to arrive.

The room exploded with laughter. *I wish I could see Rick's face,* I thought.

"Ricardo," another man said, "when did you first arrive in Panama?"

Rick reached for his Day-Timer again, and again the room exploded with laughter.

Totally bewildered, Rick asked Dave, "Why are they laughing at me?"

Dave wiped the tears from his eyes and said, "I told them you keep your brains in your pocket."

Rick's serious countenance gave way to the humor of the situation, and he felt a warm wave of acceptance.

A few minutes later, I watched as Patti came into the kitchen with her little daughter. What a sacrifice she'd made, visiting us here—even to come when the plane wasn't available. The last two days must have been excruciatingly long and hard for her, especially with such a young child. But here she was, ready to join me for the day.

After breakfast, Patti, Dora, and I went visiting in the village. Our first stop was Nanzhel's house.

"Nanzhel," I called out. "I'm here."

"Come in," Nanzhel called. The old Kuna woman's gray-streaked hair fell limply around her shoulders. Passing into the hut, we stood next to her. The top of her head barely reached the height of my chin. Being only five-foot-two myself, it still felt strange to tower over most of the women in this village. "Sit down," she said, brushing off a bench.

"Nanzhel," I said, "this is Patricia and her daughter, Dora."

"Ah," Nanzhel said, "Patricia. Dora, little white girl with curly hair. How old is she?"

"She is two and a half years old," I replied.

"Would you like a drink?" Nanzhel asked.

"Yes," I said politely. I held out my hand for the cup.

Patti looked at me uncertainly. I knew this would be hard for her—it was hard for me, too, at first. But she took the cup that was offered to her. The stained old cup contained a warm banana drink. Patti tentatively held the cup to her lips and bravely took a sip.

Nanzhel, our dear Christian friend and neighbor, with her granddaughter.

We finished our visit and moved on through the village. Everyone was pleased to be visited by our new guests. Dora was friendly to the adults and children alike. Everyone fell in love with her.

Dave and Rick called on Benito, who was blind. Since he was the oldest person in the village, it was important to honor him with a visit. Besides, Dave had become very close to this dear Christian man, often going to his home to teach him from God's Word, as best he could.

Dave told Rick a story. "About six months ago the village men were holding a work party, building a new house. I had been studying so hard, but I just couldn't get the Kuna words out smoothly yet. I went to guide Benito to the work party. As we drew close to the group of men, some of them noticed us coming. I couldn't help but laugh. I pictured those men thinking, *Here comes the deaf-mute leading the blind man.*"

Rick hesitated, but Dave's infectious laugh overtook him, too. Both men roared with laughter at Dave's joke on himself.

Then, Rick's inquisitive nature prompted him to glean more information. "Why would a blind man want to go to a work party of men building a house?" he asked.

"That is a very good question," Dave replied. "Actually, the socialistic structure of their society demands that everyone participate. But, on the other hand, all of the Kuna people are valued in this culture. We could learn a lot from them. Each person is expected to work according to his age and ability. For example, when they're building a house, the younger men are the ones who stand on the rafters, tying the thatch with vines to make the roof. The older men pass the materials up to them. The younger boys watch and learn, running errands as needed. Benito often stands by, shouting out helpful reminders, such as, 'Are they making sure the thatch is thick enough? I remember when . . .' Benito is a valued member of society. They recognize that, although age brings physical limitations, it also brings much-needed wisdom.

"I've been thinking about that a lot, actually," Dave continued. "It seems to me that our own society could learn from that part of the Kuna culture. We compartmentalize everyone too much—even in our churches. We have youth groups for teenagers, separate Sunday school classes for each grade, children's church, toddlers, and nursery, and usually only the adults attend the church service itself. Granted, adults or older teens teach the children, but the class itself is usually composed of one age group. Peers are watching and learning from their peers, instead of learning from those who are older and wiser than they are.

"Anyway, it's something I've been pondering," Dave finished as they reached Benito's hut. Dave enjoyed having another man to share his thoughts with.

• • •

The week went far too quickly. Thankfully, Chad and Sarah would be arriving on the plane that would be taking our friends back to the city. *It is lonely without partners*, I thought with a sigh.

The press of people was exhausting. Many women wanted Dora to be their little girl's "good friend." Small children, with beaded necklaces in their tiny hands, were shoved gently toward Dora and encouraged to hand over the gift, hopefully to seal the "friendship."

Once Dora accepted the gift, the happy mother would say the familiar words that grated so much against the values that our own culture had ingrained within us.

"Now they are good friends. Send back a gift when the plane comes back in," repeated each one, almost word for word.

"How many good friends can one person have?" Patti asked anxiously. "Can we choose just one or two?"

I smiled at her question and sympathized inwardly with the pressure she was facing.

"By sending back a gift," I informed her, "you'll be accepting the friendship. You will have to decide which one, or how many to accept."

"What kind of gift do they expect?" Patti asked again, her detailed mind needing to know all of the facts.

"I've been learning about that the hard way!" I replied. "We think too 'American.' I have gone from one ditch to the other and back again, trying to figure out how much to give people. They 'borrow' things daily. Sometimes I have given so much that we've run out of supplies. Other times I've felt so used that I won't give anything at all. Finally, I've realized that I can give them half a cup of sugar or flour when they ask, not a whole pound. I give them a small can of kerosene instead of a quart. Being able to communicate in their language has helped more than anything, though. For example, when a baby is born, sometimes the parents ask for kerosene. They need it so they can keep a smudge lamp lit all night, to keep the vampire bats away. Knowing that makes us want to give even the last drops available from our supply of kerosene.

"It's the same thing with these gifts. Those little girls would be delighted with barrettes for their hair or a pair of panties. They would love to have any clothes that Dora has outgrown."

"Thanks, that helps," Patti said as she tied the necklaces around Dora's neck.

I knew that Patti would carefully weigh the information I had given her. Whether or not the Lord directed her and Rick back to Púcuro, she would faithfully develop those friendships in the proper Kuna way.

"The plane is coming; the plane is coming!" chorused some of the crowd as they rushed toward the door.

Cecilia and her girls hung back with us so we could walk over to the airstrip together.

Dave and Rick rushed in to gather the suitcases. Other young men waited eagerly to help carry things across the river.

Excitedly, I locked the door behind us. *This time I will be able to meet Chad and Sarah at the plane!* With a lilt to my steps, I felt the glad anticipation of having my children near me again.

Little did we know then, nor would we know for some time, but standing by the airplane while waiting to embark, Patti leaned toward Rick and said, "I enjoyed spending time with Dave and Nancy. But I'm sure the Lord doesn't want us working in Púcuro, because the airstrip is on one side of the river, and the village is on the other."

Our routine changed. With our children here with us in the village for three weeks, Dave continued with his regular hours of language study, but I gave up on it and spent the time with the kids.

I cooked and baked lots of the foods that were special to them. Sarah and I sang duets while we did the dishes together. The three of us played the board game Life. These were fun days.

Chad spent as much time as he could with the guys. He visited hut to hut, sat around their fires, and enjoyed whatever food or drink he was offered. The Kuna people accepted Chad and bonded with him very quickly. We were told many times that Chad spoke very good Kuna. And soon he had a new name.

"Machi Nakpe is my new name," Chad proudly announced at our noonday meal.

"That sounds like a dubious honor," I replied.

"Why?" Sarah asked. "What does it mean?"

"Snake Boy," Dave translated for her.

"Yuck!" Sarah exclaimed.

"I like it," Chad said, still pleased.

"Don't you have nicknames?" Chad asked us.

Dave chuckled. "My name means 'His head is so hard, it rings like a bell.' I think it means that I'm smart. I think, though, the truth of the matter is that my head is too hard to learn their language!"

"Dad, you are smart," Chad said.

"What's your name, Mom?" Sarah asked.

I scowled at Dave, who was grinning mischievously.

"Her name is Moo," he smiled. "It means 'older woman,' kind of like a generic term for grandma, but not necessarily a blood relative."

"It means 'old lady,'" I said, still rather put out by the expression. "Besides, I'm not nearly old enough to be a grandmother. It isn't funny," I said, not willing to endure their laughter.

"Actually, it is a sign of respect in this culture," Dave explained. "There appears to be a generation nearly missing here in Púcuro. They may have died during an epidemic. Only five or six people here are older than we are, and they appear to be from ten to thirty years older. The rest are nearly our age or younger. However, because we aren't still having children, they view us as older than we are."

"Can we call you Moo?" piped up Chad with a grin.

"No! It's bad enough when you call me 'Mom' in here," I said, and we all roared with laughter.

Mam, a Kuna word that is pronounced just like "Mom," is the name of a root vegetable. To the Kuna people, every time Chad or Sarah called me "Mom," it sounded like they were calling me "Yucca."

After the meal Chad left again to go spear-fishing in the river with his friends.

It was good to watch Sarah playing UNO with a group of girls in the front room. She was adjusting and making friends in her own way.

"Do you girls want to go with me to the river to bathe?" I asked.

People in Sarah's bedroom.

They all jumped up excitedly. The Kuna bathed in the river, morning, noon, and night. But rarely did they get to use soap and shampoo, so it was a treat for them to go with us.

Sarah and I donned our swimming suits and, according to Kuna custom, wrapped our Kuna skirts around us. We searched the riverbank, checking to see if our neighbors were finished with their bath time. We each had our own area at the river, and privacy was respected.

As we sat in the cold, clear water, the heat of the day washed down the river with the flow of the stream.

I squirted shampoo on the four girls' heads. They lathered it up and giggled as they played with the suds before letting the river rinse the bubbles downstream.

The soap was very slippery and I lost my grip. Instantly all three of the small brown bodies sprang into action—diving down and swimming after the coveted bar. Much to my amazement, one of the girls rescued it and brought it back.

• • •

In the jungle latitudes, nightfall comes quickly. No twilight here. We were all tired and glad to be making final preparations for the night.

I turned on my flashlight and followed Sarah through the back porch and outside toward the outhouse, lighting the path in front of us.

"I don't like coming out here after dark," Sarah complained.

"I know, but there isn't anything that we can do about it," I said.

Grabbing the outhouse door, Sarah pulled it partway open, then hesitated. "I think I see a cockroach or something," she fussed.

My first thought was to nudge her gently toward the door and tell her to stop being so silly. I was tired, but that was no reason to be impatient. Instead, I shone the light at the crack in the door, to assure her that nothing was there.

The beam of light reflected back from the eyes of a snake. On the inside board that braced the door, the snake was coiled—inches from Sarah's hand. Letting go of the door handle, Sarah turned and ran back to the house in a flash, while I watched the door close again, taking the snake inside with it. I turned and ran quickly back to the house, too.

Chad and Sarah leaving to go back to school.

Through her sobs, Sarah had not been able to communicate clearly to Dave what was happening. He held her in his arms, and, with concern in his eyes, he looked over her head at me for an explanation. I quickly told him that there was a snake in the outhouse. Dave grabbed his machete and we ran back outside. Through an opening on the hinged side of the door, Dave was able to kill the snake without endangering anyone by opening the door again. The ruckus drew a small audience. The snake that lay dead on the ground, we were told, was a very deadly pit viper. We thanked the Lord for his protection.

That was the first of many encounters I had with snakes. My intense dislike of the creatures increased, but my determination not to be ruled by my fear increased even more. Many times in the future, I would again have to give that fear over to God.

Chad and Sarah's departure day arrived far too quickly. Sadness wrenched our hearts as we watched our children go off to school again, without us. In our hearts, we committed them to God. We prayed for peace and strength to continue the job that he had called us to.

• • •

Dry season was upon us. With it came hikers—adventurers—some of whom seemed to think that they were the first to brave the famous Darién Gap. Almost all of them found our house—and needed a good meal, a place to sleep, and a translator.

"Dah-veed, Dah-veed!" called a voice from the front door. "An American is coming!"

"It must be a hiker," I said wearily.

"I'll go," Dave said as he set his glasses down and pushed his chair away from the desk. Even though the hikers were an interruption to our language study time, Dave looked at their arrival as an opportunity. I have heard Dave tell many a hiker that God must really want him to hear the good news about Jesus Christ. "After all," Dave would say, "God sent you to a missionary in the middle of the jungle, thousands of miles from home." Dave endeavored to present God's plan of salvation as clearly as he could, to anyone God sent his way.

"Come in, Chipu," I could hear Dave say. "Where is the American?"

"Out on the trail. Gabriel and his son are coming with him now. The American says he is starving, hasn't eaten in days. He was lost," Chipu explained.

I rose to my feet. There wouldn't be any more studying this morning. I entered the kitchen as the house filled up with people. Two Kuna men were helping a young American-looking man into the living room. He staggered in, telling us that he was starving to death. Quite theatrically, he flung himself into Dave's hammock. When he put his feet, muddy boots and all, into the hammock, I could hear our laundry lady gasp. I looked over at Cecilia. She was scowling at this inconsiderate man who didn't have enough sense to keep his feet off the hammock that she had worked so hard to scrub clean.

The aroma of chocolate cake in the oven filled the room, signaling that it was done. I was glad that I could at least serve this young man a snack before fixing the noon meal. I took the cake out of the oven and cut a large piece for him.

"Here's a piece of chocolate cake that you can eat now," I said, holding it out to him.

"No thanks," he said. "I don't eat sugar. What else do you have?"

I looked at Dave. He was sitting on a bench near the hiker, who was lounging in Dave's hammock. My look told Dave that I wasn't going to have much patience with this man.

"We'll eat lunch at noon," I told our new guest. "Would you like a drink of water?"

"Yeah, water would be great," he said. "I tried to find leaves with dewdrops on them this morning. I sure am hungry, though."

I turned away so he wouldn't see me rolling my eyes. I returned with a big glass of ice water for the hiker, who said his name was Steven.

I decided to make a pot of coffee for the rest of the people who were all talking excitedly about this American. As I filled the coffeepot with water, I was wondering what I should make for lunch. Our food supply was getting pretty low. Our old refrigerator was huge on the outside, but the space inside was limited. The freezer was very small and we usually stayed in the village for ten weeks at a time before going out to the city. I opened the small freezer door inside the refrigerator and found four ice cube trays and two pounds of hamburger. I would have to make that meat last for another two weeks, and now we had another mouth to feed.

"Nahn-cee, Nahn-cee," called Hilda as she entered the crowded room.

"Come in," I replied as I looked in her direction.

"Here," she said. "My dad killed a wild pig today. Dah-veed gave him the bullets. My dad said to bring you this meat."

"Thanks," I replied. "We needed some meat. Tell your dad 'thank you.'"

"Mom says, do you have any onion?" she asked.

"Sure," I told her as I cut an onion and handed her half of it.

"Thanks," Hilda said. "I'm gone."

I cut the rest of the onion and fried it in some oil. I chopped the meat into bite-sized pieces and browned that in the oil with the onion. Then I added water to make it into soup. Looking around the room, I spotted Cecilia again.

"Cecilia," I called out.

"I'm here," she said, coming into the kitchen and sitting at the table.

"I need some vegetables for my soup. Do you need any onions or oil? Would you like to trade?"

"Yes," Cecilia said with a smile. "I'll go get some for you."

"Thanks," I told her.

Cecilia quickly rose to her feet and went for the vegetables that she had stored at her house. She was a beautiful young lady. Her black hair was full of body and flowed down her back to her waist. She had a dimple in one cheek, an unusual marking for a Kuna. Even though she was only nineteen years old, she was expecting her third child. When her husband, Tomás, became a believer, Cecilia was very angry—and so was her father, Tony Henry. Their family was from one of two Kuna villages across the border in Colombia. Cecilia once told me that she had been in love with a young man in her own village. But when Tomás came from Púcuro to visit, Cecilia's father promised Tomás that he could marry her. Cecilia was heartbroken. They were married,

Tomás with his mother, Nanzhel, and his wife, Cecilia, and their two children.

and Cecilia moved to Púcuro to live with her new husband and his mother, Nanzhel.

Moving away from her mother was very much against Kuna culture. The Kuna are a matrilineal society. When a Kuna couple marries, the man leaves his parents' house and moves into his wife's house, with her and her parents. The man works hard to supply for the wife's family. Usually, after the young couple's second baby is born, they build their own place, next to the family home. Their lineage is marked through the mother. Girl babies are, therefore, very desirable.

In Cecilia's case, however, her mother-in-law, Nanzhel, was a widow. She had no living daughter or son-in-law—no one to care for her except Tomás. At fourteen years old, Cecilia married a man whom she didn't love and was taken away from the only family she knew. Cecilia was a high-spirited and feisty young lady, however, very much the opposite of her husband, Tomás. Eventually, her mother and father also moved to Púcuro, along with some of her siblings.

"Nahn-cee," Cecilia called as she came through the house and set a huge quantity of root vegetables on my countertop.

"Oh, thank you," I said. "That is a lot! You didn't have to bring so much."

I'm sure they couldn't understand why I cooked such a small pot of soup. When a Kuna woman cooked, she made enough to last for three meals, and she fed about ten people at each meal.

I went into the pantry for oil and another onion to give to her. Cecilia's eyes lit up as I handed her the prized food items. We were both very pleased with the trade.

"I'm gone. I am going to go and make some soup, too," she said as she made her way back through the crowded living room.

Looking at my watch, I realized that time was getting away from me. I was sure that, even though I knew our guest was not starving to death, he must be very hungry. I looked out at the people again and spotted a couple of girls.

"Gladys, Hilda," I called.

They scampered to me with bright smiles on their pretty faces.

"Would you go to the river and take some of these vegetables and peel them for me?" I asked. "I'm making soup."

"Okay," they answered in unison, picking up the vegetables, two knives, and a bowl that I had set out for them. They left through the back door and took our path down to the river.

When I turned around, two more girls appeared at my side. "Sandra, Alejandrita," I said, nearly running into them. "How are you two?"

"I'm fine," said Alejandrita.

"I'm fine, too," said Sandra in her gentle little voice.

"Can we put the plates on the table for you?" Alejandrita asked with a hopeful voice.

"Yes, I need help today. I'm glad you are here," I told them.

"Is the American going to eat with you?" Alejandrita asked.

"Yes," I replied.

I didn't need to give them any more instructions. The girls prided themselves in knowing exactly where I kept the dishes and silverware. They mimicked the way I set the table. They knew precisely where I would put the knife, fork, and spoon, and how I folded the napkin and put it under the fork. They watched everything we did, and they seemed to remember it all. *What fun to have such sweet helpers,* I thought.

I opened the back door for the other girls, who had just returned from the river with their hands full. The wet feet that padded across my kitchen floor no longer bothered me. I had long since learned that a house with dozens of people a day tracking through it would not remain spotless. People were more important than a clean floor.

I added the vegetables to the soup and then put rice in a pot to cook.

"Dah-veed," I called out in Kuna, "lunch should be ready in twenty minutes."

"Good," Dave answered. "I'm very hungry." He got up from the bench, stretched, and walked into the kitchen so he could talk in English. "I never got a piece of that cake that smelled so good."

"I know. I'm sorry," I told him. "There were too many people to share it with everyone." I cut off a bite-sized piece of cake and popped it into his mouth. He grinned—his mischievous little grin that I loved so much—that grin that always reminded me of the smile on the face of "the cat that caught the canary."

I filled the plates with rice and the bowls with soup and set them back on the table. The Kuna adults took that as their cue to leave. In their culture it is impolite to stay while your hosts are eating, unless you are hungry and don't have food to eat at home.

The four girls who had helped me were still in the house. "Girls," I said, "would you like some candy or some food?"

"Food!" they all replied in unison.

"Okay," I said, returning to the stove with four more plates and bowls. There wasn't enough room at the table, and the Kuna people don't eat together around a table in their own homes anyway, so I filled their plates and set them on the countertop.

"It's time to eat," I told our guest.

"Oh, good," he said as he hoisted himself out of the hammock and ambled in.

We sat down. Dave said, "Let's pray. Heavenly Father, thank you for this food that you have provided, and for Nancy, who fixed it for us. Thank you for sparing the life of this man who has come our way. You have spared him for a reason, and I ask that, because of the experiences he has been through, he will think about his eternity. We love you, Lord. Amen."

When I looked up, the four girls were raising their heads, too, even though the prayer had been in English. They smiled and took their food to separate benches in the front room.

"There's a town meeting today," Dave said. "You should go with me," he told Steven.

"No, I'm too tired," came the reply. "I'll stay in the hammock and sleep."

"No, you can't stay in the house while I'm gone," Dave told him. "It's against the culture here."

"What do you mean? I don't get it," he said.

"It means you have to go to the meeting with me," Dave said again.

"Oh, all right," came the less than enthusiastic reply.

"Did you both get enough to eat?" I asked.

"Yes, it was delicious, honey," Dave said. "Thanks."

"I'm full. Thanks," said Steven.

"We need to go now," Dave said to me. "We'll be back in a couple of hours."

"A couple of hours?" repeated Steven in dismay.

"You can leave your backpack in the front room. It will be safe there," Dave said. "Come on, let's go."

Having Steven here is going to be like having a strong-willed child in the house, I thought.

The four girls brought their empty dishes to the kitchen. "Can we wash the dishes?" Gladys asked.

"Yes," I told them as I began to put the leftover food in storage containers.

After the dishes were done, the girls went to play with the UNO cards in the living room.

"Nahn-cee, Nahn-cee," Gladys called out in an excited tone. "That American is coming. He has a feather in his hair! It looks like the tail feather from Silvino's parrot!"

No! I thought as I rushed toward the window. Sure enough, Steven had a headband around his forehead, with a feather sticking up in back. He was doing a little war dance.

Before he could try to come inside, I walked to the screen door and locked it. I went to the back porch door and the side door and locked both of those, too. Steven might not be dangerous, but he definitely had some problems. I wasn't going to take any chances.

"Here come Silvino and Dah-veed," Alejandrita informed me.

I drew closer to the window so I could see and hear whatever was going to happen next.

"Steven," Dave said sternly, "this man is the owner of the parrot whose feather you plucked."

"I didn't pluck the feather off the bird," Steven said belligerently. "I found it on the ground."

"Steven," Dave said again. "Take the feather out of that headband. Give it to me. Okay, now, come with us. The people want to talk to you. The village may require you to pay a fine for this."

"A fine?" he whined. "I found the stupid feather on the ground. I won't pay any fine to anybody."

"You had better come. They could make you leave the village. Someone saw you pluck the feather, Steven," Dave said as though he were reasoning with a child. He looked up at me through the window. "Are the doors locked?" he asked in Kuna.

"Yes, they are," I answered.

"It would be a good idea to keep the girls in, too. I don't trust this guy," Dave said as he led him back to the meeting house.

By the time the last person left our house that night, we were both exhausted. We blew out the lantern and sat in our hammocks in the dark to unwind a little bit.

"Well, Nancy," Dave said, "you got your wish."

"What wish?" I asked.

"You've never liked having hikers sleep in our house. I always believed that the Lord would protect us, so I didn't worry about it. Today the village decided that we can't keep the hikers in our house overnight any more. They will let them sleep in the meeting house," Dave said. Then he chuckled and continued, "And they'll charge them two dollars a night."

"Well, good," I said. "I like that idea."

"I thought you would," Dave said as he smiled affectionately at me from across the room.

We were good for each other, and we worked well together. But we both realized the need for another couple to join us in God's work among the Kuna.

• • •

Through the months that followed, Rick heard Patti say many times that she didn't think that God wanted them to work in Púcuro. They visited the various mission stations in Panama and diligently completed their language study. Well into their immersion time in Chepo, the moment finally came when God confirmed to them both that Púcuro was, indeed, where he wanted them to serve. The Tenenoffs and the Mankinses would form a team—even though the airstrip was still on the other side of the river from the village!

7

The Longest Night

January 31, 1993

Patti, Tania, and I looked at each other from around the wooden table. The minutes had been ticking by, seemingly in slow motion, since Tito left the house.

We launched into the accounts of what had happened that night in each of our homes. The conversation then turned to planning a course of action for the next day.

"I'm so sad that the guerrillas confiscated the radio," Patti said. "Darío was trying to hide it for us."

"I'm so thankful that Darío wasn't harmed," Tania said compassionately.

"Yes," Patti agreed. "That's the most important thing."

"It's amazing, really, that nobody was shot or killed tonight," I said.

The silence around the table was filled with private thoughts of possibilities that none of us wanted to verbalize.

"I asked Stan if he would take us downriver tonight," I said.

Both ladies' heads jerked up.

"Tonight?" Tania said for both of them.

"Don't worry; he said no. He told me that it was too dangerous to leave the village. Guerrillas might be downriver, and he thought we should wait at least until daylight."

"Will the plane fly in tomorrow if we don't respond on the radio at our usual time?" Tania asked.

"No," Patti said. "I think they would wait two or three days; don't you, Nancy?"

"I think so," I said. "The government finally allowed us to have two-way radios, and look what has happened when we desperately need one. We have to get downriver tomorrow. We need to send a message to the mission from Boca de Cupe, asking them to have our plane meet us in El Reál. We have to warn them not to allow the plane to land here. The guerrillas could easily be monitoring the mission's radio frequency now. Part of their plan could be to come back and kidnap the pilot and steal the plane." All of us remembered well when two New Tribes Mission pilots in Colombia had been kidnapped and their plane stolen. The pilots had flown into a tribal location where, unknown to them, a missionary couple was being held by Colombian rebels. We did not want a repeat of that incident.

"There isn't an airstrip in Boca de Cupe?" Tania asked.

"No," I said. "Well, there may be an old airstrip there, but it can't be used anymore. The closest airstrip where the mission's plane can land is either El Reál or Yaviza. But there is a telegraph office in Boca de Cupe. From there, we can radio the mission office in Chame."

"I've never made a river trip before. How many hours does it take to get there?" asked Tania.

"It will take us about three hours to arrive in Boca de Cupe," I answered. "Of course, that varies, depending on how low the river is. Then it will be another three and a half hours or so to go downriver to El Reál."

Tito entered the house again. We faced him expectantly.

He launched into rapid Kuna. "I waited and waited. The guerrilla spokesman finally came back. He told me that they did not want to talk to you, and they do not want to talk to me, either."

Turning toward Tania and Patti, I realized that they hadn't fully understood him.

"He said the guerrillas didn't want to meet with him after all," I said with disappointment in my voice. I turned toward Tito again.

"Tomorrow we are going to hold a town meeting," Tito said.

"Nahn-cee, we want you to be there. We are going to decide what you three need to do. Be there at dawn."

"Okay," I answered. "We are going to bed now. We are going to try to sleep."

"Until tomorrow, then," Tito said. He turned and strode out the door.

"What did he say?" Tania asked.

"What was he saying about a meeting?" asked Patti. "He was talking too fast for me to understand everything."

"He said they are going to have a town meeting at dawn. They are going to tell us what to do," I said flatly.

"Can they do that?" asked Tania, incredulously.

"What will we do if they tell Estánislau that he can't take us downriver?" Patti asked.

"I don't know," I said. "Let's just keep praying that they will let us go. I'll try to figure out some alternatives, just in case. For now, though, I think we all have to try to get some sleep. I need to go to the outhouse first."

Two pairs of wide eyes stared at me in disbelief.

"What?" I asked. "We have to have the freedom to go to the bathroom. Come on, let's go together. Besides, Estánislau and Trigo are right here."

• • •

We left the kitchen lantern burning low. The house was deathly quiet. I lay in the bottom bunk in the guest room, thinking that resting must be the next best thing to sleeping. My mind went back to our conversation around the table and Patti's account of what happened when Rick was abducted.

Rick had been in his hammock, visiting with a Kuna man. Patti had finished getting the children ready for bed. Connie scurried happily down the hall, with Lee closing the gap as quickly as his little legs would allow. Evening visitors to the Tenenoff house were quite familiar with this scene—the nightly ritual of kissing Daddy good-night. Rick excused himself from his guest to give his full attention to Connie and Lee for a few precious moments. Reluctantly, Rick sent them on their way again, back to their bedroom for the night.

Patti finished reading a bedtime story to the children and then tucked in the mosquito netting around Connie's bed. She glanced up at the empty top bunk. Eight-year-old Dora was away at the mission boarding school in Chame, and Patti missed her. She picked up Lee to place him in his bed. From the front room, an unfamiliar scuffling sound reached their ears.

She heard Rick say in Spanish, "Why?"

Patti wasn't too sure what to make of it. She heard more scuffling.

"Why?" Rick called out again.

"My wife is in the back of the house!" Rick said loudly in Spanish.

Patti realized she was sitting on the floor near the doorway, with both children in her arms, but she didn't remember getting there. The fact came to her mind that there were some Latinos in the village, and she thought that perhaps they were drunk and were responsible for this confusing disturbance. *Rick can handle drunks,* she thought.

Then Rick called out in English, in the midst of more scuffling, "My wife is in the back!"

Patti wondered why he kept saying that. *Did Rick want her to go out there?* she wondered. Cautiously, she leaned her head out the doorway and peered down the hall.

Dim lantern light, from the center of the kitchen table, would not allow Patti to see clearly into the darkened front room. In the shadows she could see the outline of a man, leaning over Rick. The man had a gun slung over his back. She couldn't see all of Rick's body, but he was lying facedown on the floor.

No, she thought as she leaned back inside the room, *Rick would not want me to go out there. No,* she confirmed in her mind, *Rick would not want his children to see him like that.*

Patti heard more shuffling noises and footsteps. *There's more than one man out there with Rick,* she thought. The screen door slammed shut. Then silence. *They're gone,* Patti thought. *Rick and the men are gone!*

Gunshots resonated from the direction of my house, from the direction of Tania's house, and from across the river. Patti remained motionless on the bedroom floor.

The voices of Kuna men and their footsteps running through her house startled Patti into action. She rose up off the floor with both children in her arms and walked toward the kitchen.

"Bad men, bad men," they were saying in Kuna. "Nahn-cee and Tania have been taken, too!" they informed her.

"No!" Patti said, again dropping to the floor. "Don't you tell me that! I don't even want to know that!"

"No, no, it's true," they said.

I'm in the jungle with four children, she pictured in her mind, *my two and Tania's two.*

"The radio, the radio," the Kuna men's excited voices were demanding her attention again. "You have to do something about the radio."

Patti stood up. Three-and-a-half-year-old Connie spotted one of Rick's best friends and held out her arms to him. The Kuna man picked her up and held her. Patti, with eighteen-month-old Lee still in her arms, made her way through the group of men, toward the two-way radio.

Methodically, Patti began unplugging wires, paying close attention so she would be able to plug them back in again.

"Hide it! Hide it!" Kuna voices frantically advised her.

"Get a plastic bag for it," another voice called out.

Patti went to the kitchen for a plastic bag, to protect our only link with the outside world.

She handed the bag to Darío and watched numbly as he slipped the radio into the bag and disappeared into the night.

Piercing through the numbness came the realization that she didn't want to stay in her house alone overnight. Her mind began to make a list of the things she would need to take with her to one of the Kuna houses. She went to get the new mosquito net that was still in a bag and a double sheet. *This should be large enough for the three of us*, she thought. Then she remembered again that she not only had Connie and Lee to care for, but also Tania's two children. She shuddered at the enormity of it all.

Unfamiliar footsteps drew her back out to the kitchen. Two guerrillas entered the house. The Kuna men vanished quietly into the night.

One of the camouflage-uniformed men was younger and taller than the other. Both were shouting at her about food, batteries, and the radio! It was all very confusing. Patti began to focus on the older man, who appeared to be the one in charge.

"We are taking your husband into the jungle," said the older man, gruffly. "Pack clothes for him, clothes for the jungle."

Patti followed his orders by walking to the bedroom to get Rick's suitcase. Connie was holding on to her mommy's skirt, staying as close to her side as she could. Lee was still in Patti's arms. Patti returned, placing the open suitcase on the kitchen table near the lamp. She then walked back and forth with each item, folding and packing things neatly for her husband. She packed dark-colored shirts so he could escape. She remembered a pair of safety glasses that he might need. She put in the Bible that he had given her on their honeymoon, and even a recent picture of their family. Connie walked back and forth with her, never uttering a sound.

The guerrillas systematically searched the house and continued to demand the radio. Patti decided to act as though she didn't understand them. Instead of a radio, she brought a tape recorder out to the man.

Angrily, the guerrilla smacked the tape recorder and said, "Stupid woman!" But the radio was not asked for again.

"Money! Give me your money!" he demanded loudly.

Immediately Patti thought about her purse, which contained quite a bit of money. It was in a drawer under her side of the waterbed. Walking to her desk instead, she located some cash and handed it to the man.

Spotting the drawers under Rick's side of the bed, the man's search continued as he opened each one and riffled through its contents.

The thought crossed Patti's mind to attempt to get her purse out of the drawer and hide it in a place where he had already searched. Then the guerrilla went around to the other side of the room. Patti held her breath. But he continued on through the doorway and across the hall to the children's bedroom.

Patti breathed a sigh of relief, knowing she would need money to get back to Panama City. *Thank you, Lord,* she prayed silently.

Toys crashed to the floor in the children's bedroom. Connie looked at Patti. "Mommy," she said, "they are leaving things all over the floor."

"I know, Connie," Patti answered her. "They just never learned how to pick things up."

The younger guerrilla continued his search by foraging through the kitchen cupboards. The older man flung open the refrigerator door and spotted a Pepsi. Patti watched as he popped open the can and guzzled the drink. It was a very special treat that she had been saving carefully—for just the right moment to enjoy it with Rick.

Connie spoke up again. "Mommy, he isn't closing the doors to the cabinets."

"I know, sweetie," Patti said. "Let's help him out. Let's close the doors for him." As they shut the door together, the thought occurred to her that the older man might not realize that those cupboards had already been searched. Not wanting them in her house any longer than necessary, Patti changed her mind. "Connie, let's just leave it open a little while longer," she said, and they opened it again.

"Lady," the older guerrilla barked, "get some boots for your husband."

Patti headed for the back porch where Rick's boots were. She carried them back and set them in the middle of the kitchen table, by Rick's suitcase. *I can't believe I'm putting boots on the table,* Patti thought, *but I don't want them to be forgotten. I want Rick to have his boots.*

"What else should I pack?" Patti asked.

"Underwear, lady, underwear," came the reply.

Patti went back into the bedroom and brought out all of Rick's underwear and added it to the contents of the suitcase.

"Lady, I told you one suitcase, one!" the older man yelled. "Those boots won't fit in that suitcase."

Patti promptly walked to the pantry and pulled out a plastic bag. She took it back to the table and set the boots in the bag.

Immediately, the two men began throwing things into the bag—even a loaf of homemade bread—right on top of the boots. Patti said that she felt like telling the guerrillas to go get their own bag. That one was for her husband. But of course, she didn't.

Patti followed the men to the front door. The younger man quickly strode outside. The older man was heading in that direction, also.

Before he could leave, Patti asked, "When will I see my husband?"

"Soon, very soon we will arrange it," he told her as he closed the screen door behind him.

Patti looked outside. Armed men in camouflage uniforms appeared to be posted around the house. Kuna men were standing around in a group. Darkness swallowed up the guerrilla as he trudged toward the river with Rick's suitcase.

• • •

Patti's story was ringing in my mind. *Darkness*, I thought. *What is that verse? "For God, who commanded the light to shine out of darkness, hath shined in our hearts, to give the light of the knowledge of the glory of God in the face of Jesus Christ. But we have this treasure in earthen vessels. . . . We are troubled on every side . . ."*

Little Tamra's cries interrupted my thoughts. The bed squeaked as Tania got up to comfort Tamra. Jessica began to cry, too.

I stood up and went toward their bedroom, calling softly so I wouldn't startle anyone. "Tania, I'm coming." I entered the room and asked, "Do you want me to stay in here with one of the girls?"

"Yes, thanks," she said wearily. "Will you sleep with Tamra? I am so exhausted, but I just can't sleep."

"I know," I said, crawling into the bottom bunk. "I'm hoping that just lying still will be restful, but it sure doesn't feel like it. Good night."

"Good night," Tania said.

• • •

Dogs began to bark. *I wonder what time it is?* I thought. The bed squeaked as I rolled over carefully, trying not to wake up Tamra.

"Nancy," came Tania's whisper from across the room, "are you awake?"

"Yes," I whispered back.

"Can we make another trip to the outhouse?" she asked.

"Sure," I said, working my way gingerly out of the bed.

"I wonder why all of the dogs are barking," Tania said, once we were in the hallway.

"Maybe the guerrillas are leaving the village," I said.

We made our trip to the outhouse, thankful again for the two flashlights and two new batteries that, providentially, had been left behind for us to use.

"There's a trail to Balsál," I informed Tania. "The trail goes past my house. I've never been on it, but I think we could hike to the Tuíra River in a few hours. If the village won't let Stan take us downriver, maybe he can sneak us out of the village, and we can hire someone at Balsál to take us downriver in a canoe."

"Nancy, no." I could hear the anxiety in Tania's voice, even though I couldn't see her face in the dark. "I don't think we can do that. What if they catch us?"

"Never mind, Tania," I said. "Don't worry about it. I'm sure the village will let Stan take us downriver. What time is it?"

Aiming the flashlight at her wristwatch, she said, "It's three o'clock."

"I don't think this night will ever end," I said as I crawled back into bed and snuggled against Tamra's tiny body.

The trail to Balsál is the second best option, I thought to myself. *I wonder what our husbands are doing right now. Are they hiking toward*

Colombia? Oh, dear Lord, I prayed, *please protect Dave, Mark, and Rick. Lord, please help us to get downriver tomorrow. I love you, Lord. I'm sorry I'm so fearful. A spirit of fear does not come from you, Lord. I reject this spirit of fear. God, please give me your strength, your calm, your wisdom for the hours and days ahead. Thank you, Lord.*

8

Partners

March 1987–November 1991

In the months that followed, plans came together for Rick and Patti to join us in Púcuro. They would need a place to live. Years of exposure to the jungle had taken a toll on the Simmonses' house—it was no longer inhabitable. We decided it should be torn down after the Tenenoffs' house was built.

Dora, Patti, Rick (sitting sideways), and several Kuna men traveling by canoe in 1988.

The village granted permission for Rick and Patti to move in and offered several locations where they would be allowed to build. Rick and Patti made a trip in to pick out the place they preferred.

Dave helped the Tenenoffs design their house and then drew up the plans for them.

Later, a short-term missions team would come and help them build.

Dave and I were very thankful to have partners joining us. But with new partners also came new responsibilities. We struggled to balance those new responsibilities with the ongoing task of language study.

Also on our minds was the fact that Chad would soon be graduating from high school and returning to the United States. Chad planned to attend New Tribes Bible Institute before going on to Liberty University to pursue a degree in linguistics. We were making arrangements to accompany him back and help him get settled in at school. The thought of him being so far away was nearly unbearable to me. It would be a new phase in all our lives. With our minds filled with the many details of upcoming events, it was hard to concentrate.

In the meantime, life went on for us in Púcuro. We continued to hold church meetings and strove to build strong relationships with the people. Some of them desperately wanted us to know their language well enough so that we could clearly and consistently teach them from the Word of God.

One day, while Dave was entertaining his early morning guests, and I was propped up in bed drinking my coffee and reading my Bible, our bedroom curtain opened and Nanzhel walked through.

"Nahn-cee," said the frail, but spunky, little woman with her wrinkled skin and gray hair. "How did you greet the dawn?"

"Good," I said, a little surprised at her sudden, unannounced appearance in my bedroom.

"What are you doing?" she asked.

"I'm reading God's Word," I told her, holding up my Bible.

She motioned for me to move over and she sat down next to me on the bed. I must have looked so comfortable that she decided to make herself at home. But being more familiar with hammocks than beds, she found herself lying down flat, looking up at me rather helplessly. So I helped her prop herself up—on Dave's pillow.

"Teach me," she said. "I want to know what God is telling you in his Book."

"Oh, Nanzhel," I said, "I have been studying your language for so long! I want to teach you. But the words are hard to say. Someday I will be able to."

"Teach me!" she said again, not to be put off.

The curtain was pulled back again, and Dave walked in with coffee for Nanzhel. He shook his head at the sight before him and chuckled as he went back out the door.

Then I told this dear friend whom I loved so much, "Okay, Nanzhel, I will try to tell you about what I read this morning."

During the next months, Nanzhel joined me several times in my morning routine, but she did not make it an everyday occurrence.

• • •

The twenty-three-member short-term mission Summit Team, composed mainly of teenagers, would arrive soon. We would host them for the first two weeks, and then the Tenenoffs would fly in and take our place, while we went back to the States for two months with our children.

Two woodcutters from Colombia were hired to cut lumber from a huge fallen tree near the village. Materials were brought upriver

Woodcutter sawing large block of wood from fallen tree.

by canoe. Other supplies and materials had to be flown in. It was a huge project, requiring all of our attention to accomplish the job.

Since Chad and Sarah were out of school, they joined us in the village. We appreciated their help so much. We set up the Simmonses' house for the boys and the Summit Team leaders. And we prepared our house to accommodate the ten girls, including Sarah. Using all of the tables, desks, and benches from both houses, we turned our front room into a dining hall.

The airplane arrived with food for the team, and Sarah and I began to cook. Dave and Chad strung more clotheslines across the backyard to hold the laundry that would need to be done daily.

Soon our house was filled with teenagers and villagers. Chad and Sarah were such a blessing—helping to translate for the teens. Sarah helped me in the house, while Chad worked very hard right alongside the Summit Team members.

We held church meetings and many of the team members gave their testimonies, which we translated into Kuna. During the course of the two weeks we could see God working in the hearts of these American teens—their lives were being changed. Most had never witnessed another culture or poverty of any kind. For many of them, it was a wonderful and life-changing experience. They were a tremendous blessing to us, also, as they labored hard to build the Tenenoffs' house.

• • •

We returned to Panama without Chad. Sarah entered the dorm for her sophomore year of high school, and Dave and I flew back to Púcuro.

Four months after we returned, Rick, Patti, and Dora moved into their new house in the village. The Kuna people enjoyed watching them. Everyone wanted to know what these new Americans were like.

Rick and Patti needed to learn about village life, to begin Kuna language study, and to bond with the Kuna people.

Rick, Patti, and Dora at the airstrip in Púcuro.

Rick was a former police officer, dedicated to helping people. During the time when Rick had served as a policeman, Patti had worked as a police dispatcher. Now they were dedicated to helping the Kuna people, spiritually as well as physically.

Both of them were very detail-oriented and organized. Those qualities were a help in some ways and a hindrance in others. Highly organized people tend to like routines, and Rick and Patti were soon to find out that a village full of people seldom fit into anyone's schedule.

One morning at breakfast time in the Tenenoff home, three-and-a-half-year-old Dora was sitting on her booster seat at the table, head bowed, as Rick led the family in prayer. Before the prayer was finished, however, a voice called out at the door.

"Ricardo."

"Come in," Rick said, getting up from the table to meet the guest in the front room.

Sitting down on a bench, the man did not state the reason for his presence. Rick glanced back at the kitchen, trying to decide whether to go and eat or to sit and talk. Not knowing what was proper in this culture, Rick sat down on his hammock.

"What are you going to do today?" Rick asked his guest.

"Later all of us men are going to cut the weeds around the village," Silvio told him. "Dah-veed works, too. When you hear the conch shell sound, come and bring your machete."

"Okay," Rick said.

"I'm gone," Silvio said, standing up and heading for the door.

Rick returned to the kitchen.

"I wish I knew how much time I have. I need to set up my desk area so I can start language study. I have no idea how long it takes to clean the village." Rick said, looking at his now-cold breakfast.

"Why don't you write a note to Dave?" Patti suggested as she washed Dora's face and hands.

"Patricia," came a woman's voice at the door.

"Come in," Patti said, surveying the tableful of dishes that she hadn't had time to rinse and stack at the sink.

Patti joined her guest.

"Who is going to wash your clothes?" the lady asked her in Spanish.

"I don't know yet," Patti said.

"I will do it," she said hopefully.

Patti hesitated. It wasn't easy to make a decision like that. "What is your name?" Patti asked.

"Cecilia," she laughed. "But I am not the same Cecilia who does Nahn-cee's laundry."

"I will let you know," Patti told her.

More ladies came into the house with their children. Dora brought some of her toys out into the front room and the children began to play together. Patti made a mental note to ask if it would be rude to go to her kitchen and work while visitors were in the house.

The unusual tone of the conch shell sounded, calling the men to work. Rick appeared from the bedroom in navy blue shorts, a red T-shirt, and work boots. Machete in hand, he smiled broadly at all of the women and said in Kuna, "I'm gone."

They all smiled their approval and talked about Rick joining the men at work.

A couple of hours later Rick came back. His sweaty face reflected his exhaustion. Dirt covered his arms, legs, and clothes.

"I'm thirsty," he said. "Do you have any iced tea made?"

Patti went to the refrigerator and poured a glass of tea for him.

Rick downed half of the glass before speaking again. "That is hard work!" he said. "It'll take some practice, too. I'm going to the river to bathe."

After eating lunch Rick went into his office to set up his desk. Patti put Dora down for a nap and decided to take a shower while her little one slept.

Having finished her shower, Patti was refreshed and ready to get her own little desk organized.

"Patricia," called out a young girl's soft voice from the door.

"Come in," Patti said, coming out of the bedroom and walking toward the door.

Sandra walked in with a small piece of white paper in her hand. She held it up to Patti.

"Thank you," Patti said, reaching for the note.

Patti gave Sandra a piece of hard candy and then read the note: "Patti, the ladies will sweep the village soon. When you hear the conch shell blow, meet me by the meeting house. Bring a broom. —Nancy."

Sandra looked at Patti, wondering whether she would send another note back to me. Patti looked at Sandra, wondering why she was still standing there.

"Thank you," Patti said again.

"I'm gone," Sandra said, deciding to leave.

The conch shell sounded.

"Rick, Dora is still sleeping. I'm leaving now to sweep with the ladies."

"I'll take care of everything. Be careful not to work too hard. You aren't used to this heat," Rick said, concerned for his wife.

"I don't know what to expect. I'm glad that Nancy will be there, too," Patti said.

The sun beat mercilessly on her head as she walked the path to the meeting house. Ladies were milling around in the shade with small, short homemade brooms in hand.

"Hi, Patti," I said, joining the group.

"Hi," she said.

"How is everything going?" I asked.

"Pretty well, although I don't feel like I've accomplished anything today," she said.

"Believe me, I understand," I sympathized. "Some of these things just can't be helped."

Seemingly without a signal, the ladies all bent over and began to sweep the weeds and grass that had been cut, leaving bare dirt. Clouds of dust filled the stifling air. The younger women scooped piles of debris into baskets, hauled them to the river, and dumped them in.

With sixty or more women and girls working together, the project was finished within an hour or so. My face was flushed from the exertion and the heat. Patti looked as hot and tired as I felt. Dirt clung to our clothing and hair.

"Now I need to go take another shower," Patti said.

"I'm sorry I didn't let you know sooner," I told her. "I assumed that Dave and Rick had talked about it."

"Never assume anything," Patti said with a little laugh.

Dora Tenenoff coloring with some Kuna friends.

Heading in opposite directions, we each returned to our own house. I changed into my swimming suit and went to the river for a refreshing bath. Patti preferred her shower.

Rick plunged into language study. Patti guarded his time as best she could. Her own study hours were limited, because her primary job was to care for Dora.

On many occasions Dave and I were invited to lunch at Rick and Patti's house, often for pizza—the Tenenoff family's favorite meal. Their generosity was evident—Rick and Patti even shared their Pepsi with us when it was available.

Our first six months together as partners sped by quickly. Dave and I were leaving for a year of furlough. Rick and Patti would be left alone in the village. We had tried to pass along to them as much information and advice as we could. But much of missionary life is simply taking one day at a time—and there wasn't any such thing as a typical day.

• • •

One day, after we left, Rick spent an afternoon visiting with several families. He loved getting out and talking to people, and they loved having him come to their homes. His sense of humor was coming out more and more, and he faithfully attempted to use whatever Kuna phrases he had been studying. He returned home, happy and hungry.

"Something smells good," he said, walking into the kitchen. He stood behind his wife and bent over to kiss her. He complimented her on how pretty she looked in her Kuna clothes.

Leaning against the countertop, Rick took out his Day-Timer and said, "Day after tomorrow, Silvio is going to teach me how to pole a canoe. We're going to try to get together once a week for a while. I'm looking forward to it."

"It seems to me like poling would be very hard to do," Patti said. "But I'm sure it would be useful to know how."

"Let me set the table for you, honey," Rick said, always willing to help her.

Lesson day arrived quickly. Silvio, with a big smile on his face, showed up at the house. He and Rick left together for the river. They weren't alone, however. A dozen or more young boys followed excitedly—to watch Rick get his lesson.

Silvio's canoe was waiting at the river's edge. A long pole lay in the bottom of the boat. Silvio directed Rick to stand in the front end of the canoe. He showed him how to hold the eight-foot pole and explained to him how to plunge it into the water.

Rick carefully held the pole, following all of Silvio's directions.

"Now, plunge it into the water and push your weight against it," Silvio directed from the shore.

As Rick plunged the pole into the water, he felt his weight shifting and knew he was losing his balance. *My Day-Timer!* he thought, and he attempted to toss it to shore as he sailed out of the boat and into the water. He quickly retrieved his Day-Timer and got out of the river.

The boys, who had been practicing the art of poling since age five, hadn't experienced this much entertainment in their entire lives. They followed the drenched and dripping American back to his house, laughing and talking excitedly the whole way.

Rick entered through the back door by the shower so he wouldn't track water through the house. He tried to air out the pages of his precious Day-Timer.

Silvio (left), the Kuna man who gave Rick "lessons," and Rick looking at molas.

A week later, an even larger group turned out for the "lesson." Much wiser, Rick was wearing his swimming trunks and a T-shirt—and his Day-Timer was at home, sitting on his desk.

The spectators were not disappointed. The second lesson proved to be as entertaining as the first. The "lessons" also made very good fireside conversations in many huts for weeks to come.

• • •

Rick and Patti had times of discouragement, but they persevered through that long and lonely year.

We returned from furlough rested and refreshed. Sarah moved into the dorm, ready to begin her senior year of high school. We were excited to move back in to Púcuro and to get started again on language study.

Patti was expecting a baby in three months, so we all thought we would have a month in Púcuro before they went out to the city for the birth. After her doctor's appointment, however, Patti and Rick had to remain in the city, and Connie was born three weeks early. Rick and Patti returned to the village six weeks after Connie joined their family. Then, after four months in the village, they went on furlough—leaving us to work alone again, for another year.

We all began to pray that the Lord would send a third family to join our team, so that at least two couples could be working together, most of the time.

• • •

Dave and I progressed quickly in the Kuna language during that year, even though there were many interruptions to language study.

One morning, as we were studying, Dave heard a boy cry out. Quickly Dave ran to the front door. Looking out, he saw a young boy writhing on the ground. Rushing outside, he scooped him up and carried him in to our wooden couch.

He was an Emberá Indian who attended school in Púcuro and

Dave and Rick studying with Estánislau and Darío.

stayed with Tomás and Cecilia. He had been walking from the river, carrying a log over his shoulder, when the log slipped out of his hands and landed on the calf of his leg. The deep horseshoe-shaped gash was bleeding quite badly.

The house filled up with people. Tomás and Cecilia arrived.

"Someone go get Nestor," Dave said.

"Nestor is out hunting," Tomás informed him.

"Nancy," Dave said, "I need to clean and suture this cut."

"Okay," I said, entering the pantry where I kept our medical kit.

Setting down the kit on a wooden bench near Dave, I began filling a syringe with lidocaine to numb the boy's wound, while Dave cleansed the area with Betadine.

"Nahn-cee, Nahn-cee," a girl called at the back door. "We're back from the river and need help."

"The girls washed a foam mattress for me. I have to go help them put it on the clothesline," I told Dave.

"Can't it wait?" Dave asked. "Nancy, don't we have a larger-sized suture? This is not going to do."

"Maybe I do have a Tupperware container with extra supplies in it," I said. "I'll go look."

The crowd parted for me, even though we were talking in English. I hurried back into the pantry and located the container of sutures and took a medical book off the shelf, before returning to Dave and his young patient.

"Nahn-cee, Nahn-cee!" came an urgent cry from the back door, before I could assist Dave further.

I hurried to the door, where my neighbor stood.

"Hurry, come! My husband fell through the roof!" she said frantically.

"Dave," I called back over my shoulder. "Gabriel fell through the roof. I'm going to check on him."

"Good grief," Dave mumbled. "What else can happen?"

I ran over to our neighbors' hut, followed by several people who had been in our house. I found Gabriel lying in his hammock.

"Where are you hurt?" I asked him.

"My side," he said, pointing to his ribs. "I was repairing the roof," he said, pointing up. "I fell through and landed here."

"You may have broken some ribs," I told him, relieved that he was conscious. He looked pale but didn't appear to be in serious condition. "Rest until Dave can come and see you."

"Okay," he told me.

I walked back to our yard where the two girls stood with the foam mattress still across their heads, water dripping from it and from them.

"I'm sorry, girls," I said. "Here, let me help you." We struggled to wrestle the mattress over the clothesline, and in the process, water drenched me, too.

I quickened my pace and ran into the house.

"Is Gabriel okay?" Dave asked.

"He may have broken some ribs, but he's in his hammock resting. I told him you'd come to see him when you're finished here."

"I'm almost done," Dave said.

Finally, the boy's leg was stitched and the crowd left.

When Dave returned from the neighbor's house, I dished up three plates of food and handed one to our patient, who was lying on the wooden couch with one pillow under his head and another pillow under his leg. We sat down wearily and ate our meal.

Afterward, Dave went back into his study to work with his language helper.

I began clearing off the table, stacking the dishes in the sink. Then I went into the pantry to put the medical book back on the shelf. I slid it into its spot. I stopped. I pulled it out again. My eyes widened as I saw the shiny, smooth scales of a creature slithering behind the books!

I turned and got out of the pantry as fast as I could and ran into the office. "Dave, there's a *nakpe* in the pantry!" I said—in my haste, using the Kuna word for snake.

Both men jumped up from their seats.

"Where is the snake?" Chico asked in Kuna.

"In there," I said, pointing to the little room.

"Go get the machete," Dave said as he went into the pantry with Chico.

"And a stick," Chico called out.

"*¡Máchi!* (Oh boy!)" I heard Chico exclaim in Kuna.

Running back in, I handed the machete and stick to the men and left again as quickly as I could. Wanting to throw myself on the bed and cry, I paced the floor instead. *I hate snakes! I'm angry that a snake could be inside my house. It's bad enough that I've seen them in the outhouse, but inside my house! Lord, how can I live here if I'm not even safe in my own house? I hate snakes! I am never going into that pantry again.*

"Nancy, we killed it. From what I can tell, it was a coral snake. Chico said it was very poisonous, and the markings look like a coral snake to me—only it seemed lighter than the ones I've seen in pictures. We buried it. We'll check out the pantry to make sure there aren't any babies," Dave informed me.

Babies? There could be more? Lord, I am really not happy about this. I paced back and forth a few more times.

"We're through," Dave said. "It appears to be all clear."

"Appears to be?" I asked.

"Nancy, we checked it out. We took everything off the shelves and didn't find any more snakes," Dave said.

Well, I'm never going in there again, I thought, stubbornly. Feeling very miserable, I knew I had to seek God's help in order to find peace. *Lord, I'm sorry,* I prayed. *Help me through this. I want to feel safe in my own house.* Peace filled me as I realized that my safety is in God's hands—it never depended on the walls of my house. *Thank you, Lord, for your protection.*

• • •

Rick and Patti returned from furlough. We were very happy to have them back in the village with us. They were now expecting their third child.

They had been back in Púcuro for only two months, and Patti was five months along in her pregnancy, when, one morning, as Dave and I were sitting at the table eating our breakfast, a voice at the door called my name.

"Nahn-cee, Nahn-cee," a young girl's voice called out.

"Come in," I replied in Kuna.

"Ricardo sent a note," she informed me, holding up the small folded paper for me to see.

"Thank you," I said, handing the note that was in Rick's handwriting to Dave.

"It sounds like Patti is having some problems, maybe even labor pains or contractions," Dave said. "They want you to come over and see what you think. I'll go, too."

"Thank you," I told the little girl, handing her a piece of candy.

"Do you want me to take a note back?" she asked.

"No, just tell Ricardo we are on our way," I told her.

Going into the pantry, I grabbed my medical books. Coming out again I met up with Dave, who had locked the back doors. We abandoned our half-eaten breakfast, which still sat on the kitchen table, and we walked out the door.

We were both praying silently for Patti, Rick, and their unborn child as we walked quickly to their house.

"Rick," Dave called out from the front door as we entered.

"Oh, good, you're here," Rick said, coming out of the bedroom to meet us.

"Nancy, go on in," he told me.

Dave and Rick sat down in the hammocks to discuss the situation. Nearby, Dora and Connie were playing with dolls on the floor. I walked on in to Patti and Rick's bedroom where Patti was lying down.

"Patti," I said, "what's happening?"

"I've felt several very strong contractions. You know that with Dora I didn't feel any contractions, all through labor," she told me.

"I remember, you told me," I said. "I'd never heard of that before."

"With Connie I felt a few, but this morning I felt several, and they were very painful," she said. "Nancy, I'm only five months along. What should we do? Do you think this could be false labor? I just don't know what to compare it to, because I felt so little before."

"Well, let's pray and ask God for wisdom. I know Rick and Dave are out there praying, too."

"Dear Lord," I prayed, "please calm our hearts. Lord, please give us the wisdom and peace that can only come from you. We commit this precious baby into your care, Lord. Show us what we need to do. Amen."

"Patti, what are you feeling now?" I asked.

"I just feel the baby moving," she said.

"Is the baby kicking?" I asked.

"No, kind of rolling-like," she said.

"Okay, tell me every time you feel that sensation," I told her. "Where can I get a piece of paper and a pen?"

"I feel the baby now," she said. "There is paper on my desk and a pen."

Looking at my watch, I noted the time and then walked over to retrieve the pen and paper. I pulled a chair over alongside the bed and sat down, writing the time she felt the baby move.

"When did all of this begin?" I asked.

"Several hours ago. I just didn't feel very well. Then I felt a pain—I actually cried out it hurt so bad," Patti said.

Thirty minutes passed, and Patti said, "The baby is moving again." So I noted the time on my paper.

"Do you mind if I keep my hand on your stomach while we talk?" I asked.

"No, that's fine," she said.

We talked for the next half-hour. I could feel her abdomen contract again.

"Mommy, Mommy," came Dora's voice as she entered the bedroom. "Why are you in bed, Mommy? Aren't we going to have kindergarten today?"

"Mommy's not feeling very well today, Dora," Patti informed her. "You get a vacation day from school. Thank you for playing with Connie; you are being Mommy's big helper. I love you, sweetie."

"Okay, Mommy, but I'm hungry," Dora said.

"Go ask Daddy for a snack, Dora. Daddy will take care of you today," Patti said.

"Okay," Dora said, her blonde curls bouncing as she ran out of the room and down the hallway.

We talked some more. Thirty minutes later I felt another contraction.

"I'm going to go talk to Rick and Dave. I'll be right back," I said.

"How's my wife?" Rick asked nervously. "Do you think she is in labor?"

"She may be. I don't know for sure," I told him soberly.

"Her doctor gave us some medication for premature labor, just in case. He was concerned because Patti had to be in bed the last two months of her pregnancy with Connie. He knows how isolated we are here. Should we start giving her that medicine?" he asked.

"Did he tell you specifically when to give it to her? Should it be given even as a precaution?" I asked.

"I don't think he was very specific," Rick said.

"Where is it? I'd like to see what it is and read about it," I said.

"It would sure be nice to have a two-way radio right now," Rick said. "I'll go find the medicine."

"Nancy, what do you think?" Dave asked me.

"Dave, it's really hard because she doesn't actually feel the contractions. That is very unusual. But, from what I can tell, she is having contractions at thirty-minute intervals. If that keeps up regularly, she needs to go out to the city."

Returning with the medicine, Rick proceeded to read all of the side effects listed on the information sheet. I read what I could find in my medical books. The three of us prayed some more.

"What should we do?" Rick asked again.

"There were some Latino men in the village last night," Dave said. "They're heading down to Boca de Cupe. Let's ask them to telegraph the mission and have them send the plane in today."

"That's a good idea. I'll go find them," Rick said. He got up in a flash and went out the door.

"I'll go monitor Patti," I said. "She needs to go out, regardless, but if the contractions keep up this way, or get closer together, Rick will have to make a decision on the medicine."

"Hey, kiddos," Dave said to the girls, "bring me a book and I'll read to you."

"Hooray!" Dora said, running down the hall to her bedroom for some books.

Connie went over to the hammock and held out her arms for Dave to pick her up. I went back to Patti's side.

"Patti, I think that what you're feeling are contractions, not the baby moving, because they are happening at regular intervals. Rick went to give a message to some people who are going to Boca de Cupe. We've sent for the plane," I told her.

"I feel it again," Patti said.

I marked the time on my paper.

"Do you want me to read to you from your Bible?" I asked.

"Yes, that would be nice," she said.

Another hour went by. Walking out to the front room where Dave and Rick sat in hammocks and both girls sat on the floor playing with toys, I directed my question to Rick. "What do you want to do about the medicine? The contractions are closer together now, about every twenty minutes."

"The doctor gave it to us to use if we needed it. I think we should give it to her," he said.

"Okay," I said. "Why don't you go talk to Patti about it and give her the medicine? We'll just sit here with the girls for a while."

When Rick returned, I asked, "Did Patti agree about taking the medication?"

"Yes," Rick answered.

"I'll make some lunch if you want me to," I told Rick.

"That would be nice," he said.

After the meal Rick busied himself by putting the girls down for their naps, while I stacked the dishes in the sink.

"Nancy," Patti called from the bedroom.

Quickly, I walked to her room to see what she needed.

"Nancy, my heart is just racing. Could it be from the medicine?" she said.

"I'll go read about the side effects. How do you feel other than that?" I asked her.

"The same, I guess. But I really don't like the way my heart feels," she answered.

Returning to the kitchen I located the information sheet about the medicine and started reading it.

"Rick," I said, "this medicine shouldn't be given to anyone with heart problems of any kind. Does her doctor know that she has a heart murmur?"

"Yes," Rick said, "I'm sure he does."

"Maybe a heart murmur isn't considered a heart condition," I said. "I wish I were a doctor. Rick, it is really scary giving medications like this when we know so little. You have to make up your mind on this if you want to continue to give it to her. I don't know enough about it."

Returning to the bedroom, I picked up a book and started to read it out loud to Patti, to pass the time. We continued to monitor her contractions. The hours ticked by slowly. Late afternoon soon turned to evening, ending our hopes for getting Patti out to the doctor that day.

I surveyed my paper, which tracked the past four hours of contractions. They were now down to five minutes apart, even with the medication she had been given.

The evening was still and quiet. Uncharacteristically, the house was void of visitors. Rick, Dave, and I prayed together once more—committing Patti and her unborn child to God.

Returning to Patti's side, I rested my hand on her abdomen once more. Ten minutes went by—with no contractions. *Thank you, Lord.* Fifteen more minutes passed, and we had hope that the contractions had stopped, at last.

Dave said, "I've been wondering about seeing if the village would send a man over to Paya. The Panamanian police should have two or three men guarding the border, and they have a two-way radio. We could have them contact our mission pilot to see whether they received our first message, and we could request an emergency flight."

"That sounds good to me," Rick said.

"We'll go talk to the chief on our way home," Dave said. "Come and get us if Patti needs us during the night. We'll be praying that you both can sleep through the night."

"Thanks," Rick said with feeling. "I really appreciate all you've done for us."

"You're welcome, Rick," I said. "Good night."

"Dora Beth, Connie," Rick called, "it's time for bed. Let's go kiss Mommy good-night, and then I'll read you a story."

Rick raced with the children down the hall toward their bedroom, and we went out into the night.

Early the next morning we ate our breakfast quickly and returned to Rick and Patti's house. Esteban and another young Kuna man left at dawn to hike the three hours to Paya, the neighboring Kuna village, to deliver the message for us.

Rick, Dora, and Connie were sitting at the table eating cereal when we entered.

"Good morning," Dave said. "How's it going?"

"We slept pretty well, actually," Rick said, "but this morning the contractions started in again. Go on in to see her, Nancy."

"Good morning," I said to Patti, pulling the chair to the side of the bed. "How are you feeling?"

"I did better last night, but I think the contractions are back to every five minutes again. Do you think the plane will come this morning?"

"I hope so," I said. "Probably the earliest it could arrive is ten-thirty. We have been praying that you will be okay and that the plane will get here soon."

Reading a book aloud helped somewhat, but the hours still passed by slowly.

"Nance, I hear something. Is that the plane?" Patti asked.

I lowered the book and strained to hear. "I do hear something," I said.

"It sounds like a helicopter," Rick called out from the other room.

"A helicopter?" Patti said. "Did they send in a helicopter for us? Rick, did you pack clothes for the girls, too?"

"Yes, honey," Rick said. "I'm going to meet the helicopter."

Two sets of tiny feet brought the two little girls into the room. Sensing the raw nerves, they were frightened and confused.

"Mommy, Mommy," Dora said, leaning on the bed.

Connie quietly leaned her head on my lap, so I picked her up. She was so tiny for her eighteen months. Her light blonde hair was straight instead of curly like Dora's. Connie's personality was quiet and reserved, while her sister's was busy and outgoing.

Soon the house filled up with people. A man came into the room with Rick. Because of prayers, swift Kuna feet, a radio message, and, most of all, God's mercies, an emergency medical helicopter had come for Patti.

"What do you mean?" Rick asked. "You are taking all four of us, aren't you?"

"No, we are supposed to take only the patient," the man informed us.

Patti's eyes grew wide with apprehension.

"I have to go with my wife," Rick insisted.

"I guess we can take you, too," the man said, "but we cannot take your children. We are only supposed to transport the patient."

"We'll keep the girls with us, Rick," I said. "You can fly back in as soon as possible. They'll be fine. Right now, Patti needs you more."

"Okay," Rick said.

The medics put Patti on a stretcher and carried her from the house. Rick grabbed the suitcase. He hugged and kissed his girls and ran after the stretcher.

"Mommy! Daddy!" Dora cried out as she grabbed my leg.

With Connie in my arms I couldn't pick up Dora, too. So Dave scooped her into his arms and we walked outside toward the helicopter. We were each explaining to the child in our arms what was happening. We reassured them that their daddy would come back as soon as he could and take them to Panama City. In the meantime, they would get to sleep at our house.

"Wave at Daddy," I told the girls.

Dora and Connie waved their little hands at their daddy, who waved back until the helicopter was too far away for us to see him. We turned away from the soccer field and walked back to Rick and Patti's house to get the girls' things.

"Will you teach me school, Aunt Nancy? Will we have class?" Dora asked.

"Sure," I said. "You'll have to show me where your books and papers are, though. We'll take them to our house."

With two small children in our house, the next three days were very busy. Connie was happiest when she was with Dave. Often she sat on his lap, while he somehow worked at his computer. On the fourth day we heard the plane in the distance. Rick returned with news that Patti was still in the hospital. She hadn't miscarried the baby, but she wasn't out of the woods yet. She would be discharged the next day but would remain medicated and have to stay in bed, most likely for the rest of her pregnancy.

The girls were excited to have their daddy back and to go see their mommy. As the plane took off down the airstrip, we waved good-bye. We had learned that our mission had received a message the first day, but it wasn't clear to them who had requested the flight. Was it Ricardo Tenenoff, the missionary, or was it a Kuna man named Ricardo, who lived in the village of Paya? The mission plane was being repaired, and even though the pilots began working as quickly as possible, it would still take another day before they could fly in. The next day they received the message from Paya, clearing up who was requesting the flight. The second message sounded more urgent than the first, so arrangements were made for a helicopter to fly in and evacuate Patti.

Sixteen weeks later, a beautiful, healthy baby boy was born, only three weeks before his due date. Richard Lee Tenenoff II was welcomed as the newest member of their family.

• • •

Six weeks later, Rick and Patti, along with Dora, Connie, and baby Lee, returned to Púcuro. We were ready to begin again, working as a team.

Dave and I passed our final language check. We were now able to

Nanzhel holding Lee Tenenoff.

begin translating Bible lessons from the Old Testament into Kuna. Beginning with Genesis, we would build a foundation from God's Word. We wanted the Kuna people to know more about God's character before we presented the gospel to them.

Having longer periods of time in the village, Rick began to make good progress in the language. Patti was progressing, too, even though she had small children at home to care for—along with all of the visitors, as well as the cooking and cleaning. With few modern conveniences, everything took more time to accomplish.

One day Patti was sitting in her front room with some Kuna ladies. Connie and Lee were sharing their toys with several Kuna children. Dora was in first grade at the mission school, living in the dorm. The ladies were all looking outside, watching the men clean the trail near Patti's house.

"Look, Silvio has a new machete," someone commented.

"Yes, and there is Ricardo. He is still learning how to cut," said another.

"He is trying to keep up with them," another one chuckled.

"Does your husband have a new file?" one woman asked another.

"Yes, he sent money out with Ricardo, and he bought it for him in the city," she replied.

As the men cut the weeds leaving only dirt, chickens followed behind them, eating the bugs that were often dislodged along the way.

The conversation continued among the contented little group of ladies, until a strange noise made them turn their heads again toward the trail outside. It was an odd squawking sound. A headless chicken soon came into view—running and then flopping around in the dirt. Rick stood frozen, machete still in midair.

"Ricardo killed a chicken!" Bielka laughed.

"Isn't that your chicken?" one of the ladies asked her, laughing at the unusual sight.

"No," Bielka said. "Yes! It is my chicken!" she realized, her tone changing as she ran out of the door to recover the fowl.

The women all howled at her as she picked it up and stomped home to prepare it for their supper.

Rick was still standing with machete in hand, calling after Bielka, "I'm sorry. It was an accident."

Wisely, Patti went to the kitchen and prepared a peace offering for Rick to take to Bielka's house: oil, onion, garlic, and a couple pounds of rice. *At least they will have a delicious meal,* Patti thought, still chuckling at the sight.

God was blessing the ministry in Púcuro. Three nights a week, from thirty to eighty people gathered to hear Dave present Bible lessons. People were interested in knowing how God created the world. They were fascinated to learn about Adam and Eve. Noah's Ark and the Flood were of special interest, especially when Dave taught about the rainbow. According to Kuna culture, if you point at a rainbow, you will get a boil. They were amazed and relieved to know that the rainbow actually signifies God's promise that he will never again destroy the earth by a flood.

These were busy and profitable days. Dave and I spent our time translating and teaching new lessons. The church met on Sunday afternoons. We were encouraged with the work God was doing in Púcuro.

9

Decision at Daybreak

February 1, 1993

I watched as the room slowly turned from black emptiness to gray shadows. The shadows gradually gave way to the soft pinkish dawn. My eyes burned from lack of sleep, but I could wait no longer to get out of bed.

As soon as my feet touched the floor, I realized that I was not the only one. Patti and Tania were as anxious as I to end the agony of the long night. However, the dawning of this new day, or the next, or the next, or the next . . . would not end our agony.

We headed for the kitchen. Estánislau and Trigo were sitting in the front room, and I greeted and thanked them. They left.

"I need a cup of coffee!" I said. "Patti, you do have coffee, don't you?"

"Actually, I do," Patti replied. "We bring it in to give away, but we don't have a coffeepot. How about a cup of tea or some hot chocolate?"

"I guess hot chocolate will be okay," I said, trying not to sound too disappointed. I really needed a cup of coffee.

"Nahn-cee, Nahn-cee," Chico, one of the Kuna church leaders, called from outside the screen door.

"Come in," I replied. "I'm ready to go to the meeting. Has it started?"

"No. We have already talked it over and decided," Chico replied. "We have decided that we can't make the decision for you. The guerrillas told us not to leave the village. They told us not to go upriver, not to go downriver. Your husbands' lives are in danger, so we can't tell you what to do. We don't want that on our hearts. You need to tell us what you want to do."

Thank you, Lord, for this answer to prayer, I thought. I told Chico, "We want to go downriver."

"Are you sure?" he asked again. His eyes showed the weight of this decision.

"Yes," I said. "Dave told me that is what we should do."

"Dave told you?" Chico's face brightened with my words.

I was able to say that to Chico because of a conversation Dave and I had—nearly a year prior to that time. One evening, long before the Riches had moved into the village, Dave and I were sitting in our hammocks. The thought *What would I do if Dave were captured by guerrillas?* had planted itself in my mind. There wasn't any known guerrilla threat in Panama at that time. It seemed ridiculous. Yet the thought of guerrillas continued to plague me. I had to take care of it.

So I said to Dave, "Honey, I have a question for you."

"Yes?" Dave said, looking up from the book he had been reading.

"Dave, I want to know what I should do if guerrillas were to come across the border from Colombia and capture you and Rick," I told him.

Dave rolled his eyes and looked back down at his book again, saying, "Oh, Nancy, we aren't going to be captured by guerrillas."

I knew that Dave hated hypothetical questions, but I persisted.

"Honey, I'm serious," I said. "Just say, for instance, that they took you away and told us not to go downriver—and said that they would kill you if we leave the village. I don't want to have to make a decision like that. I want to know now what you would want me to do if that ever happens."

Dave put his book down again and humored me. "Nancy, I don't think that we are in any danger of being kidnapped by Colombian guerrillas. But, even if we were, I should think that we would all be captured. They wouldn't leave you wives and just take us."

"Well, if we were all captured, I wouldn't have any decisions to make. But, just say that you were taken away, but we were left behind. Then what should we do?"

"If they only took us, you would probably be forced at gunpoint to call in our mission plane. We wouldn't want our plane to fly in. They would probably confiscate the plane and kidnap the pilot, too. If you had a choice, you would have to go downriver. We wouldn't be in any more danger than if you stayed in the village," he finished and looked back down at his book.

"Thank you," I told Dave.

Am I dreaming all of this? I thought. *No, that conversation with Dave really did take place. That incident the night when we first moved into the village wasn't a dream, either. Could those "bad men" have been guerrillas, scouting the area, preparing for last night's attack? No, that was seven years ago.* My mind reeled. Then Chico's voice drew me back to the present.

"Patricia," he said, "and you? Do you have peace in your heart that you should leave and go downriver?"

"Yes," Patti said.

"Tania," Chico said, looking her way, "and you, too?"

"Yes," she answered.

"All right then," Chico declared. "It is decided. I will tell Estánislau to get the motor and canoe ready."

"Thank you, Chico," I replied with relief. "We will get ready for the trip."

"I'm gone," Chico said, leaving.

Kuna women and children had filled the house. They had heard our conversation and knew we would soon be leaving.

My heart ached as I looked into Sandra's eyes. She had just turned eleven. How close together we had grown during these past seven years. How could I leave her here? She had become my little girl, and we were as close as many a mother and daughter. I held her close and remembered how frail her little body had been when she was so ill, only two years ago.

At that time, due to government restrictions, we were without two-way radios. Sandra came to our house, her face flushed with fever. The medic was out of the village, so I took her temperature. It was well over 104 degrees. I gave her some Tylenol and put her in Sarah's bed. She stayed with us overnight so that I could monitor her.

The next day some Panamanian doctors arrived by canoe. I didn't know why they had come, but I took Sandra home and told her mother that she needed to take Sandra to the doctors while they were in the village. I feared that she was very ill.

Sandra was taken downriver with the doctors when they left, and then they flew her out to the city. She had a collapsed lung and was put into the hospital. I prayed for God to protect sweet little Sandra, who must be scared to death and feel so alone in such a strange place. She knew very little Spanish.

The public hospital in Panama City was not like our hospitals in the States. The patients needed to have relatives with them, to help. Toilet paper, towels, and washcloths were not provided. Bedpans were not brought or emptied. Sandra had no one.

She was in the hospital for three weeks before we could fly out to the city to help her. She still had a tube draining her lung, so she was bedridden. The Lord had provided some caring people who were attending their own children in the same ward. But, even so, she was very frightened and lonely.

As soon as our plane landed in Panama City, I took a taxicab to the hospital. It was hard to locate her ward, but I finally found her. When I came through the door, she cried, a rare occurrence in the Kuna culture. I ran to her and hugged her and cried with her. I stayed with her all day and told her I would come back early the next day.

The doctor wanted to keep Sandra in the hospital several more weeks, because she lived in the interior. Promising him that she could live with us for the next two months and that we would bring her back for a checkup, he finally released her into our care.

During the next few months Sandra grew healthy and strong. She went home whenever she wanted, but she ate her meals and spent the nights with us. She accepted the Lord as her Savior and learned to read the Bible in Kuna. During those months we grew to love each other very much. She wanted to be our little girl forever, and I would have liked nothing better.

"Sandra, I love you," I told her. My heart ached.

Adding to the burden of leaving Sandra was the sight of Bielka, who stood before me. Pleading with her eyes, Bielka stood holding her baby, Michelle, out to me.

Dear Lord, I prayed, *how can I leave this baby here, too*?

Two months earlier, Michelle had come into the world. Mark and Tania were alone in the village.

Dave and I were in Chame, working hard on last-minute preparations for the annual field conference. That day, however, I was in the middle of rolling a colleague's hair in perm rods. A knock came from the front door. Another missionary had driven from the mission office to deliver a message.

"Nancy," he said, "Tania radioed from Púcuro. She needs to have you or Dave radio back. It's something about a sick Kuna baby. Do you want me to wait for you, so I can drive you back to the office?"

"Yes, thank you," I replied.

Briefly explaining the situation to my friend Maria, I asked her to pray and left her sitting with a head full of curling rods.

Dave had left the house earlier, so I had to go alone. My heart was pounding and I was praying.

I radioed Púcuro. Immediately Tania answered and spilled out the events of the day. Much earlier in the morning than usual, a man had called out at their front door.

"Marcos, Marcos."

Tania explained that Mark rose from the chair at his desk where he was reading his Bible and went to unlock the screen door.

"Come in, Pablo," Mark answered.

Pablo entered and sat down. Uneasiness filled the room.

Tania handed a cup of coffee to Pablo. She, too, sensed that something wasn't right. Silence hung thick in the air.

Finally, Pablo spoke. Even though Mark was learning Kuna very rapidly, he couldn't understand everything Pablo was saying.

"Pablo," Mark said in Spanish instead of Kuna, "I don't understand what you are saying."

Pablo shifted uncomfortably in his seat—whether from embarrassment, from not knowing the Spanish words for what he needed to say, or from cultural taboos, they did not know.

In halting Spanish, Pablo continued, "My wife has given birth. Something is not right. Will Tania come and see?"

"I'll watch the girls. You'd better leave right away," Mark told Tania. "Hon, I will be praying for you."

Nine-month-old Jessica howled as her mother sat her down on the floor near Tamra, who was playing with some toys. Tania hurried outside. Two-and-a-half-year-old Tamra followed her mom to the door, pressing her little face against the screen.

Tania walked quickly to the hut with Pablo. They stepped through the doorway into the darkened hut. Her heart began to pound as she was ushered into a smaller room. A tiny baby girl lay on banana leaves in the middle of the floor, crying. *Why is she just lying there?* Tania thought. *Why doesn't someone pick her up?*

An older woman spoke rapidly in Kuna, jutting her chin toward the child. Walking closer, Tania could see the infant's cleft lip. She knelt down and picked up the shivering baby, still damp from birth. Tania asked for a cloth. She wrapped the baby, then cradled her in her arms.

Tania looked at Bielka, who had just given birth and was lying in a nearby hammock. Bielka had a hard, cold look in her eyes—she stared off into the distance. Tania wondered, *Is her culture telling her that she has to reject this baby? Is she trying to steel herself against the inevitable? Or, is her heart simply breaking for her newborn daughter?*

"Nestor told us to take her downriver to a doctor," Pablo said. Concern was etched in the lines in his face.

He loves his baby and wants her to live, but hidden fears and cultural strongholds are obviously at war with him in his heart, Tania thought with great insight.

"That is a good idea," Tania said.

"Do you have a box?" he asked.

"A box?" Tania replied.

"We need a box to take downriver," Pablo said.

"Yes, we have a box you can have."

They placed the baby in the box. They wouldn't hold her. They couldn't feed her.

Eight hours later, Pablo arrived at their door again—box in hand. The fragile cry from the dehydrated infant tore at Mark and Tania's hearts.

The helpless expression on Pablo's face spoke louder than his words.

"She can't suck. She needs an operation. Take her or she will die," he said.

Tania picked the baby up out of the box and took her into her own daughters' room. With tears streaming down her face, she tried desperately to nurse her with precious drops of nourishment from her own body. The baby could not nurse.

"Nancy, what should we do?" she asked over the radio waves.

"It's too late today for the plane to pick you up. We'll send it in tomorrow," I told her, having to make the decision without Dave. "Bring her out and Dave and I will care for her until we can figure this all out."

"She can't suck. How will we keep her alive? She is already dehydrated, and she's very tiny."

"Try putting a cotton ball into formula and squeezing that into her mouth," I told her. "There's a can of formula at our house. We will be praying for her and for you."

The following day Dave and I arrived at the small airport in Panama City to meet the mission plane. Tania handed me a four-and-a-half-pound bundle, and I immediately fell in love with this precious baby girl. Her parents had given her a name—Michelle.

For hours we drove around the city, trying to get help for Michelle. We went to the hospital, where they told us to buy a special nipple for a bottle and to bring her back in three months for surgery. Finding the nipples took three more stops at various pharmacies. Nearly another full day had gone by, feeding Michelle by dipping cotton balls in for-

Sarah with Michelle (Kuna baby with cleft lip).

mula. Finally, with the special nipple, she was able to drink several ounces of the life-sustaining liquid from a bottle.

With one radio message our life had changed. We attended field conference with a week-old baby, and we were on the conference committee—with many responsibilities.

Michelle suffered from a severe case of thrush that week, yet, in answer to our prayers, she continued to eat well. She began to flourish, quickly doubling her weight.

After Christmas, only one month ago, we had flown back into Púcuro with Michelle. The plan was to keep her with us for one more month, until her operation. We believed her parents would take her back after the surgery to repair her lip.

Bielka was at the airstrip when we landed. She looked at her daughter, asleep in my arms, and I handed the baby to her. She held Michelle, and then she said she was going to take the baby to Pablo. A few hours later Pablo and Bielka brought Michelle back to us.

But in the meantime, I felt strongly that the Lord wanted us to give the baby back to them now—to make them bond with her, even before we took her out for the operation. I told Dave what I was sensing from the Lord. He was quite surprised, but he heartily agreed.

Dave told Pablo and Bielka that we would supply formula for them, but they needed to keep Michelle with them until we left

Nancy with Michelle the day before flying back to Púcuro with her.

again for her operation. They were not happy with the situation and tried to persuade us to keep her, but we said, "No."

And now I know why, Lord, I thought.

"Bielka," I said, "I have more formula at my house, and I will leave it with you."

Tears spilled from Bielka's eyes. I could no longer look at her or Michelle. I wanted so badly to take Michelle with me.

"We are never going to see you again," wailed one of the women.

Others in the group began to sob. I looked at these ladies. Many of them hadn't become Christians yet.

"God sent us here to give you a message," I said. "Dave taught you from God's Word. He told you about Jesus dying for your sins—how he died, was buried, and rose again. You can have the new life that God is offering you, by believing in Jesus—by accepting his death on the cross for your sins. You have had the opportunity to hear the message that God wanted you to hear. Now it is up to you."

I could not leave without telling them the gospel again—that was the reason we were there in Púcuro. Only God knows whether any of them put their faith in him that day.

I forced myself to think about what we needed to do before

going downriver. *Last night, time seemed to stand still,* I thought, *and now it seems to be racing by. We have too much to do.*

Turning my attention to Tania and Patti, who were feeding the kids their breakfast, I said, "We need to get ready as quickly as possible, so we can go downriver. I've been thinking about it. We need to turn off the gas to our stoves and refrigerators and then give away the food that will spoil. Let's quickly pack the few things that we need, lock up our houses, and go. As hard as it is, I really believe that we should not allow ourselves to think about things that we want to take with us. That would slow us down too much."

"That sounds like a good plan to me," Patti said.

"Fine," said Tania. "Patti, may I leave Tamra and Jessica here with Gilbertita?"

"That will be fine," Patti said. "Connie and Lee will enjoy playing with them while I pack."

"Tania," I said, "will you be okay, going back to your house alone?"

"I'll be fine," she assured me.

Then, looking around the room, which was still crowded with women and children, she said, "I don't think any of us will be alone."

"Nancy, you haven't eaten anything," Patti said.

"I'm sorry," I told her. "I just can't eat."

Tania and I each hurried to our own homes.

With trembling hands I unlocked the front door and stepped inside. Dave's flip-flops sat underneath his hammock. My eyes welled up with tears.

Dave should be lounging in that hammock, I thought. *I cannot think about it now. I must remain focused on what I need to do.*

My house filled with neighbor ladies. Most were crying softly—such an unusual thing for the Kuna people to do.

Memo, a close friend and neighbor, was appalled at the sight of books and papers strewn all over the floor.

"Nahn-cee," she said, "I will clean it for you while you are gone."

"Thank you," I said. "Memo, will you look for any food that will spoil and take it? Divide it up however you want or keep it. I don't care. I just don't want food to spoil."

"Yes," she said as she followed me to the refrigerator.

I opened the door and told her what certain items were. "This butter won't keep. Give it to the neighbors. Use it like oil."

We moved to the pantry. "These are for Bielka's baby," I said, setting cans of formula on the countertop.

"Look in all of these buckets. Do whatever you think is best."

"I will," she said.

"Memo, I don't know how to turn off the gas! Dave always does that," I said, with my eyes filling up again with tears.

"The men know how to do that. My husband has watched Dave many times. I will have my husband do that for you," she said, her eyes welling up with tears again, too.

My tote bag was already at Patti's house. I remembered the packet of important papers that I had hidden under my pillow the night before, so I climbed the stairs and got it. Quickly, I descended the stairs again, willing myself not to look around at the mementos that I knew I would miss so badly in the days to come.

I left the house quickly, locking the door behind me. I faced Memo and handed her the keys to the house. I hugged her. Even though it wasn't a common practice for the Kuna people, I felt her hugging me back.

As I trudged back to Patti's house, the decisions of this day were pounding in my head with each throbbing beat of my heart.

10

A Time to Sow

December 1991–August 1992

Field conference rolled around again and we were in Chame, making last-minute preparations. It was always a refreshing time of fellowship with our coworkers, a time we really looked forward to. This year, we had a new family to meet.

Mark and Tania Rich were the newest members of our field. Tania's father, Tim Wyma, was a field committee member of our mission in Panama. Tim and Betty had worked in Bolivia during Tania's growing-up years, so she and Mark were new to us. At twenty-two years old, they were very young but incredibly wise, enthusiastic, and energetic.

Mark had grown up in Peru, where his parents worked as missionaries. He spoke fluent Spanish. He and Tania would be an asset to any team on our field, and nearly every mission station needed another couple to join them.

After our field conference, Tania began language study to brush up on the Spanish that she, too, had learned while growing up. Mark began developing friendships among the local people. Soon he led a young man to the Lord and began teaching him chronologically through the Bible. Mark also read aloud the Spanish *Building on Firm Foundations* chronological Bible lessons, recording audiotapes that would be a blessing to many, for years to come.

Mark and Tania's little girl, Tamra, was eighteen months old, and they were expecting their second child in four months.

Our daughter, Sarah, had graduated from high school a year and a half earlier and had spent one year living in the United States with Dave's mom, Lois. Now, back in Panama, Sarah was the secretary in our mission office in Chame. She quickly became good friends with Tania and Mark.

Soon, Mark was visiting all of the mission stations, seeking to know where God was leading them to work. Being in the last trimester of her pregnancy, Tania followed her doctor's orders not to make the trips in our small aircraft. She stayed at home and prayed for the Lord to guide Mark to the place he wanted them to work. Sarah stayed with Tania when Mark was away.

After several trips to other locations, Mark scheduled a flight to Púcuro. It was dry season, and the weather was hot and windy with no rain. Children were spearfishing in the clear river, which was lower and calmer than during rainy season.

"I hear the plane," I said to Dave.

"Yep, I do believe you're right," Dave said, pushing his chair away from his desk. "And is that chocolate cake I smell?"

"It is," I said with a smile.

"You're too good to me, sweetheart," Dave said as he kissed me. "I love you."

"I love you, too," I told him. "Invite Mark over for cake, after he gets settled in at Rick and Patti's."

"Okay," Dave said. "See you in a little while."

Later, Dave and Mark entered the house, along with several young Kuna men. Sitting down in the front room, they were all talking happily. *Mark is a "natural" with these people,* I thought. *He reminds me a lot of Chad.*

"Mark, it's good to have you here in Púcuro. Would you like a piece of chocolate cake?" I asked.

"Yes, thanks," Mark said enthusiastically.

"Mark, you remind me a lot of our son, Chad," I told him.

"I know Chad; we went to Bible school together," Mark said.

"I didn't know that," I told him.

"Yes, I've even met his grandparents. They are your dad and

mom, right? Chad rode with Tania and me down to Florida, and we dropped him off at Grandpa Jim and Grandma Jean's house on one of our breaks from Bible school," Mark informed me.

"It sure is a small world," I said. "I had no idea that you had met so much of our family."

I cut pieces of cake for everyone in the room and poured cups of coffee. Then I started cooking lunch.

Mark enjoyed the river that afternoon. In the evening we all went to the Kuna meeting house, where Dave taught a Bible lesson.

The meeting house is the largest building in Púcuro, and it sits in the center of the village. There, the Kuna hold regular town meetings, once a week. Men, women, and most of the children attend. They discuss issues such as which house needs to be repaired, they consider requests for permission to leave the village, they schedule workdays, and sometimes, they discipline a person for poor behavior. The discipline may consist of a fine or work, such as cleaning a trail.

In the town meeting, we were given permission to teach Bible lessons in the meeting house. It's a typical Kuna structure with palm-bark walls, a thatched roof, and a dirt floor. Benches line the inside walls, with more benches in rows from side to side—room to seat most of the 250 residents of Púcuro.

Dave picked up his notes and a copy of the final revision of the New Testament in Kuna. We grabbed our flashlights and walked out the door. Sandra was with us as we strolled over to Nanzhel's house and greeted her before walking on. Sandra darted into her own house as we walked by. Before we reached our destination, she had caught up with us.

The Tenenoffs arrived next, along with Mark. Soon the village people were arriving and taking their seats. Following Kuna custom, the women sat on one side and the men sat on the other. Small children wandered back and forth at will.

Rick lit a lantern and Dave began by reviewing the last lesson. Thirty-five people were sitting around the room, listening. They had a hard time answering questions about the last lesson. It was difficult to know whether they weren't understanding, they weren't remembering, or calling out answers was a foreign concept to them. We realized we still had so much to learn, and we had much more work to do to make the lessons more understandable. We knew, too, that language learning would continue as long as we were here.

Dave finished the lesson and we all stood up. Feeling stiff from sitting on the hard bench, I stretched and walked over to the group of ladies who were chatting nearby. After several more minutes of visiting, while Dave and Rick talked to some of the men, someone blew out the flame in the lantern and we walked toward the door.

"See you tomorrow," I said.

"See you tomorrow," was repeated among the ladies.

Once outside, Rick said, "Dave, would you and Nancy like to come back to our house? It's late enough that maybe we could have some time with Mark, discussing the work here, without too many visitors."

"That's a good idea," Dave said.

Dave followed Rick, who had Connie riding on his shoulders. Mark and two young Kuna men talked as they walked along. I walked next to Patti as she carried eight-month-old Lee, who had fallen asleep in the meeting.

The people who usually followed us home hesitated when we started walking off in a different direction—we had disrupted their routine.

"Old man, where are you going?" one of our neighbors called out to Dave. Most of the people had switched to calling him Tad, "old man," in the same way they called me Moo, "grandma." I'm not sure that the term seemed quite as funny to Dave when they first started using it, but now we had both grown accustomed to these endearments.

"We are going to Ricardo's house," Dave called back.

"Ah," came the voice. "See you tomorrow, then."

"See you tomorrow," Dave called back.

At Rick and Patti's house the men visited with the people who had followed them home, while Patti put Connie and Lee into bed for the night. When the conversation began to lag, the visitors took their leave.

Moving to the kitchen, we all sat around the table. The dancing shadows of the dim lantern set the mood for a nice conversation, and soon Patti joined the group.

"Does anyone want iced tea?" she asked.

"That sounds wonderful," we agreed.

"Where is the work at right now, here in Púcuro?" Mark asked. "I mean, aren't you far enough along that you don't really need a third family to join the team?"

"Actually, we have been praying for another couple to add to our team," Rick said. "We need a third family so one couple can go on furlough and we can still have two families here. There probably will still be short periods of time when one couple is alone, but hopefully those times would be few and far between. It is very difficult to work without partners, and there is plenty of work for three families to share."

"Mark, one thing that I've learned," Dave said, "is that church planting is a long-term job. The work here in Púcuro was actually begun in the seventies."

"Oh, really?" Mark said. "I didn't know that."

"Yes, two missionary families moved in then. They built two houses, ours and one that has since been torn down. At that time, the village was in quite a turmoil.

"A Latino man had come into the village several years earlier. He was very forceful and strong-willed. He fit right in with the Kuna system of intimidation. He became a leader, of sorts. Then he started his own little harem, devastating the Kuna culture and way of life. Apparently, he had "wives" and children many places in the Darién. After several years he was killed by a man in a town downriver.

"Shortly after he died, the first missionaries came to Púcuro on a survey trip of the area. The village invited them to come and live here. Some of the Kuna men spoke limited Spanish. The two missionary families had such a heart for people's souls that they began to preach in Spanish.

"I can't remember how long the families stayed here, but they had a small group of people who were really interested in God and the Bible. They held church meetings and really helped the people with medical needs. Eventually, however, they left Púcuro."

"Jim and Polly Brown moved in next," Rick said.

"I remember hearing a lot of the Browns' stories from their time in here," Patti said. "They have such a gift for hospitality, and they sure were able to use that in here."

"Jim and Polly lived in the village for three years, I think," Rick said.

"They were without partners, weren't they?" Patti asked.

"I believe that sometime in their last year is when the Simmonses joined them," Dave said.

"At one point, Jim was really sick. I think it was kidney stones," Rick said.

"I remember Polly telling us that Nanzhel was so upset because Jim and Polly had helped them so much—she wanted desperately to do something for Jim," Patti said.

"Praise the Lord, they were able to go out to the city and get medical attention," Rick said. "They came back, though. And after a while Brian and Candy joined them."

"Then the mission desperately needed another set of dorm parents, so Jim and Polly left Púcuro to fill that need," Dave said.

"Brian and Candy were the first missionaries in Púcuro who learned the Kuna language. They taught through several New Testament books and had a good ministry here in the village. Then, six and a half years ago, we came," Dave said.

"Wow!" exclaimed Mark. "That is quite the history of missionaries for one little village. How do you think all of this has affected the people here?"

"Every missionary who lived here had an effect on the village. There were many personalities and a lot of love shown to these people," Dave said.

"We are committed to learning their language and their culture so that we can present the gospel to them in a way that they can fully understand," Dave continued. "Unfortunately, a lot of things need to be retaught. Because they misunderstood some of the teaching that was done in Spanish, they took what they thought was being said and mixed it with their own belief system. The resulting syncretism is a very works-oriented religion. I'm afraid they didn't really understand that the only way to be accepted by God is through faith in Jesus Christ and his finished work for us on the cross."

"I can see where that could have happened easily, because their Spanish is very limited," Mark said. "Considering those I've talked to, it seems that they would have a difficult time fully understanding biblical concepts taught in Spanish."

"At this point we are in phase one of the chronological teaching, in their own language. In this phase, we acquaint them with God's character and man's need for a Savior. Then we present Jesus Christ as the only Savior from Satan, sin, and death. We want them to hear the gospel clearly before we go on to teach them how believers should live, in the power of the Holy Spirit. We have so much more to tell them, but we want this first part to be clear, so we can build on Christ as the only foundation. To fully equip the church, we hope to teach nine more phases. Twenty-five or so believers attend church.

"Keith and Wilma Forster, who are Wycliffe missionaries, have completed the final draft of the New Testament in Kuna. They are in the final process of editing it. In fact, they have scheduled a trip to come in soon. They plan to read it through with various people and to revise it as needed.

"We need to begin a literacy program, to teach the people here how to read in their own language," Rick said. "The village has an elementary school, first through sixth grades. The classes are in Spanish. This younger generation is learning to read, and they should be able to switch to reading Kuna fairly easily. However, most of their parents and grandparents cannot read at all. The adults could really benefit from literacy classes. We want them to be able to read their New Testament in Kuna."

Dave said, "Along with language study, Rick is updating the Kuna dictionary and compiling into our culture file the information that we each gather. And with her language study, Patti is eliciting information to add to our genealogy file. She also transcribes stories that could be used later for primers. Nancy is doing text analysis. And she is making recordings of the chronological Bible lessons, reading them aloud herself, in Kuna, so people can listen to the tapes in their homes. At Nanzhel's house, Nancy has a special class, teaching the older women who have a hard time getting to the meetings. She is helping me with the lessons, too. I am translating lessons and teaching them three times a week. Soon Rick will be far enough along in the language that he will begin to share the teaching responsibilities with me.

"It will probably be another ten years before we have a functioning church. Then we will begin to phase out, eventually leaving the Kuna church in the hands of their own capable elders," Dave said.

"Having at least two families in here most of the time could speed up the process, and it certainly would make it easier on all of us," Dave continued. "We would love to have you and Tania join us, if this is where you believe God wants you. We will be praying for you, that God will direct you unmistakably where he wants you to go. I believe you would be a great asset here, but you would be an asset at any of our stations. I want you to go where God wants you to be."

The next day we all gathered again for a church meeting.

"We are meeting at Nanzhel's house," Rick told Mark as they walked along the trail.

"Do you always meet there, or do you go to different homes?" Mark asked.

"We have been gathering at Nanzhel's house since she injured her hip and hasn't been able to walk," Rick said.

"Nanzhel," Rick called out at the door to her hut, "we're here."

"Come in," Nanzhel said from her hammock. "Sit down."

Pointing to some benches next to where Dave and I were sitting, Tomás indicated where they should sit down.

Tomás's wife, Cecilia, gathered their three children and headed out the door. "I'm gone," she said. Cecilia—who was either being pressured by her parents or was still resisting the gospel in her own heart—walked toward her parents' house, where she would stay until the church meeting was over.

Chico arrived next, carrying a Spanish Bible and a copy of the final draft of the Kuna New Testament. Close behind him, his wife and their four small children entered the little hut. Tomás carried another bench inside and set it nearby.

"Good afternoon," Estánislau said to Nanzhel as he entered. As they came in behind him, his five daughters and one of his sons began greeting people. Sandra immediately came to my side with little Esther. I picked up Esther and she contentedly sat on my lap, while Sandra squeezed onto the bench with me.

Estánislau and his wife, Mambo, with some of their children: Alejandrita, Sandra, Esther, Candi, and Estánislauito.

Darío, Chipu, and a few other young men straggled in last.

"Let's pray," Chico said, bowing his head and praying a long prayer in Kuna.

Afterward, Darío, a young Kuna man who had translated some Christian songs from Spanish into Kuna, began to play his guitar.

Sandra dressed up for church.

I handed the song sheets to Sandra, and she quickly got up and passed them out.

Darío began playing "When the Roll Is Called up Yonder." Children and young adults who could either read or had the words memorized sang along. Older people sang a few words behind everyone else. Thankful that God loves to hear the joyful noise we make, because it is from our hearts, we went through most of the nine songs that had been translated in Kuna. We ended with "Jesus Loves Me."

Darío's and Chico's Spanish abilities appeared to be the best in the village.

Chico began teaching us from God's Word. To prepare his message, he had laboriously studied Scripture in his Spanish Bible. Then he read the same verses in the latest revision of the Kuna Bible. He preached a message to us in Kuna. Chico had taken over the preaching when we went on furlough. We were all very excited that the Kuna New Testament would be completed soon. In the meantime, we appreciated the few draft copies that we had.

A chicken walked in the door and was shooed out again by some of the children. Chico continued talking, seemingly oblivious to the minor disruption.

If Nanzhel didn't understand all that Chico was saying, she would call out questions, and Chico would attempt to clarify things for her.

A dog ambled in and Nanzhel threw her sandal at him. He scurried back out the door with his tail tucked between his legs. My mind began to wander from the Kuna words that I was trying so hard to concentrate on. I looked over at Mark, who was surveying the small gathering. Sandra was fanning us with the small home-made fan I brought. Even though the late afternoon sun began to recede in the western sky, the heat was still oppressive. Men and women alike were fanning themselves as they listened to Chico.

Almost an hour later the meeting ended with another prayer, this time from Estánislau. Standing to our feet, we bade our farewells to Nanzhel and left.

Mark's days in Púcuro went by very quickly for all of us. All too soon the plane was landing again, to take Mark back to Chame.

In Chame, Mark walked through the door to greet his wife. Tania took one look at him and knew that they would be joining the Púcuro work. That gleam in his eye had not been present when he returned from any of his other trips.

They prayed for God's will in the matter and realized that he had already confirmed in their hearts where he wanted them. So, soon after he returned from Púcuro, Mark and Tania met with the field leadership and told them they believed that God was directing them to join the Púcuro team.

Tania's father, Tim, spoke for the whole committee at that meeting, saying, "Mark and Tania, we want you to know that God has been confirming to our hearts, also, that you join the Púcuro team. We want you to be aware that there will be times in the future when things get hard—they do in every work. Opposition and hard times will come, so now is the time for you to make sure in your own hearts that the Lord is the One who wants you on this team. Knowing clearly that God wants you to be there is what you will need to look back on, when times get tough."

Shortly afterward, Jessica was born into the Rich family. Tania finished the language study course, and then they began the process of planning for their move to Púcuro.

Mark and Tania happily agreed to move into our house, instead of building another home that size in Púcuro. Because of the translation work we were involved in, we decided to build a small house on the outskirts of the village, allowing us a little more isolation and, hopefully, a little less interruption.

Once more the building process began. We again hired woodcutters from Colombia to cut the lumber for our thirty-by-eighteen-foot house with its small loft bedroom.

Tania and the girls went to the United States for her two sisters' weddings, while Mark flew to Púcuro to live with us and help us build our house. Four friends from a church in Panama City flew in for four days to help frame in the house. The hard work was overshadowed by the wonderful fellowship we all shared together.

Dave's post and beam fit together beautifully.

Dave enjoyed the building process, especially the day the main beam was raised. From the hand-hewn lumber, Dave had chosen the two-by-eight-foot girder with care. He planed it by hand and then laboriously hand-sanded it. It was a beauty. The moment arrived when the notched posts would be fitted into the beam. The usual audience of men stood by. Earlier, they had watched Dave measure and notch the posts carefully. The beam was raised—everyone seemed to hold their breath. The posts were lifted up to the beam. Silently and easily the wood slid perfectly into the notches. "Ahhh . . . " A collective gasp of awe escaped from each of the amazed and impressed onlookers. The hours of labor and the long nights with aching muscles were well worth it—especially in that one moment.

Even though much work remained to be done on the inside of our house, we were very thankful to have the frame, screen, and roof completed.

Dave turned his attention to getting our old house ready for Mark and Tania. He decided, with Mark's and Rick's help, to build a shower and make provision for an inside bathroom (which could be added later) on the back porch of the house that would soon be Mark and Tania's. The old shower was badly in need of repair, and an inside toilet would be a wonderful addition for the young family—and a first for the village of Púcuro.

Forming a new bucket brigade, a group of girls smiled and giggled as they went to the river for small pebbles. Rick and Mark began to mix cement. When they had mixed it sufficiently, they shoveled it into the forms Dave had made. He troweled it smoothly into place. Next came the pebbles—Dave's idea for a surface that wouldn't be too slippery. The bucket brigade handed their buckets to Dave, who poured the small pebbles on top and troweled them in.

Rick and Mark were mixing another batch of cement for the rest of the floor area.

Leaning on the frame of the porch, totally absorbed in watching them, Dave smiled and asked, "Isn't this fun, guys?" He was enjoying the project immensely.

Two hot, red faces dripping with sweat scowled up at him, contemplating handing over their shovels. But they had to laugh at his hurt look, and they continued mixing cement until the project was finished.

The plane arrived, bringing Wycliffe missionaries Keith and Wilma Forster and their son, Steven. Keith was ready to do the final check on the Kuna New Testament that he had translated.

Dave set up a place where various Kuna men could come in to hear Keith read the New Testament to them. This way, Keith could check for understanding and make any corrections that were needed. Wilma and I made extra iced tea and snacks to serve the men while they worked.

Keith spent hours reading aloud. Wiping the sweat from his

brow periodically and drinking tea or iced water, Keith looked encouraged.

"Do you understand? Is it clear to you?" he would ask.

"Yes, it is very clear. It is very good. The words make sense to me," were some of the encouraging replies. A cross section of people were asked to participate, in order to ensure accuracy. Sometimes the Kuna men would add a word or change a word that would make more sense to them. At those times a discussion would ensue, until they were all satisfied that the proper meaning was being conveyed. It was a long and tedious process but with a very encouraging outcome.

"Wilma," I said one day, "would you go to Nanzhel's with me? I've been trying to get her to walk with the crutches Dave made for her. I took her out to the hospital and they said her hip wasn't broken, but she still can't walk very far. Since you are a nurse, maybe you could teach us some exercises that would strengthen her legs again."

"I'll be glad to help," Wilma said.

Even though we had to walk only a short distance to Nanzhel's house, we still gathered a crowd of women. We all entered the tiny hut.

"Nanzhel," I said, "how are you feeling today?"

"No different," she replied. "Sit down."

"Nanzhel," I said, "Wilma wants to show you some exercises that may strengthen your leg."

"Okay," she said.

After the exercises Nanzhel stood up with the crutches and walked a few steps to the end of the room.

"Nanzhel," I said, "walk with us out to the coconut tree and back. It will be good exercise for you."

"No," she said, sitting down in her hammock.

"Nanzhel," I said, "every day I ask you to walk with me to that coconut tree. I really think you can do it."

"No!" she said again adamantly.

I couldn't believe my ears when I heard the Kuna women whispering together in the background.

"Nahn-cee is going to get Nanzhel killed," one woman said.

"What are you talking about?" I asked incredulously.

"Nahn-cee," another woman said, "look at that tree. The coconuts are ripe. If Nanzhel walked over to that tree, she couldn't move fast enough to get away if one started to fall!"

I laughed. "Nanzhel, why didn't you just tell me that? You know I'm a dumb American. I never look up at the trees."

Everyone laughed heartily, agreeing with my last statement.

"Okay, Nanzhel," I said. "Will you try to walk halfway to Isabelita's house?"

"Okay," she said, standing up from the hammock.

She walked successfully to the designated spot and back again.

Wilma and I went back to my house, still laughing.

"The hospital that you took Nanzhel to did take x-rays, didn't they?" Wilma asked.

"Yes, and they said her hip wasn't broken. Nanzhel was so glad to leave there, I don't think she cared whether her hip was broken or not. It was quite an experience," I said. "It seems that some days she can walk pretty well, and then other days she can't walk at all."

"She may need a hip joint replacement," Wilma said.

"She told me she never intends to go back there—she'd rather stay right here in her village and live out her days the way she is," I told Wilma.

"What happened in Panama City?" Wilma asked.

"An ambulance met us at the airstrip and took us to the public hospital. They took Nanzhel into the emergency room and told me I couldn't go in. My Spanish is pretty pathetic, since I speak only Kuna here, but Nanzhel doesn't speak any Spanish at all. I stood at the door, praying for her, knowing it would be a very frightening experience. A few seconds later the man who told me I couldn't come in rushed back out and told me to get in there; they couldn't communicate with her.

"The emergency room had ten or twelve beds, all filled with sick or hurt people. I answered the questions for the nurse who wrote up Nanzhel's chart. She told us that someone would come in and take her to the x-ray department. It was very hot in the room, so I fanned Nanzhel with a small homemade fan she brought with her.

"Every time something unusual was happening, I found myself fanning her more rapidly. Nanzhel kept asking, 'What's happening? What is that noise? What's wrong with him?' I tried to answer her questions.

"The man in the bed next to us went into cardiac arrest. It was just like in the movies. A doctor with paddles in his hands yelled, 'Clear!' I felt trapped, trying to stand free from the metal rails of his bed and get as close to Nanzhel's bed as I could.

"Next, a woman was brought in on a stretcher, but she was dead. Rigor mortis had already set in, and the doctor was exclaiming about how many hours they must have waited before calling an ambulance. It was scary for me, but I can't imagine how Nanzhel felt.

"Finally she was taken to get an x-ray. Her bed was rolled outside, across the street, and into another building. I walked behind her. She kept asking, 'Nahn-cee, are you still there?' I told her, 'Yes,' that I would stay with her as long as they would allow me to.

"In the next building a blind man with a cane almost ran into her bed while she was waiting in the hallway. She asked, 'What is wrong with him?' I told her that he was blind.

"Another man had his neck in traction. It all looked very strange to both of us. Then some men rolled her into the x-ray room. When I tried to follow, a man said, 'No! You wait here.' A few seconds later the same man rushed back out and looked around anxiously for me. Spotting me, he said, 'Come in here; she can't talk to us.'

"We were taken back to the emergency room and waited there for several more hours. Ricardo, your language helper, arrived then. What a blessing he was. Nanzhel was so glad to see him.

"Finally, a doctor came and looked at her x-rays. He said her hip wasn't broken, and he released her from the hospital.

"Ricardo hailed a taxi for us, picked up Nanzhel in his arms, and put her into the cab. We went to the guesthouse for the night. The next day we flew back here.

"Quite a few months have passed since then. Dave asked her whether she would like to go back out—not to the hospital, but to a different doctor. But she refused. She would rather die right here in her own village, even if she never walks again. Poor thing," I said.

The day arrived for the plane to come in. Mark was returning to Panama City to meet Tania and the girls, who were arriving from the States. Soon their whole family would return—moving in with us until our house was finished.

Keith, Wilma, and Steven flew out on the same flight.

• • •

Another death occurred in Púcuro. Wailing could be heard throughout the village. The family prepared the customary farewell meal and served it to the entire village. We joined them for the meal. Afterward, the tiny coffin of the eighteen-month-old was taken across the river and carried to the cemetery.

While walking to the grave site with the child's mother, who is a Christian, I was able to remind her that she would someday see her little boy again in heaven. I told her that he was not alone right now, but he was with God.

She squared her little shoulders and walked on—she stopped her wailing. At the grave site she asked Dave to pray.

What a difference we were witnessing between this funeral and the first! There was sorrow, yes, and there was wailing. But in the village of Púcuro we were witnessing a change. God's message of eternal life through Jesus Christ our Lord had brought new life and hope to those who believed. Light was shining in the darkness—in the hearts of people who live in the midst of the dense rain forests of Panama.

11

Daylight—the Harsh Reality

February 1, 1993

I continued to walk quickly to Patti's house—followed by all of the ladies and children who had accompanied me to my house. As I climbed the steps and entered Patti's door, I saw Tania coming, too.

Patti had packed two small suitcases and placed them inside the door. Tania entered and picked up Jessica. I went into the guest room and grabbed the overnight bag that I had brought with me the night before, and then we left the house. Patti locked the door behind her.

Ladies and girls carried our things for us, and we all began to move—in one large group—toward the riverbank. After only a few steps, however, the former chief's wife came running up to us.

"You can't go! You can't leave!" she said in near panic.

We all stopped in our tracks.

"There are bad men, just outside the village, downriver a little way. They might capture you, too!" she exclaimed again.

Tania looked at me and asked, "What did she say?"

"She said the guerrillas are downriver and might capture us, too," I translated for her.

Tania, Patti, and I looked anxiously at each other. The peace that I had felt a few seconds earlier had vanished. Fear gripped me, and my stomach tightened into a knot.

Patti said, "Let's pray."

We huddled together and bowed our heads.

Patti prayed, "Lord, please give us wisdom to know what to do. Help us, Lord; we're afraid. Amen."

"We need to find one of the Christians," I said.

The group of ladies parted to allow me to pass through. I spotted Chico standing nearby, and I walked toward him.

"Chico," I said, "Arturo's wife says there are guerrillas downriver. She says we shouldn't go on. What should we do?"

"Guerrillas had the village surrounded last night," he said. "Some of them went across the river with your husbands, and the rest stayed here. In the middle of the night another group of them crossed the river—we heard all of the dogs barking. This morning at dawn the rest of the group left the village. I don't think any of them are downriver. They all crossed and went upriver toward Colombia. It is daylight now, anyway, so even if a small group is there and sees you leaving, I think they will just fire a warning shot in the air and make you turn around and come back. In the daylight I don't think they would shoot you. It is safe for you to go."

I went back to Tania and Patti and told them it was safe for us to go. Amazingly, a sense of peace and calm filled our hearts again as we headed toward the canoe at the edge of the river.

Reaching the center of the village, however, I remembered Nanzhel. Since she had hurt her hip a year ago, she could walk only with the crutches that Dave had made for her. She barely managed to make her way to and from the river to bathe. I had to go and tell her good-bye. I just couldn't leave without telling my dear friend Nanzhel good-bye.

I broke off from the group and called over my shoulder, "Go on ahead without me. I am going to tell Nanzhel good-bye. I'll meet you at the river."

Walking as quickly as I could, I reached Nanzhel's hut.

"Nanzhel, I'm here," I said, entering the familiar doorway.

Nanzhel sat in her hammock. The lines in her weathered face appeared even deeper this morning. Her head hung down.

"You are leaving us," she whispered sadly. "I will never see you again."

"No, we may never see each other here again, Nanzhel," I replied. "But I will see you one day in heaven, my good friend. I love you."

I hugged her frail shoulders and left. At the doorway I turned, for one last look.

"See you later," I said.

I hurried down the path toward the river. Kuna men and women lined the bank. Estánislau sat in the back of the canoe, ready to run the motor. Chino, one of Tito's sons, sat in the front. Patti was in the next seat with Connie and Lee. Tania and Gilbertita were sitting in the middle with Tamra and Jessica. I stepped in near the back and sat down.

"Wait!" called out a Kuna lady.

She was wearing a wraparound skirt over a work dress, so she took off her skirt and draped it over Tania's blonde head.

"Cover the girls, too," she said. "You look too American!"

Then Patti and I were handed skirts from other dear, precious women who loved us so much. We, too, covered our heads. Knowing how important their skirts are to them, and how hard to come by, their thoughtfulness meant all the more to us.

The memory of a dream I'd once had filled my head instantly. I had dreamed that Dave had been captured by guerrillas. I had to escape downriver in a canoe. I painted my face and arms with a dye that the Kuna sometimes use to paint themselves with. And I covered my head with one of their skirts and fled the village.

I shivered. *Lord, have you been trying to warn me? Could I have done something to prevent this?* Yet, I knew we could not, based on a feeling or a dream, have left the ministry God had called us to.

Chino plunged his pole into the water and pushed off into the current. We waved good-bye to the sad crowd at the bank and silently floated downstream.

Large trees lined the banks. Because the river snakes back and forth, the view ahead was usually blocked. An unspoken thought hung heavily in the air: *Could guerrillas be around the next bend?* And yet, paradoxically, we were floating along peacefully. Four children—children three years old and under—sat quietly, without making a sound. Occasionally, a bird swooped down for a fish, and turtles' heads ducked down under the water as we passed. Water rushing swiftly along sounded so peaceful, but inwardly a war was raging in each of our hearts.

After about twenty minutes, Stan and Chino poled the canoe to the bank of the river and Stan stepped out. He looked around the ground and then he climbed back into the canoe.

"Estánislau," I said, "what were you doing?"

"Looking for footprints," he informed me. "I see only our people's footprints. The guerrillas haven't been here."

I passed the news along to Tania and Patti.

Tania then asked him in Spanish, "How do you know that the footprints you saw are Kuna footprints?"

"Because we don't wear boots," Estánislau called back to her as he started the motor and dropped the propeller into the water.

Tania began laughing at herself. Her laughter turned into crying—and her crying gave way to sobs.

Lord, you gave Mark to me, Tania's mind battled with God. *He is my husband and I need him. You have to bring Mark back to me, Lord. You have to!*

Her heart and mind battled with the Lord until she finally gave up her own will and was able to pray, *Okay, Lord. I know that you are God. I know that Mark is yours and you can do whatever you want with him. Your ways are perfect, even if I can't understand them. I give Mark to you, Lord. Amen.*

Watching Tania's body heave with sobs was more than my strong resolve could handle, and I quickly joined her in tears. In my own mind, I began to fight the same battle with the Lord, for my own dear husband and for Mark and Rick.

Finally, our tears were spent. Our energy was gone. We sat numbly, listening to the drone of the motor.

I looked toward the front of the canoe, at Patti, Connie, and Lee. Fortunately, they had been oblivious to our tears. For the sake of her children, Patti had locked the pain and raging battle inside her heart.

Two hours passed slowly. The sun was beating down on our heads.

We had long since removed the coverings. I licked my dry lips, wishing I had thought to bring some water. My stomach growled. *I didn't eat any breakfast,* I thought, *but food still doesn't sound very good to me.*

The Púcuro River ended, spilling out into the Tuíra River. We veered toward the right and headed for Boca de Cupe. It wouldn't be long now.

My mind began formulating a plan of what we should do when we arrived at the little town.

Buildings came into view on the left-hand shoreline. Estánislau expertly guided the canoe toward the cement stairs and turned off the motor.

Chino hopped out and tied the canoe to a post. At my end, Stan stepped out and took my hand to steady me. Tania and Patti began handing their children out, one by one, and soon we were all walking up the cement steps to the small outpost.

We stopped at the top of the stairs.

"Patti, will you and Gilbertita take the children to the bathroom and buy us all some soft drinks? The water here is not good to drink. Tania and I will go to the telegraph office and get a message to the mission in Chame for our plane to pick us up in El Reál. Meet us at the telegraph office," I told Patti.

"Where is the telegraph office?" Patti asked.

"To the right, down this sidewalk—it's that little building there on the left-hand side. Can you see it?" I asked.

"Yes, I see it. We'll meet you there," she said.

"Tania, let's go to the telegraph office. I've never done this before. I'm glad your Spanish is better than mine," I said.

Walking into the telegraph office, we felt very conspicuous. I let Tania do the talking.

"We need to get a message to our office in Chame," Tania said.

"Do you have the phone number?" the man asked.

Tania told him the number and we exchanged quizzical glances. *Surely there aren't any telephones out here,* we both thought.

Picking up a microphone in one hand, the clerk spoke into it. From a speaker came the sound of a telephone ringing at the other end. The microphone was shoved toward me. *Please, Lord, let Bryan Coupland* [the field chairman] *be in the office today. Please, Lord, don't let Sarah answer the phone.* (Sarah had graduated from high school two years earlier. After living in the States for a year, she had returned to Panama and was a secretary in our mission's office in Chame.)

"Hello," came the voice of the other secretary in our office.

Crackling and static prevented my answer from being heard at the other end.

"Hello," she said again. "I can't hear you . . ."

More static prevented me from hearing the rest of her sentence.

"This is Nancy Mankins. I need to talk to Bryan Coupland," I repeated.

"Nancy Mankins?" the voice questioned.

Then, "Hello, this is Sarah Mankins. I'm Nancy's daughter. I could take a message for her."

"Sarah, this is your mom. Sarah, your dad . . ." My voice cracked. I could not go on.

I handed the microphone to Tania.

" . . . Mark, and Rick were captured by Colombian guerrillas. We need the airplane to meet us in El Reál in three and a half hours. Tell Bryan Coupland and the pilot. Have the plane meet us in El Reál. Do you understand?" she finished for me.

"Did I hear you correctly?" Sarah asked, confused because she thought she had heard my voice, but then she heard Tania's, confused because she didn't know if all three men had been captured. "My dad, Mark, and Rick have all been captured by Colombian guerrillas, and you need the airplane in El Reál in three hours?"

"Yes," Tania said. "And tell Bryan Coupland."

"Okay," Sarah said. "I will."

"Good-bye," Tania said.

"Good-bye," Sarah repeated.

I had not dissolved in tears. I was afraid to lose control of my emotions, because I knew it wouldn't be just a few tears. I found myself sitting in a chair that must have been offered to me. Tania was sitting in another chair by my side.

"Here," the clerk said again in Spanish, shoving the microphone back into Tania's hands. "This is the U.S. Embassy. It is too dangerous for you to go on. Tell them you are U.S. citizens and you need a helicopter."

Tania explained our plight to the man who answered the call at the U.S. Embassy. He asked what had happened, and then he told her he would be working on it. He asked her to call back in an hour.

"Tania, I guess we'd better call the office back now and let them know we may not need the plane. But make sure to tell them that it isn't for sure whether the helicopter will come and pick us up," I said.

Tania made the second call to our mission office.

Looking around the small room, we realized it had filled up with curious people. An uneasiness settled in our hearts—a feeling of not knowing who were our friends and who were our enemies. An hour—it seemed like an eternity to wait.

Patti, Gilbertita, and the children entered the crowded room. "I hope Pepsi is okay. I forgot to ask what kind of sodas you wanted," Patti said, handing each of us an ice-cold drink.

"Thank you," Tania said.

"Thanks," I said. "Patti, we talked to Sarah in Chame. She's calling the pilot. But we've also talked to the U.S. Embassy and we asked them to bring a helicopter in to pick us up."

"The U.S. Embassy? A helicopter?" Patti asked.

"It's a long story. These people here all know what's happening now, so the clerk thought we would be safer going out by helicopter. It just happened. He called them without asking—he just handed the microphone to Tania. She talked to them, and they told us to wait and call back in an hour."

"An hour?" Patti asked, echoing our feelings exactly.

The large round clock on the dirty, cracked cement wall ticked off the minutes laboriously. I couldn't tolerate sitting there any longer.

"Tania, Patti," I said, "I know some Christians here. I'm going to go visit one of them. I'll be back soon."

I walked out of the door and into the noonday sun. All eyes were on me as I walked through the small town to a little house on the next block.

"Maria," I called out at the structure that was little more than a shack.

"Nahn-cee!" exclaimed the thin black woman coming to the door. "Where is Dah-veed?" she asked, looking around. "Come in, come in."

"Oh, Maria," I said, searching for the words I needed in Spanish. "David, Marcos, and Ricardo have been captured by guerrillas."

"I will pray for you. I will have all of our brothers and sisters in Christ pray for you. I am so sorry," she said with compassion.

We visited for a while, and then I bade her farewell and walked back to the telegraph office.

At last it was time to call back the embassy. With microphone in hand, Tania conversed with the man from the embassy. Again we heard the words, "We're working on it. Call us back in an hour."

My shoulders drooped. *Dear Lord,* I prayed. *What do you want us to do? We're hungry and tired. Should we have called the embassy? How long do we continue to wait? Help us, Lord.*

"Nahn-cee," a lady's voice brought me out of my silent prayer.

"Yes," I said, standing up and shaking her outstretched hand.

"I'm Lydia," she said. "Your husband, Dah-veed, preached to us on some trips he made here. Come and eat dinner with us. I have fixed some rice and fish. Come, eat."

"Thank you," I said, relieved to do something—anything but listen to the clock ticking away the minutes.

"We have three Kuna people with us," I told her. "There are six of us, plus four children. That is a lot of people to feed."

"No, come," she said.

I walked out behind Lydia as Tania and Patti gathered their children and followed. "Estánislau," I said, "we are going to Lydia's house to eat dinner. Come with us." Stan and Chino fell into step. Our large group followed this kind lady to her house.

Tamra and Connie were so hungry that they, uncharacteristically, began eating before we prayed. Tania and Patti took hold of their little hands as we all stood in a circle around the table and prayed. It was a long prayer. This dear Christian woman, who was so concerned about our husbands' welfare, prayed earnestly for them and for us. We dished up our own plates and sat down to eat the meal.

"Patti, Tania," I said in English when our hostess left the room, "I've been thinking. When this hour is up and we call back again, we really don't have any more time to wait. If the embassy can't pick us up in a helicopter and our plane still needs to come, we have to leave here soon in order to get to El Reál and fly to Panama City before the sun sets." (Small airplanes in Panama must land by sunset.)

"What should I say?" Tania asked.

"When you talk to them again, if they tell you to call back in an hour, tell them we can't. Tell them we'll have our mission plane pick us up in El Reál," I said with more peace than I'd felt for the last two hours.

"Okay," Tania agreed.

"What time is it?" Patti asked.

"I hate not having a watch," I said. "I can't tell you how many times I have looked at my wrist. Every time I see my watch gone, I feel a stab of pain in my heart, remembering last night."

"We have fifteen more minutes," Tania said.

"Let's all go to the bathroom so we'll be ready to get back into the canoe after the call, in case they still don't have an answer for us."

We gathered the children again and took them to the outhouse. We were all very glad to have something to do.

"Thank you so much, Lydia," I said. "Good-bye."

"Good-bye, sister," she said. "God bless you all. God bless you. I will pray for you."

Walking back to the telegraph office didn't seem as difficult, knowing we had another plan of action. Once again we entered the now-familiar structure.

"We are ready to call again," Tania informed the clerk.

"Here," the man said, handing the microphone to her again.

I looked around the crowded room. Many of the faces appeared to be lined with concern for us.

"Never mind," Tania was saying into the microphone. "We don't want the helicopter anymore. We are now leaving here and going to El Reál. We will have our mission plane pick us up there."

"I thought you told us you were in danger," came the voice at the other end.

"We *are* in danger," Tania said in frustration. "But we feel that it would be more dangerous for us to be stranded here in Boca de Cupe all night long than to travel on the river and have our plane pick us up." (We would learn in the days to come that many caring people had tried desperately to get permission to send a helicopter to pick us up. It was, however, out of their hands. A political power struggle prevailed.)

The conversation ended. The three of us looked at each other, all of us realizing at the same time that we needed to contact our mission office again.

Our plane would meet us in El Reál in three and a half hours. We were in the canoe again. The motor hummed along as Boca de Cupe disappeared from sight.

Once more, my heart felt peaceful. I knew that we should be on this river, and it felt good to be traveling again. Glancing toward the front of the boat, I saw that all four children were sound asleep. *How I wish I could curl up and sleep, too,* I thought. I felt weighed down with exhaustion. My eyes felt gritty and dry from lack of sleep. My mind moved in slow motion, yet in fast forward, all at once—as though I were entering a time warp. *Perhaps,* I thought, *perhaps this really is a horrible nightmare. Wake up, Nancy,* I told myself, wishing it truly were only a bad dream.

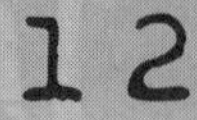

Little Did We Know

August 1992–January 1993

Mark and Tania arrived at the hangar at eight o'clock in the morning. The pilot was already loading boxes into the cargo pod on the belly of the Cessna airplane. Using the large scale inside the hangar, Mark and Tania weighed themselves along with two-year-old Tamra and six-month-old Jessica.

The Riches had spent many hours in Panama City buying the materials needed to fix up their house. They also planned for and bought supplies for their first ten weeks in Púcuro. Space at the hangar was filling up, and they had to decide which boxes needed to go in with them and which boxes could be brought in gradually over the next months. The pilot could only haul a certain amount of weight on each flight, so, at the last minute, more calculations were made, along with final decisions about things that needed to be left behind, to be brought in on future flights.

Dave and I were spending a month in Chame while the rest of the field committee and their wives went to Florida for a leadership conference. The Tenenoffs and Riches had both been in Chame, too. The Tenenoffs had planned to stay for two weeks and then return to Púcuro.

Rick and Patti's flight to Púcuro was scheduled two days before Mark and Tania's. The Tenenoffs had hoped to get settled in and have a nice meal prepared for the Riches on the day they moved in. Plans had to be changed at the last minute, however, due to a rescheduling problem with a doctor. The Tenenoffs had to delay their flight by several days.

Eager to move to Púcuro, Mark and Tania had decided to keep their scheduled flight, even though it would mean being in the village without partners for a few days.

Once the plane was loaded, Tania climbed up into the middle section of the plane and buckled her seat belt. Mark handed Jessica to her and then went around to the other side of the plane and lifted Tamra up into the seat next to Tania. Mark fastened Tamra's seat belt around her. Then he sat in the front, next to the pilot.

Mark, Tania, Tamra, and Jessica in Púcuro in 1992.

The one-hour-and-fifteen-minute flight was uneventful. They were able to land in plenty of time for the pilot to return to Panama City before the usual afternoon rainstorms.

Excited villagers crowded around the newest residents of the village. Children vied for the opportunity to hoist boxes onto their heads and carry them across the river. Heavier items were left for the older ones to transport. In previous years, everyone had to slip and slide down the muddy bank. But now Púcuro had cement stairs. As they walked down the steps to the river, Mark and Tania each carried a child in their arms.

Mark unlocked the front door of their house, and he and Tania and the girls went inside. Soon the front room filled up with boxes and people. Mark found a bag of candy and handed out pieces to the willing helpers. His warm and enthusiastic smile was returned by the happy faces around him.

Tania looked around the house, wondering where she should start. It all felt more overwhelming than she had expected.

Tamra began playing with other little girls in the front room. But Jessica cried when Tania set her on the floor near her feet.

"Tania," a girl said, coming into the kitchen.

"Yes?" Tania asked in Spanish.

"My name is Gilbertita," the girl said in Spanish. "Can I pick up Jessica? I can watch her for you."

"Yes, thank you, Gilbertita," Tania said, relieved.

Gilbertita picked up the chubby six-month-old with big blue eyes and soft blonde hair that fell into ringlets at the nape of her neck, and she took her into the front room. She shooed other children out of the hammock and sat down to swing baby Jessica, who hushed immediately. Gilbertita looked quite proud of her accomplishment—and the job she'd been honored to do.

Tania looked at Gilbertita, amazed that Jessica had quieted down so quickly. *The contrast of Jessy's milky-white cheek against Gilbertita's beautiful dark arm is striking,* she thought.

While Tania set up the portable crib in the girls' room for Jessica, Mark hooked up the gas tanks to the stove and refrigerator. Then they both moved boxes into the bedrooms and started to unpack.

"This is working out nicely," Mark said, "to be able to use Dave and Nancy's appliances and everything, until all of our things are flown in."

"It sure is," Tania said. "We can gradually unpack our things, and what we don't need until they move into their house can be left across the river in the shack on the airstrip, right?"

"Yes, as a matter of fact, there are already a few things stored over there," Mark said. "And we'll keep extra propane tanks there all of the time, I guess."

Mark wiped the sweat that was dripping from his face and neck. The tin roof was so hot that it made small tapping sounds as it expanded.

Tania opened the boxes that were filled with food, looking for a fresh loaf of bread and some lunchmeat. She made sandwiches while Mark searched the cupboards for plates and glasses.

Tamra, whose appearance favored her father, had already run squarely into the language barrier. She scampered into the kitchen to inform her daddy that she couldn't understand these children.

"They talk funny, Daddy," Tamra said.

"They speak their own language, Tamra," her daddy explained. "They think you talk funny, too. But, soon, you'll be able to talk to them and understand them. You get to learn the Kuna language, just like your mommy and I will learn it! Won't that be fun?"

"Yes, that will be fun!" Tamra said, her large blue eyes sparkling with delight and her impish little grin animating her face.

Mark always had an exuberant way of making things very fun and exciting for Tamra.

When the little family sat down at the kitchen table and prayed, the room grew quiet. Afterward, quite a few of the remaining children took their leave, with a quick "I'm gone" and a slam of the screen door. Several girls remained, quietly swinging in the hammocks and looking at books. Mark and Tania graciously accepted the beloved Kuna guests who had become a part of our home in Púcuro.

"Tamra looks like she is going to fall asleep at her plate," Mark said.

"I know, but look how dirty she is," Tania replied.

"Jessica is, too. Why don't we go to the river and bathe before putting them down for their naps?" Mark said.

"That sounds very good to me," Tania replied.

Mark and Tania put on their swimsuits. Tania remembered to wrap her skirt around herself—the Kuna custom for propriety—before she grabbed soap, shampoo, and towels. Then she and Mark headed out the backdoor toward the river. Each with a child in their arms, they walked down the steep trail, with its dirt steps that Dave had carved into the riverbank.

Tamra and Jessica loved the cold, rushing water. Jessica giggled and kicked her feet as Tania struggled to hold on to her slippery, wet body. Balancing the children, holding the soap, and shampooing their heads was all quite a feat. Yet, it was hard to get out of the cool, refreshing water and walk back into the noonday heat of the house. Tamra, with one pacifier in her mouth and another in her hand, rubbing her nose, soon fell fast asleep. Jessica cried when she was laid down in her crib, but she soon lost the battle and slept, too.

As Mark and Tania unpacked boxes and visited with people who came, the remainder of their first day went by quickly. Soon, another meal was over and lanterns were lit, softly illuminating the darkness that had descended on their little house by the river, deep in the jungle.

Little by little, evening visitors began to arrive, and Tania followed tradition by making coffee for them. Mark sat in the hammock and talked and laughed with his new friends. The women who came in sat at the kitchen table near Tania. The younger women, who spoke some Spanish, carried on a little conversation with her, but the older ones just sat quietly. Everyone accepted the coffee that was offered to them.

Adults as well as children picked up and inspected Tamra's toys, and Tamra, playing in the front room, chattered to anyone who would listen. People laughed because they couldn't understand her, yet she persisted. The children taught her words that she quickly repeated, and soon they seemed to get along quite well, despite the language barrier.

Tamra enjoying her new friends despite the language barrier.

Tamra yawned and Mark looked at his watch, deciding her bedtime had arrived.

"How do you say good night in Kuna?" Mark asked one of his guests in Spanish.

"*Panmal,*" his new friend said in Kuna.

"Tamra, say '*Panmal*' to everyone. That's how they say 'Good night,'" Mark instructed her.

"*Panmal,*" Tamra said.

"*Panmal,*" all of the pleased guests repeated.

Tania appeared from the kitchen to take Tamra to her bedroom. Jessica was already asleep in her crib.

When the last person left the house, Mark blew out the flame in the lanterns, and he and Tania walked toward their bedroom.

"I am exhausted!" Tania said.

"What time is it?" Mark asked.

"Eight-thirty," Tania laughed. "But it feels like at least ten o'clock."

Lying in bed, they listened to the night sounds. Bats flew by the window, and insects sang their harmonies in the night. The river rushed swiftly over rocks and around bends. The village lay quiet and peaceful in the moonlight.

Yet, in Tania's heart, a fear began to grow—a fear she hadn't expected and didn't understand. Finally, she decided to voice her fear to Mark.

"Mark, I'm really afraid," she whispered to him in the darkness of their room.

"Hon, what are you afraid of?" Mark asked.

"I don't know for sure, but it is overwhelming—like, could we be in danger here? I'm sorry, honey, I don't know why I feel this way. I'm just very afraid," Tania said, trying her best to put her feelings into words.

"Let's pray together and commit it to the Lord," Mark said.

They held hands and prayed together, committing themselves and their children into God's hands. They prayed until God lifted from Tania's heart the burden of overwhelming fear for their safety and replaced that burden with his peace.

Two days later, Rick and Patti returned to Púcuro and began to help Mark and Tania become accustomed to life in the village. Many notes were passed between the houses, much like the first days that we each had spent in Púcuro.

Then Dave and I returned. We moved in with Mark and Tania until our house was ready with the basic necessities.

One day, just after we finished eating lunch, we were all still sitting around the table, and it began to rain. This was the first time Tamra had heard rain pounding on a tin roof. She looked around the table, unsure whether to be frightened or not.

"Tamra," Mark said, "what is that noise?"

"What is it?" Tamra asked, her whole face seeming to move animatedly around each word.

The rain pounded even harder on the tin roof. Her large, beautiful eyes widened even more.

"It's rain," Mark said.

"Oh," Tamra said. Then turning to Dave she added, "Turn it off, Uncle Dave!"

We all roared with laughter.

Five days later, we moved—partially, at least. We worked at our house all day and slept there at night, but we ate our meals with Mark and Tania, or Rick and Patti, until our kitchen was equipped.

Finally, our house was completed, and we were ready to translate and teach again. Mark and Tania began Kuna language study. Rick and Patti were already progressing well with their studies.

One morning a young voice called out at our door, "Nahn-cee, Nahn-cee."

"Come in," I said.

Note in hand, a little girl walked in.

The note read, "Question #5,264—How much do you pay for eggs? And how do you know who is selling them?—Tania."

Chuckling, I said to Nelsi, "Tania needs some eggs. Will you go buy some for her?"

"Yes," she said.

"Here's a note to give back to her. She will give you the money for the eggs," I said.

Nelsi took the note, along with the piece of candy that I handed her, and walked back to Tania's house.

Tania read the note, which said, "Tania, eggs are worth ten cents each. Just give the money to one of the girls and she will go around and ask people for eggs. Sometimes, it is nesting season and you won't be able to buy any at all, but right now they should be available. Nelsi said she would buy some for you today.—Nancy."

Later that morning another note arrived. It said, "Nancy, would you and Dave like to join us for lunch? Our neighbors brought us some meat called '*oos*.' I found a recipe for roasting wild meat in my *Wycliffe Cookbook* and thought I'd try it.—Tania."

"Hey, Dave," I said "do you want to eat lunch at Mark and Tania's house? She'll be cooking *oos*."

"She'll be cooking *oos*, you say?" Dave said with a slight smile on his face. "I take it she didn't see it first?"

"I doubt it," I said.

"Sure, maybe they'll need some encouragement to get through that meal," he smiled.

I sent a note back to Tania, accepting their invitation. At noon we left our house and walked the trail to Mark and Tania's place. We called out at the door, "I'm here," and entered our old house.

Surprised by the delicious aroma, I said, "Are you sure you're cooking *oos?* That really smells great. It actually smells like roast beef.

"My *Wycliffe Cookbook* said to roast wild meat in two cups of strong coffee. I thought I'd try it. What is *oos*, anyway?" Tania asked.

"Well, we haven't quite figured that out, but let me help you put water into the glasses."

After the prayer we all sampled the *oos* and were pleasantly surprised by the wonderful roast beef flavor.

"I may need to borrow that cookbook from you," I said, very impressed.

"Why don't I just finish the wiring for your solar panels while I'm here?" Dave offered.

"We didn't invite you to dinner to make you work, but it would be nice to be able to listen to music without going through so many batteries," Mark said.

Tania put the girls into their beds for their naps while I started doing the dishes. Soon Tania joined me and the job was finished.

"I'm going on home," I told Dave.

"Okay," he said. "I'll be there soon. This shouldn't take me too much longer."

Dave finished the wiring and then looked through the music tapes on the shelf. He inserted one of the contemporary Christian tapes into the portable stereo, turned the volume on high, and quickly headed for the door—with his "cat-that-caught-the-canary" grin on his face.

As he headed out the door, he said, "There, now you can listen to your music as loud as you want to and you won't wear out your batteries."

Mark and Tania looked at each other in amazement. *Dave isn't such an old stick-in-the-mud after all!* they thought and then broke into laughter.

• • •

Tania found herself recalling long-forgotten words from the Ayoré language, words that she had heard growing up as a missionary kid in Bolivia. Living in Púcuro seemed to her almost like going home. And yet, along with the familiarity of village life came the unfamiliarity of the Kuna language and culture. The unknowns and the new routines and way of life here brought many stresses.

One day, as Tania was cooking the noonday meal, she looked around for Tamra.

"Tamra," she called.

No answer.

"Tamra?" Tania called out again.

Silence.

"Mark," Tania said, walking into the office with Jessica on her hip, "is Tamra in here?"

"No," Mark said, getting up from his desk.

With panic rising in their hearts, they quickly searched the house.

"Tamra!" they both called out. Running outside, they looked around. Soon neighbors and other children were calling out and searching for their little girl.

Gilbertita, Jessica, and Tamra "licking a bowl."

Looking toward the river, Mark saw two tiny girls playing in the water at the river's edge—Tamra and a little Kuna girl! Mark ran down the bank with Tania close at his heels. Tamra was whisked up into her daddy's arms, and the other little girl was escorted back up the bank, too—even though she probably went to the river regularly by herself.

"But, Daddy," Tamra said as they headed for the house, "I was with my older friend."

"Tamra," Mark said, "Doris is only four years old, and that isn't old enough."

Thanking God first for Tamra's safety, they then proceeded to instruct Tamra *never* to go to the river without their permission. The realization of how quickly Tamra could get out of their sight sent chills down their backs. *Thank you, Lord. Thank you for keeping Tamra safe,* was repeated many times in their hearts that day.

Another night, as we were swinging gently in our hammocks, reading books, we heard Mark call out from the trail.

"Dave," Mark called.

Surprised to hear Mark's voice, Dave and I looked at each other.

"Come in," Dave said.

Mark entered the house and said, "Jessica is sick. She's been crying for well over an hour. No matter what we do she won't stop. Will you come and see what you think?" he asked.

"Sure," Dave said.

"Let me get my medical book," I said.

We walked single file down the dark trail, lighted only by our flashlights. Dogs barked as we walked past huts. A neighbor called out, "Where are you going?"

"We are going to Mark and Tania's house. Jessica is sick," Dave answered.

"Ah," came the reply.

We could hear Jessica's crying before we reached their house. Walking through the back door, we saw Tania's silhouette as she stood in the kitchen, rocking Jessica back and forth in her arms. Jessica's face was red and hot from crying.

Tamra and her "older" friend Doris went to the river together.

"She has a low-grade fever, about 99.2 degrees," Tania informed us. "She's been crying for over an hour. I've tried looking in her ears with an otoscope, but because she's been crying for so long, both ears look red. It seems, though, like it's her stomach that hurts. She keeps drawing her legs up, and when I try to straighten them out, she screams. Is it possible for babies to get appendicitis?"

"It seems unlikely, but I can look it up," I said, opening the medical book. "Appendicitis is rare in children under two, it says. Hold her so that I can press lightly on the right lower side of her abdomen."

Jessica screamed out, seemingly in pain. We all looked at each other.

"Did you press on her ears?" I asked.

"Yes," Tania said. "But you can do it again and see what you think."

As I pressed on her left ear, her cry didn't change. Then I pressed on her right ear and she cried out harder.

"I had her right side against me when you pressed on her stomach—maybe it was her ear that hurt then, too," Tania said. "I pulled her ear, instead of pressing like you did. It does appear to be an earache."

Tania tried holding the baby in various positions, and her cry changed whenever her right ear was affected. Relieved, we decided that giving her an antibiotic would be best, along with a decongestant.

"We'll be praying that you both will get some sleep tonight," I said.

"We'd better go now," Dave said. "Good night."

"Good night, and thank you," Mark said.

"Thanks," Tania said. "I'll try sleeping with her in the hammock tonight."

We walked quietly home, but once inside our house we discussed the situation.

"Tania looks so tired," I said.

"Yes, that's a lot of stress to have a sick baby, along with all of the other adjustments they've had," Dave said. "They need a little break."

"We could watch the girls and let them float down the river on our inflatable rafts," I suggested.

"That would be nice for them. Why don't you talk to Tania about it tomorrow?" Dave said.

Two days later Mark and Tania brought the girls up to our house. Jessica had responded well to the antibiotic. That first night was a sleepless one, but the following night both she and Tania slept fairly well.

Mark and Tania both looked eager for their little getaway together. We handed them the folded plastic rafts that they would inflate once they hiked to the head of the river.

Mark and Tania crossed the river and found the trail. They hiked for about forty-five minutes, feeling a little uncomfortable that they possibly could have missed a turn but enjoying each other's company nonetheless.

"These are huge trees," Tania said, the farther they walked.

"Yes, and look at the orchids that are growing out of the crooks in the branches of that tree over there," Mark said.

As they trudged along, the forest grew denser and the trail grew steeper.

"Maybe we should have brought someone with us," Tania remarked, her uncertainty beginning to grow.

"Yes, but it is nice to be alone," Mark said with a twinkle in his eyes.

"It is, but how long should it take before we get to the head of the river?" Tania asked. "I've seen quite a few little trails that we didn't take."

"Dave said about forty-five minutes," Mark informed her. "And he told us to just stay on this main trail."

They walked on for a few more minutes. Then they heard the water. Relieved, they quickened their pace. The trail ended at the river. Looking thirty feet across the expanse, toward the other shore, they could see a trail begin again and disappear into the trees on the other side.

"Dave said this is the Tapalisa River. Right here it flows into the Púcuro River. The trail on the other side leads to Paya and on into Colombia. The men in our village clean this trail halfway to Paya twice a year. The men in Paya clean the trail the rest of the way to their village. We'll get in here and float down to Púcuro," Mark explained.

After inflating the rafts, they stepped into the cool, swift water. Climbing onto the rafts was a struggle, but finally they were floating downstream. Soon, however, the clear water began turning brown and rushing more swiftly than usual. Large sticks floated near them. A log rushed swiftly past them, and they realized that the river was rising.

"Oh, there must have been a big rainstorm upriver somewhere," Mark said.

Surveying the jungle on either side of the river, they knew they didn't have any options, so they continued to float down the river—looking back cautiously, and often, to avoid the objects that were being carried swiftly through the rising water.

At a wide, deep area shaded by trees, the river slowed its pace somewhat. A creepy feeling descended on Tania as her thoughts turned to alligators and snakes. She tightened her grip on the air mattress, making sure she wouldn't slide off.

Mark gazed up into the branches of the overhanging trees. The only sound that could be heard was the rushing water.

The river narrowed again, and Tania and Mark found themselves hurling through rapids as the river rushed swiftly downstream over the rocks.

"I'm not so sure this is relaxing," Tania said.

"No, but it is a change of pace," Mark said, smiling, "and we are alone together."

They laughed, but their laughs were laced with tension and uncertainty.

Soon, our house came into their view, but they couldn't maneuver their rafts close enough to shore to stop. They began paddling toward the left-hand bank as they passed Silvino's hut, then Arturo's. At last, near the bank, they slipped off their rafts and stood up, walking toward the shore by their neighbor's house. They walked the few feet to their own landing near their trail—they were home!

Mark and Tania changed into dry clothes before walking to our house to get their children.

Several days later, we had a team meeting at Rick and Patti's house. Rick led the meeting and opened it up with prayer. We each discussed how our study or work time was progressing, and what goals we had for the weeks ahead.

Afterward, Dave said, "I've been thinking, would you guys like to meet every Saturday morning for a prayer breakfast at our house?"

"That sounds great," Rick said.

"It sounds good to me, too," Mark said.

"In three days, Nancy and I are flying out for committee meetings. When we return, we'll start meeting every Saturday morning at six o'clock," Dave said.

"Six o'clock?" I asked. "And who's going to make this breakfast?"

"I will," Dave said. "I can fry an egg, ya know."

"Well, okay," I said, relieved that I wouldn't be cooking breakfast that early every Saturday morning.

"Nancy, do you still make Dave a hot breakfast every morning?" Tania asked.

"Yes," I said.

"Mark hasn't been happy with toast and cereal since he lived with you guys for that month," Tania laughed. "He said you made hash browns, eggs, and bacon. Sometimes even steak and eggs. Before that, he never knew what he was missing."

"Well, yes. Dave loves his breakfast. When we get wild pig or venison, I make small butterfly steaks and fry that with eggs. I almost always make hash browns, too. See, Dave, you really are quite spoiled," I said.

Rick and Mark looked at their wives, and Patti and Tania scowled at me. I shrugged my shoulders innocently.

"Nancy also serves large pieces of cake," Rick said.

"At our house we always say, 'Do you want a regular piece, or a Mankins-sized piece?'" Patti said. "Don't worry, Tania, we have a hot breakfast only once or twice a week."

After several more minutes of small talk, Mark picked up Jessica, and Tania took Tamra's hand to head for home. Dave and I said our good-byes, too, and we left.

That night Mark said to Tania, "Dave thinks that we should fly out with them for a short break."

"I don't need a break," Tania said, bursting into tears. "I don't know why I'm crying. I don't need a break."

Mark held her close as she sobbed. When her tears slowed down, she looked up at him. "I guess I really do need a break. It would be wonderful to get away for a few days. I just feel like I shouldn't need to leave so soon. I grew up in a village like this. I didn't think it would be so stressful for me."

"Tania, there isn't anything wrong with needing a break. We have been here for nearly two months. Dave says that is good for our first time living here," Mark encouraged her.

"I'm used to being around a lot of people," Tania said, "but it has been really hard to make all of the decisions. I wasn't prepared for so many people wanting to 'borrow' flour, sugar, coffee, salt, and oil. I don't even know how much of those things we'll need ourselves for our time in here. And, as silly as it sounds, these clothes I have to wear are so uncomfortable. They are hot and tight, and I have such a hard time with these wraparound skirts!" Tania chuckled. "It feels good just to talk about it, as silly as it all seems."

"It isn't silly," Mark said. "It's been stressful for me, too. I love the people, but I find myself a little nervous, wondering whether I'm saying the wrong thing or doing the wrong thing. I want to give them batteries or fishhooks when they ask, but I don't want to give them more or less than Rick and Dave do. Sometimes I wonder whether some people are comparing the three of us. I look forward to really getting to know how they think and understanding what they're saying. It will just take us time, though."

"Actually, I feel really relieved," Tania said. "I didn't even realize how stressed I was."

Mark and Tania returned to Púcuro after a few short days in Chame. They were refreshed and ready to start back into their language study.

When we returned, I started watching Tamra and Jessica for two hours on Tuesday afternoons while Tania studied. On Thursday afternoons, I helped Tania with the language for two hours, while Mark took the girls visiting with him in the village.

One Thursday afternoon, after our study time together, Tania said, "Nancy, I thought I would get some good contact time in yesterday. I went spearfishing with Gilbertita, Alejandrita, Sandra, and Nelsi."

"That sounds like fun," I said.

"Well, we hiked up a trail first, and then we got into the river. The rocks in the river are hard on your feet and slippery, but we walked downriver until the girls found a good spot and put on their masks and grabbed their spears. They floated on top of the water and periodically smacked the water with the spears. Then they would stab a fish. You would think that smacking the water would scare the fish away," she said.

"My understanding is that smacking the water stuns the fish momentarily and makes them easier to spear," I said.

"Oh, that makes sense. They handed me a mask and I put it on, but I couldn't even see any fish, so they took the mask away from me. Every time they speared a fish, they would clean it and string it onto a vine. They decided, since I couldn't see any fish, much less spear them, that my job would be to hold the fish and the knife.

"We moved on to another spot and they speared a few more. I think we had six or seven small fish. We walked down the river a little farther and I was trying to follow them through these little rapids. I put the knife in my left hand with the fish, so I could steady myself on the rocks. Then, Nancy, I fell. The knife cut the vine and all of the fish floated downstream!

"The girls couldn't believe it. They dove into the water and swam after the fish. But, the fish were gone. None of them were happy with me, but Gilbertita was disgusted. You should have seen the look on her face as she stomped around in the water. But Sandra, somehow, had this little grin on her face. She was not happy about losing the fish, but her expression was more sympathetic, like she knew I couldn't help myself. Somehow she saw the humor in the whole situation. I kept telling the girls how sorry I was. Nobody caught any more fish. We came back with nothing. I knew that I'd lost their supper—they weren't fishing just for the fun of it. So I gave them a large can of sardines. They seemed pleased with that, anyway."

"What do they think of us?" I asked. "The things that they learn to do at age five or six, we grownups can't begin to master. One day when I went down to the river to bathe with Sandra, she asked me, 'Why does Dah-veed walk like this in the river?' She proceeded to imitate Dave flailing his arms and his peculiar walk as his tender feet gingerly pick their way to the middle of the river."

We laughed at ourselves and the oddities that we were to these people.

A few weeks later, the mission plane brought our language consultant, Jamie Enemark, to the village. Jamie came to give language evaluations to the Tenenoffs and the Riches. The usual greeting committee was at the airstrip for the landing. When the plane taxied back to the center of the strip near the shack, Dave, Rick, and Mark were waiting nearby, too.

When Jamie got out of the plane, Mark was speaking in Kuna to the guys who were standing around. With a dramatic flourish, Jamie turned around, walked back to the plane, and said, "Never mind, I'm going back. I can tell you right now I didn't bring in enough material with me to test you, Mark. You are already well past level one!"

Even though Jamie obviously was kidding about leaving, his compliment was not a joke. Mark's eyes sparkled. He enjoyed language learning immensely, but this affirmation from a respected colleague encouraged his heart in a very special way.

Rick passed the language test at a level that he could now begin teaching. We could all relate to his feeling of elation. His diligence and hard work over the years had paid off.

On our team we now had three members who were qualified to teach, and Patti was also making good progress. Mark was picking up the language by leaps and bounds, and Tania was close behind him. We were all really excited at the prospects of the ministry we could soon have together.

A few days later, however, the plane arrived again. Dave and I needed to fly to Chame for unexpected field committee business. It was so close to conference time that we ended up staying in Chame until after Christmas.

• • •

Our son, Chad, and Gary Roberts, a friend of his from college, flew to Panama for Christmas. Gary planned to shoot video footage during his visit so he could produce a video that our team could share with our supporters. Three days after Christmas, our "extended" family flew back to Púcuro. Chad, Gary, and Sarah flew in with us for two weeks, along with little Michelle, who was flying back to the village she had left when she was only two days old. Everyone was happy to see Chad and Sarah again. They were all very pleased that Chad hadn't forgotten their language. He had learned Kuna quickly and very well, especially for having been in the village only during his school breaks for two years.

Mark's brother and sister-in-law, Paul and Kim, were in Púcuro visiting Mark and Tania. They were at the airstrip, waiting to fly back to Panama City. They had hoped to spend a few more days in the village, but they had gotten word that Kim's grandmother had passed away. Paul and Kim were, however, very thankful for the time they'd had in Panama, especially for the time in Púcuro, seeing firsthand where Mark and Tania lived and ministered. Little did they know just how precious these weeks would be to them in the future.

Two nights later we all met at the Tenenoffs' house for a Christmas party. We had drawn names, and we each bought one present for the name we drew.

"Tamra," Mark said, "here, go take Uncle Dave this present you got for him."

Tamra, with a little help from her daddy, lugged the gift over to the hammock where Dave was reclining.

"Here, Uncle Dave," she said with a cute little smile. "Open it."

"Help me," he said, and they both tore into the wrapping.

"A hurricane lantern, how neat," Dave said, genuinely pleased.

Dave had designed our house to be cool in the Panama heat, but what he hadn't accounted for was the wind that blew through, making it very hard to keep a lantern lit. The red hurricane lantern remained in his lap for further inspection, but it was his turn to give his gift to Lee.

Blond-headed Lee sat on the floor with the package between his legs and pulled the wrapping off with skill. He was a typical little boy in all of his ways.

Everyone crowded in to inspect the homemade gift that sat in front of him.

"Wow, when did you make that?" Rick asked.

"I've been working on it, little by little, making it from bits and pieces of parts I had," Dave said.

"Lee, it's a little workbench," Rick said. "Look here, you can unscrew these bolts. And look, there's a latch and a hinge."

Lee didn't need any more encouragement. The eighteen-month-old began to twist, pull, and inspect his new toy.

"Do those nails come out?" Patti asked, a little concerned with some of the very real parts on this workbench. After all, their first two children were girls. It might take some time to get accustomed to little boy ways and little boy toys.

"He'll love it," Rick said.

I looked around the room. Rick was sitting in his hammock with Connie resting contentedly on his lap. He watched carefully as Lee played with his new toy. Dora was walking from person to person, enjoying everyone's company.

Jessica was snuggled in her mommy's arms, and Tamra was leaning across her daddy's knees. As usual, Mark's knees were bouncing up and down as he talked. He rarely sat completely still.

It didn't seem so long ago that our own children were the ages of these little ones. Yet here were our kids, all grown up—Chad, with his friendly, outgoing personality and love for learning, and Sarah, quiet and reserved, yet with a poise that was impressive. Working in the mission office, she had blossomed. Until recently, we hadn't known her propensity for the many new skills she was developing. *Thank you, Lord, for my family. Thank you, Lord, for our partners and their dear families, too. And thank you for sending Gary here to make a video for our team.*

All too soon, we were saying our good-nights and heading for our own homes.

"Tomorrow the village will have its annual all-night get-together in the meeting house to celebrate New Year's Eve," Dave said.

"Do they really stay up all night long?" Tania asked.

"A lot of people will, but not everyone, I'm sure," Dave said. "We'll probably go for an hour or two."

"You'll stay to see in the new year, won't you?" Chad asked.

"I don't know; we'll see," Dave said. "I've gotten used to being in bed by nine and up before dawn. Staying up past midnight doesn't appeal to me anymore."

"It's hard to believe that 1993 is beginning—I feel like 1992 flew by," I said.

"Isn't that a sign of getting older, Moo?" Rick said with a chuckle.

"That isn't funny," I countered.

The five of us walked home underneath a bright, starry sky.

One week later we all met again, this time at Mark and Tania's house.

"What do I smell?" Dave asked as we walked into the Riches' home that evening.

"Homemade doughnuts," Mark informed us with a grin.

"Did you get the recipe out of your *Wycliffe Cookbook*?" Dave asked.

"Well, yes," Tania said, chuckling.

"I want to see that cookbook," Dave said. "It must weigh at least ten pounds if it has everything in it that you say it has."

"Dave, why are you teasing Tania about her cookbook?" I asked.

"Every time I come over here, she's gotten some new information about pest control, rehydration drinks, even emergency preparations. When I ask her where she learned that, her answer is always, 'The *Wycliffe Cookbook*,'" Dave said, still amazed.

"Well, now you know what to buy me for my birthday," I told him.

Dave rolled his eyes and headed for the doughnuts and coffee.

Mark brought some songbooks into the room and handed them out. Chad and Gary were lounging in the hammocks, while the rest of us sat around on benches and talked. Sarah began looking up songs that we could sing together. Soon our voices blended as we sang familiar choruses, some in Spanish and some in English.

Taking a break from the singing, we all sat in silence for a couple of minutes.

Then Patti said, "An interesting thing happened today. You know Rick started teaching the Bible lessons at our neighbor's house. Well, after the lesson was over, Cecilia came into our house, furious—the Cecilia who does my laundry, not the Cecilia who does your laundry." Patti chuckled at our longstanding joke.

"She stormed in and said, 'Patricia, you have to tell me that Ricardo is lying—he is not telling us the truth!'

"I said to her, 'What did Ricardo say?'"

"'No! You tell me that Ricardo was lying to us!' she said. She was practically shaking, she was so angry.

"I said, 'I can't tell you he was lying. I don't even know what you think he said to you.' I began wondering whether I was understanding her correctly.

"Finally, she said, 'In our study today Ricardo told us that God knows what I am thinking in my mind! God can't know what I am thinking. Only I can know what I think in my own mind! Tell me he is lying!'

"I told her, 'Cecilia, Ricardo is telling you the truth. God's Word says that God knows our thoughts.'

"She was angry that God could know her thoughts. She turned and left in a huff. She stomped out the door."

"That's really interesting that she would react that way," I said.

"It's encouraging that they're understanding what you teach, Rick," Dave said. "You must be doing a good job."

"Do we have time for one more song?" Gary asked.

"Sure, let's sing one more before we call it a night," Dave said.

While they were deciding which song to sing, Dave kissed me.

"Look at the lovebirds over there in that dark corner," Tania said as the flash of her camera shone in our eyes.

"You young couples could take a few lessons, so you can stay lovey-dovey even when you are a 'tad' and a 'moo,'" I laughed, even though I was blushing.

Tania took another picture.

Chad, Gary, and Sarah would be leaving in three short days. It had been a wonderful two weeks, having Gary and our children with us in Púcuro.

We all sang one more song and then called it a night, ending the evening with a prayer.

The next day Mark, Chad, and Gary went to Boca de Cupe with Estánislau and his son Benjamín. It was Mark's first canoe trip since moving to Púcuro.

The following day, Mark, Chad, and Gary hiked to Paya with

Estánislau. First, they hiked up the trail to the Tapalisa River and crossed over, picking up the trail that Mark and Tania had seen on their rafting ride.

Soon the trek turned into an uphill slog through the mud. They trudged on. The jungle trail that led to Paya and then on into Colombia was shaded by a thick canopy of trees. They saw many smaller trails shooting off from the main one. Some were only faint footpaths, probably hunting trails . . . or so they thought. Little did they know the danger that lurked beyond those paths. Little did Mark know that in nineteen short days, he, Rick, and Dave would be hiking one of those paths with guns pointed at their backs.

Dave and Nancy at Mark and Tania's house.

Only three and a half hours later the tired men arrived in Paya. Estánislau hadn't slowed his pace very much for these three gringos.

They crossed the river to Paya, which is on a peninsula. The village is even smaller than Púcuro. They entered the hut of Estánislau's mother, and she offered them a banana drink, which they all eagerly accepted. The rest of the day they spent visiting many of the residents and sitting around their fires talking with them. After a meal of fish and rice, they were offered hammocks to sleep in for the night.

As they were lying in their hammocks that night, one of the Kuna men in the hut said to Mark, "Who taught you our language? Someone taught you to speak Kuna before you moved to Púcuro! You haven't lived in Púcuro long enough to speak as well as you do."

"No one taught me before I moved to Púcuro," Mark said, feeling very encouraged by the compliment on his language abilities.

For breakfast the next morning, they ate more fish and rice, and then they started back down the trail toward Púcuro.

Chad, Gary, Estánislau, and Mark returning from their trip to Paya.

January fifteenth came all too quickly. The plane arrived to take Chad, Gary, and Sarah back to Panama City. We waved good-bye as the plane raced down the runway and lifted into the air. As we looked at the plane up in the sky, we realized they had left none too soon. Rain clouds were quickly moving in, and we were in for a downpour. Those were not the only storm clouds developing, however. Little did we know that Dave was waving good-bye to his children for the last time.

• • •

We all got back into our routines. Dave began reviewing the Bible lessons. Every other day at Nanzhel's house, I taught her and some of the other older women.

One day I thought it would be nice to make a special meal for Mark and Tania and let them eat together—the two of them alone—at our house, while we watched their girls at their house. I planned the meal and Dave printed out the menu for the "Starlight Inn." We sent the invitation to them by way of one of our special couriers. The next night we left our house, with table set and food ready, and walked to Mark and Tania's house to watch their children.

A few minutes later Mark and Tania walked hand in hand—wearing "outsider's" clothes—heading for our house on their special date.

Neighbors were perplexed at this oddity. "Where are you going?" called out one neighbor, watching Mark and Tania head up the trail in their fancy clothes.

"We're going to Dave and Nancy's house," Mark replied with a smile on his face.

"But Dave and Nancy went to your house. We saw them walk by," said the perplexed friend.

"Dave and Nancy are watching Tamra and Jessica while we go to eat supper at their house," Mark told them.

The silence said that, again, our strange ways had stymied our friends and neighbors.

• • •

When Mark and Tania returned, they appeared happy and refreshed by their getaway date together. We left them and returned home. Little did we know that it would be their very last date.

The Panamanian government allowed for a representative to be elected from these remote areas. Darío, the Christian man who had translated some songs for the Kuna church, was now the representative for Púcuro and Paya. He worked very hard for Púcuro to be allocated money and materials to build a new school and a much-needed clinic.

Cement block and block layers had arrived and the new school and clinic had been constructed at the far end of the soccer field, a short distance from our house. The villagers were excited about the new buildings.

One day, Dave was visiting at Nanzhel's house. He was talking to Tomás about the new school and clinic.

"I will never get to see them," Nanzhel said sadly, with her head bent down. "I haven't seen your new house, either."

"Maybe you can see them," Dave said.

"No, I'll never walk that far again," Nanzhel said.

Dave grinned. "I'll be back," he said, walking out of their house. Both Tomás and Nanzhel stared after him, unsure what to think of his abrupt departure.

Minutes later Dave returned to Nanzhel's house, followed by a dozen curious onlookers. He went into the hut and told Nanzhel that she was going to go and see the buildings. Then he scooped her up out of her hammock and carried her outside.

Waiting for her was a wheelbarrow fitted with a foam mattress. Dave placed Nanzhel gingerly on top of the mattress. She smiled, a bit embarrassed, and then hung on tightly as Dave wheeled her around the giggling throng that had assembled to watch. Dave steered the wheelbarrow swiftly up the trail to the clinic. Nanzhel was impressed with the new building that was painted blue and white. Next, they wheeled up to the school. Nanzhel exclaimed over the size of the schoolhouse. Finally, Dave brought her up the trail to our house.

Nanzhel chuckled as Dave carried her inside and set her in a hammock. I served her coffee and cookies and we had a wonderful hour, chatting together. Noticing that she looked pretty tired, I asked her if she was ready for Dave to take her home.

"Yes," she said. "I thought I would never see your house, never see the school, or the clinic. But now I have seen them. You have a good man, Nahn-cee."

"Yes, I do have a good man," I said.

Down the trail they went, Nanzhel's head jutting forward, her hands clenching the sides of the wheelbarrow, and her long gray hair streaming out behind her.

Why didn't I take a picture of that? I thought as they rounded a bend out of sight. *Oh, well, we'll have Dave bring her back again soon.* Or so I thought . . .

The following day, Rick and Patti were walking back to their house from Mark and Tania's. Connie was sleeping in Rick's arms, and Patti was carrying Lee, who was also sound asleep.

As they walked past the small store the village had begun to operate, Rick said, "Wait a minute, Patti."

He walked to the door and looked in. A kerosene lamp on the table allowed him to see who was inside the small structure. With no further comment he walked back to Patti and they continued on home.

When they were almost there, Rick said, "Patti, in the *tienda* there were some outsiders that I've never seen before. Tomorrow, maybe you shouldn't go outside our house unless we're together."

The next day was Sunday, January 31, 1993—like any other Sunday in the village. The church met at Nanzhel's house.

Rick came in late. He had been talking to Dora on the two-way radio. Little did he know that it would be his last talk with his precious little girl.

Patti, Rick, Nancy, Dave, Tania, and Mark, two weeks before Rick, Dave, and Mark were kidnapped.

Little did we know that, in a few short hours, all of our lives would be changed—forever.

13

Escape before Sunset

February 1, 1993–April 1993

The sun was sinking in the western sky as the canoe sped down the river toward El Reál. My head throbbed as the events and decisions of the past twenty-four hours haunted my mind and heart.

We are running out of time, I thought nervously. *Our mission plane needs to leave El Reál with enough time to land in Panama City by sunset. With the guerrilla threat here in the Darién, we can't expect the pilot and airplane to wait for us past that time. Lord, why did I tell Estánislau to take us to El Reál? I've only been there once, when the plane landed for a few minutes. I've never even seen the town itself. Why didn't I say we wanted to go to Yaviza? At least I've been there before. Well, none of our missionaries live in Yaviza anymore, anyway. Lord, please get us to Panama City tonight.*

The motor stopped running. I anxiously turned back to look at Estánislau. Thankfully, he had turned the engine off in order to talk to me. Nothing was wrong with the motor.

"Nahn-cee," he said, "the branch of the river that would take us close to the airstrip is very shallow right now, but I know a trail that we can take from here. You have to decide. By trail we could reach the airstrip in about twenty minutes, but if we continue on by canoe, it could take an hour or longer."

"We'll walk," I said without hesitation.

Estánislau started the engine again and headed for the left-hand bank of the river. A small dock appeared and soon we disembarked. The trail led past a house, then under the canopy of trees. Chino led the way, with Connie on his shoulder and a small overnight bag in one hand. Patti walked behind him with Lee in her arms. Next came Gilbertita, carrying Jessica and a small bag. Tania was carrying Tamra, and I trailed behind them with my overnight bag. Estánislau, walking at the end of our procession, carried the remaining two small suitcases.

Five minutes into our hike we heard the familiar sound of our Cessna 185 taking off. I felt as though my heart would stop beating. *No, Lord, please, God, don't let him leave us here!*

Chino began to run toward a clearing in the trail—a place that didn't have the canopy of trees. Connie jostled precariously, as she rode sidesaddle on his shoulder. Patti, Tania, and Gilbertita began running, too. I picked up my pace then slowed again as my heart pounded in my chest.

I listened as the plane flew up the river and then banked and flew back down the river. *He is looking for us,* I thought. *He can't see how close we are. He doesn't know we're walking.*

Soon the plane flew over again and Chino was at a clearing, waving with the suitcase he had in his hand. The plane landed. *Thank you, Lord,* I said in my heart.

We finally reached the clearing near the airstrip, where the small red-and-white airplane sat waiting for us. What a wonderful sight it was! The tears began to flow as we said good-bye: to dear Estánislau, our faithful friend; to Gilbertita, who had stood beside us these long terrifying hours; and to Chino, who had helped us to flee from the village to safety.

Dave Chapman, the pilot, said, "Climb in. Sit wherever you want. You can let the children move around if they need to."

I climbed into the front seat. Tania and Patti sat in the middle seats with Jessica and Lee in their arms. Tamra and Connie were buckled in the back. Soon the plane ascended into the sky.

Tania, Patti, and I sobbed as the green blanket of trees below us grew smaller and we lost sight of the river. *How can I leave Dave out there? How can we escape and leave our husbands in these jungles? Oh, God,* my heart cried, *help us, Lord, help us.*

Connie and Tamra began to cry, too. Tania handed Jessica up to me. Patti and Tania let the girls climb over the seat to sit on their laps so they could be calmed and reassured. After several minutes Jessica began to cry because she was hungry. I handed her back to Tania, and Tamra crawled forward into my lap. An hour later the girls were buckled back into their seats for the landing.

Just as our little airplane landed at the small airport in Panama City, the last rays of the sun set below the horizon.

Our daughter, Sarah, and Del Coupland ran to us. We all hugged, and more tears flowed. Eight-year-old Dora was not there, however—she didn't know yet that her father had been captured by guerrillas.

We were driven to the two pilots' houses, which were side by side, a few blocks from the airport. Doug and Sharon Hefft had a room prepared for Sarah and me, and another room for Patti and her children. Tania and her girls stayed at the Chapmans' house.

Patti found Dora sitting in a bedroom watching the video *Anne of Green Gables*. Dora couldn't understand why her daddy hadn't arrived with her mommy, sister, and brother.

She had sensed all afternoon that something was up. Her dorm mom and teacher had seemed upset while they packed some of her clothes to take with her to Panama City. During the ride into town she heard Sarah telling Alane about office work that needed to be completed. Awkward pauses were filled with talk about the weather.

Dora didn't want to hear why her daddy wasn't there. She stared at the television screen. The video was paused—that scene from *Anne of Green Gables* is indelibly etched in her mind, merged with the moment she learned that her daddy had been kidnapped!

Our mission headquarters in Sanford, Florida, had been informed of the abduction and had already formed a crisis management team, which was on its way to Panama.

We spent the evening calling family in the States. I phoned Chad, who was doing graduate studies at the University of Texas at Arlington. He was at Keith and Wilma Forster's house. They were living in Dallas while preparing the Kuna New Testament for printing. Keith had been able to call Chad out of his class and tell him that his father had been captured by Colombian guerrillas. Chad was very thankful to hear it from such a good friend of his father. I filled Chad in on all of the details of the capture. Not knowing what the next few days would hold for us, we decided that he should stay in Dallas. I promised to let him know what our plans were, as soon as I knew.

I talked to Dave's mother, Lois, and to his father, Chuck. It was excruciating, having to tell them their son had been tied up and taken away at gunpoint, headed toward Colombia I told them, too, that I would call again with any new information as soon as I could.

Next I telephoned my mom and dad, Jim and Jean Van Delinder. They were very supportive and understanding. They encouraged me to stay in Panama, if necessary, so that I could do whatever might be needed.

Exhausted, I took a shower and got ready for bed. I wasn't sure how to turn off my mind, though. Sarah was ready for bed, too, so she offered to tell me all that happened since she, Chad, and Gary had flown out of the village two weeks before. Listening to her soothing voice, I was soon mercifully and soundly asleep.

The following day several men from the U.S. Embassy arrived to debrief us. Tania, Patti, and I were all questioned separately. We each relayed the events of Dave, Mark, and Rick's abduction. We were then questioned by the FBI. The following day we went to the Panamanian police station to give them a statement.

Guy Sier, Bob Klamser, and Tania's father, Tim Wyma, arrived. Tania's parents had gone on furlough a few months prior to that time, but Tim flew back to Panama to help out on the newly formed crisis team, which also included Bryan Coupland.

American friends who lived in the Canal Zone offered to house us, for our protection, and also to isolate us from any reporters. Sarah and I stayed in the home of Cleve and Bonnie Oliver, and Tania and Patti stayed at Ken and Jane Thompson's house.

We were given a book of guns to look at, so we could identify the machine guns that we had seen. Tania flipped through the pages, looking everywhere except at the guns!

Guy said, "Tania, you have to look at them before you can identify one."

"I don't like guns," she said. "I didn't look at their guns."

That day, after trying to identify the guns, the three of us looked up and saw Jessica *walking* toward us! Here she was, the very first time she had walked, and Mark wasn't there to see her. We burst into tears. Jessica, proud of her efforts, blinked at us in confusion and plopped down on her bottom. Tania hugged her and, even through her tears, encouraged her.

"You walked," she said as enthusiastically as she could. "That's good, sweetie."

The pain in our hearts was overwhelming. The immensity of the situation hit us from all sides, in wave after wave.

Every hour we hoped for news. We wanted to do something, anything, except sit and wait.

On the ninth day we learned that our crisis team had received a radio contact from the group who kidnapped our husbands. The captors demanded a five-million-dollar ransom for the release of Dave, Mark, and Rick.

Five million dollars . . . or they'll kill our husbands. Five million dollars, a ransom demand. Kidnapped, our husbands have been kidnapped. They want five million dollars. This doesn't happen in real life. This doesn't happen to normal people like us. This is a dream, where I'm playing a part in a movie. Wake up, Nancy, wake up. But, try as I might, I couldn't wake up—and it wasn't a dream.

Patti, Tania, and I knew that we could not pay a ransom for our husbands. As missionaries, we live by donations from churches and friends who support us financially. Millions of dollars was not even an option we could consider—it was an impossibility. Not only was the amount out of the question, but morally we could not even consider paying a ransom for our husbands. By paying a ransom, we would endanger the lives of other missionaries all around the world. As members of New Tribes Mission, we had agreed with their no-ransom policy. God's grace and strength enabled us not to waver on that issue. It was not an option.

Airplane reservations were made for us to fly back to the States. In a kidnapping case, our mission's policy is to evacuate family members, for their protection as well as for the protection of the hostages.

Two days later we were aboard the plane, flying thousands of miles away from our husbands, away from our mission family in Panama, and away from the Kuna people who had become such a part of our hearts and our lives.

An airline stewardess came to me at my seat and said, "I'm so sorry to hear about your husband. I hope everything will work out for you."

"Thank you," I said numbly. *How does she know?* I thought.

For the three of us, life as "hostage wives" had begun.

Patti, Tania, and I were still in a state of shock. I was feeling like I had become one of the characters in a spy novel. I felt suspicious of everyone. I didn't trust anybody outside of our circle, and I was afraid to give out any information to anyone.

Walking through the Houston airport to change planes, I found myself looking at the faces of the people who were passing by, wondering why everyone else's life seemed to be going on normally. Part of me wanted to call out to the group, *How can all of you go on with life as though it's normal? Don't you know my heart is breaking?* I felt like I was being pushed along in a throng of people, when really, my life had stopped. My mind was on overload—again I felt like I was entering into a bizarre time warp.

The next week was a blur of activity. Our mission provided us with a counselor, a doctor, and a dentist to help meet our emotional and physical needs. One member of our crisis team continued to meet with us daily, and we had regular updates and telephone calls from the other members of the Crisis Management Committee (CMC) in Panama.

Jessica turned one year old—fifteen days after her father was torn from her life. We had a party for her. Life was going on, whether we wanted it to or not. The clock would not stop ticking. Days would end and new ones would begin, even though our hearts cried out for them to stop—to wait for our husbands to catch up with us again.

Chad flew in from Dallas to be with Sarah and me. The separation and unknowns of any situation seem to me to be much worse than being a part of the situation. It was wonderful to have both Chad and Sarah by my side and to go through it together with them. At the end of the week, Chad went back to school, Sarah flew to California to be with Dave's family, and I went to stay with my parents.

Tania's mom, Betty, came to stay with Tania and the girls and took them home with her when the week was over.

Patti settled in to as normal a life as she could, homeschooling Dora and renewing acquaintances. She decided to remain at one of our mission centers in the States, thinking—as we all did—that soon this would be over and we would have our husbands back.

Our lives, however, became anything except normal. Tania, Patti, and I found ourselves afraid to leave our houses, for fear we would miss a phone call—the phone call that would end the nightmare we each were living.

Chad had missed the first several weeks of the new semester. After much prayer, we both believed he should cancel his classes until the following term. He and Sarah both flew to Florida to join me at my parents' house. The long vigil had begun.

February turned into March. March sixteenth was Dave's forty-fourth birthday. Sarah and I drove down to Sanford, Florida, to attend a weekly evening meeting at our mission's international headquarters. I was invited to share at that meeting, to give an update to our colleagues who had been praying so earnestly and diligently for us. It was the first time I had ever spoken in front of a crowd of people. Yet, somehow, their eagerness to learn more about our situation, and their love and concern, encouraged me to share with them the events that took place the night Dave, Mark, and Rick were kidnapped. Speaking to our coworkers at the headquarters actually strengthened and encouraged my own heart. This was the first of many opportunities I have had to share the story and keep it alive in people's hearts.

In early April we received a "proof of life." A message from each of our husbands was played over the two-way radio. The crisis team recorded the messages for us. Dave, Mark, and Rick each spoke in Spanish, sending their greetings and their love to us. They each told of Scripture verses that had been encouraging their hearts.

Along with the messages from our husbands came the same demand—five million dollars, or they would be killed.

Don't these guerrillas have family? I thought. *Yes, they do have fathers and mothers, most likely sisters and brothers, and possibly spouses and children. How can any human being be so cruel? Do they ever lie in bed at night and think how they would feel if someone kidnapped their own husband or father, their own brother or son? Surely they must have consciences. Lord, I don't understand. I don't understand their cruelty. I don't understand why you've allowed it.*

And so the questions in my heart began to grow. The pain and the struggles increased. How could I go on?

14

The Missing Years

January 31, 1993–

Our husbands had become "the hostages." Dave, Mark, and Rick were on the hearts and in the prayers of thousands of Christians around the world. People faithfully prayed, even though they received very little information concerning them.

We had no contact with our husbands. No conversations. No letters were delivered to them from us, and we did not receive any letters from them. What were they going through? What were their lives like after they were marched toward the river at gunpoint, with their hands tied behind their backs?

I read books about other hostages who had gone through similar circumstances. Patti, Tania, and I met with Ray Rising, who had been held by the same guerrilla group in a different area of Colombia. I lay in bed at night and imagined what they must be going through.

Crossing the river in the dark, with guns aimed at their backs . . . Dave and Mark must have been wondering whether Rick was waiting on the other side. When they stepped out of the cold water and sloshed up the muddy bank, they probably saw the three or four men who guarded Rick as he sat, perhaps on a fallen log.

Rick may have looked up at them, thankful that he wasn't alone, immediately ashamed that he could feel thankful—the same as Dave or Mark would have felt. His haunted eyes questioned his comrades and looked for some comfort. Dave and Mark returned his look. None of them knew whether to talk or to be silent. They would wait. They would watch. They would simply do what they were told to do.

They may have thought, *Perhaps these people will tell us what they want and then let us go. Could they be running drugs and arms through here? Maybe they don't want Americans in their way.*

But those are only my thoughts, my suppositions of their first few minutes as hostages. What were their lives like for the next few days, weeks, and years?

According to accounts of other hostages, they must have hiked for many long hours that first night. They may not have stopped until they reached a campsite that was already set up. Their beds may have been made of wood stretched across fifty-five-gallon drums. Perhaps tarps formed roofs against the rains and hopefully they had mosquito netting to protect them at night. They may each have had a thin blanket to cover themselves with.

But was sleep possible—with a guard shining a light in their eyes every ten minutes all night long? Could they sleep when their tortured minds wondered about us—whether we had been harmed after they left? Or could they have been so exhausted from the hours of hiking through the jungle that God mercifully allowed them to sleep when they had the opportunity? We don't know.

The campsite must have had a makeshift kitchen. They may have been served a greasy fried bread for breakfast, perhaps rice and fried cooking bananas for lunch. If their camp was near a river, the guards may have caught some fish to serve with rice for supper. From what we've heard about others, though, they probably ate no better and no worse than their guards ate.

Most likely, they didn't stay very long in the first camp. Trudging through the jungles, they probably would have moved from place to place. The initial group of guerrillas who kidnapped them was large. The group who guarded them later could have been quite small.

Six or eight young men and women, from fifteen years old to early twenties, may have guarded them for several weeks before others took their places. Young guards can be very careless with their weapons, and I can very well imagine that Dave, Mark, and

Rick were at times more fearful of accidental death than intentional execution.

While most hostages held by this group are not tortured physically, any hostage lives with a daily mental torture. Being held against your will, not having any knowledge about your loved ones, being told you will be in captivity for a very long time, and the threats of death if a ransom isn't paid for your release are only a few of the ongoing horrors that they faced. Trying to sleep on a hard board at night, hiking for hours when your body is used to sitting at a computer all day long, and eating a diet with very little protein in it would also take its toll on the hostages.

Perhaps after the first few days, or when they reached a camp where the guerrillas felt less vulnerable to being detected, Dave, Mark, and Rick may have been allowed more freedom. They may have been permitted to exercise and to bathe in the river while being guarded. Their hands were probably freed from their shackles. And, most importantly, their Bibles were most assuredly being read.

Typically, hostages have been asked for a list of a few items that they would like to have brought in with supplies—things such as a bar of soap for bathing, and maybe combs, toothbrushes, and toothpaste. I know Dave would ask for a notebook and pen, so he could continue his habit of keeping a journal.

Rick's background as a police officer would add a special dimension to this team of hostages. He would understand the captors' criminal minds and know what special dangers they might pose. Also, the first-aid training that officers must go through could be of special value to the hostages and perhaps even to their captors at times.

Dave, having been on submarines during his tour of duty in the navy, would have his experiences of long periods of isolation from family, and the coping skills he had learned, that he could share with his two comrades.

Mark, growing up as a missionary kid in Peru and speaking Spanish as his first language, was able to understand any dialogue, whether whispered, spoken rapidly, or in slang. They would all benefit tremendously by understanding what was going on around them.

Some of their guards may have been mean and angry, but others may have been more friendly and open to communicating—perhaps even to discussing the Bible. Certainly, some of their captors would be curious about the number of hours their hostages spent reading God's Word. Typically, however, if a guard begins to develop a relationship with a hostage, that guard is transferred and replaced. How many guards could Dave, Rick, and Mark have influenced over the years? How many people may have come to know Jesus Christ through our husbands' faithful witnessing and their strong testimonies under the worst of circumstances?

Dave, Rick, and Mark most likely faced some long days and many miserable nights of illness.

Dave suffered from arthritis. How could he sleep on the hard surfaces they called a bed? He had broken a tooth and was scheduled to go to the dentist in three days, when we were supposed to fly to Panama City. Did his tooth begin to ache after his capture? Without a dentist or medicine, how much did he suffer before it was, perhaps, pulled with a pair of pliers? I don't know, but I've imagined the different scenarios.

Rick had been suffering with bouts of pneumonia. A chest x-ray revealed a spot on his lung that the doctor was going to monitor in the months ahead. Did his pneumonia recur? Was he able to get medication for the long, sleepless nights of coughing? We don't know.

Mark suffered from recurring ear problems, and he didn't have hiking boots to wear like Dave and Rick had. Did he suffer with his ears? Were any boots ever provided for him?

Could they have been plagued by mosquitos and contracted malaria? What about snakes, scorpions, and dangerous animals in the jungle?

Many thousands of prayers must have been prayed for their physical needs, and I believe that God's grace was sufficient for Dave, Mark, and Rick.

I also feel in my heart that their hardest trials were probably not their own physical needs, but rather their concerns for us—their wives and children, and parents and family—the torturous unknowns that plagued them when they were too weary to hand the burden to God again. Yet, through the prayers of thousands of Christians, I believe that they were given peace and comfort and strength to accept God's grace for those trials, too.

They were being held by the Marxist-inspired Revolutionary Armed Forces of Colombia, which is the largest guerrilla force in the country. The FARC (Fuerzas Armadas Revolucionarias de Colombia) are hunted by the Colombian military and paramilitary troops, who frequently engage the FARC in combat. For this reason, FARC units are constantly on the move. Dave, Mark, and Rick were in the middle of a war. Danger threatened them from all sides.

There were probably many times when the sound of helicopters overhead began a panic in their camp, sending the guerrillas and their hostages fleeing for cover in the jungle. Dave, Mark, and Rick were in danger from the firefight that would ensue—from either side.

Perhaps, as odd as it sounds, their lives may have taken on a normalcy as they learned what to expect and how they would be treated. Stepping outside of the boundaries may have been fearful; staying within them may have seemed safe. Nevertheless, did they consider escaping? I'm sure it was never far from their minds. They may have even attempted an escape. But where would they go? Who would befriend them if they were fortunate enough to find a dwelling in the jungle byways? Are peasants in the area guerrilla sympathizers, either willingly or unwillingly?

The guerrillas have a terrible hold on the peasants. The FARC troops would not think twice about killing any person who takes a stand against them or refuses to pay them "protection money." This bribe is one of the many ways in which the peasants are forced to cooperate in order to "ensure" that they will not be harmed by the guerrillas. Paramilitary troops often come into the same areas and threaten to kill the peasants if they do pay the protection money. These innocent people are caught in the cross fire, and many hundreds are killed by both groups. Revenge killings often occur. The peasants are targeted to avenge the deaths of members from either of the warring groups. Our dear husbands found themselves in the midst of this tragic and senseless evil, which has become a way of life for thousands of other innocent people in Colombia.

The outward circumstances were grim, indeed. The more I learned about Colombia's terrorist groups, the more I realized the hopelessness that many people in this fallen world live in every day. And those who haven't accepted Jesus Christ as their Savior have nothing better to look forward to for eternity; in fact, eternity for them will be even worse. Dave, Mark, and Rick have eternity with Jesus Christ in heaven, forever. The sorrows and hardships of this life are fleeting in comparison.

Our three families believed that taking the gospel to people groups who didn't have an opportunity to hear about God was the most important thing we could do in this life. We believe that only two things will last for eternity—God's Word and people's souls. Missionaries will sometimes risk their own lives to take the gospel to people groups who are even vicious headhunters. We know from God's Word that he loves everyone and doesn't want any person to perish.

But what about these Colombian guerrillas in the isolated jungle regions? They kidnapped their missionaries. The guerrillas are an isolated group of people, without a gospel witness. No missionary would volunteer to go to them, and no mission board could send their missionaries there. But God, in his sovereignty, allowed three of his servants to go and preach the gospel to a tribe of guerrillas. I've often wondered if some mother's prayer has been answered for her child's salvation, her child who, perhaps, was conscripted into guerrilla life and couldn't escape.

Throughout their long captivity, Dave, Mark, and Rick most assuredly continued their missionary service, for God's honor and glory.

15

Portal of Faith

April 1993–October 2001

The months dragged by. Information about our husbands came in waves. Our hopes were raised and our hopes were dashed. Through the first three months I remained strong and encouraged, believing that soon Dave, Mark, and Rick would be released.

And then one day, an imaginary line was crossed—a time deadline that I had unconsciously set up in my mind—and my world began to crumble around me. I questioned God. I couldn't understand why he was allowing this to go on, and on, and on. I was hurt, I was angry, and I was miserable.

During that miserable week I received a phone call from a colleague in Panama. She wanted to let me know that little Michelle was in the hospital in Panama City. Her sister had been carrying her and tripped—the baby fell into the cooking fire and was burned very badly. Michelle had, however, undergone the operation on her lip a few months before that incident, and most likely she would recover from the burns, as well.

At first, I couldn't even pray for her. I was numb. *Should I have tried to take Michelle with me? Did I misunderstand what you wanted me to do, Lord? Why, Lord, why did you allow this, too? I can't stand the pain. Why do you allow us to go through such trials?*

And yet, I was talking to God. I knew that I needed to sort out, from Scripture, exactly what God says about trials. Was there something wrong with me that God would allow these trials into my life?

Was I not walking with him? Was this some sort of punishment?

I opened my Bible and began to read. At first the words seemed dry and of little use for my hurting soul. But I read on and began to pray for encouragement and answers. I decided to look up passages in the Bible about people who suffered. I was amazed at what I found. Suffering was not some strange thing that happened only to people who were walking in sin. Even the apostles suffered many trials and died cruel deaths.

Joseph was thrown into a pit by his brothers, sold into slavery, and while a slave in Potiphar's house, was tempted by Potiphar's wife. Joseph fled the temptation—did what was right and honorable—but was thrown into prison. He was forgotten there. Years and years of trials he suffered, yet through it all, God said he was remembering Joseph, and he was blessing Joseph.

Can we be blessed by God even while we are suffering? I was curious. I discovered that God's Word says that he will give us the grace to get *through* trials. God doesn't say that he will simply pluck us out of every trial or keep anything bad from happening to us.

I began to climb up out of the valley I had been in. The realization hit me that I had been trying to conjure up faith in what I wanted to happen. Somehow I thought that, if I could have enough faith that Dave, Mark, and Rick would come home, they would come home. And when they didn't, I perceived it as my fault, because I didn't have enough faith. But that simply wasn't a truth from Scripture! That was presumption. My faith needed to be in God—God and his Word, God and his sovereignty. And there I found peace and rest for my weary heart and mind.

By then, Chad, Sarah, and I had moved from my parents' house to Sanford, Florida, to work at our mission's international headquarters. Chad stayed for two months and then moved away to get a summer job. In the fall he moved back to Dallas to complete his graduate studies at UTA.

Shortly after Chad left, Tania and her girls moved to headquarters. Tania's mom went back to Panama to join her husband. Soon, Tania and I began to rely on one another in many ways. We became accountable to one other. We were able to share our deepest thoughts—thoughts that no one else, other than Patti, would understand. We had each other to share confidential hostage information with, when we couldn't reveal it to anyone else. And it was wonderful to call each other before going to bed at night and first thing in the morning. Our lives began to bond in a way that few friendships do.

Patti, even though in another state, was never far from our minds. We all talked on the phone quite often. Tania, her girls, and I drove up north to Patti's for a visit, and we all traveled together on many trips dealing with the hostage situation. The three of us have a very unique friendship—we are united in a very special way.

The months passed by, and sporadic radio contacts between the kidnappers and our CMC continued, but still with no resolution. December of that first year we received another proof of life, more messages from our husbands over the two-way radio. The ransom demand had continued throughout that long year. But in January there was nothing—no more ransom demand, no more radio contacts—nothing but silence.

Normally, when the FARC kills their hostages, they leave the bodies to be found—clearly showing the consequence of not paying a ransom. Many times, however, relatives pay a ransom for their loved one only to receive another proof of life, and a demand for more money. Oftentimes, people pay a ransom and receive back only the remains of their loved one.

For us, however, hope remained that Dave, Rick, and Mark were still alive. We waited. The silence was deafening.

Around that same time, I received another phone call from Panama—Michelle had died. She had recovered fairly well from the burns and had gone back to Púcuro. There, she contracted a cold and died. I can remember the sobs that racked my body and the depression that seeped in. I lacked the desire for any consolation or help. Again my focus was on my circumstances and away from God. How did I get there? How could I get out?

I had to make a choice. I had to choose to focus on God again and to read his Word. I had to choose God's will over my own. I had to choose to pray.

But how could I? I remember lying in bed at night with my fists clenched. I would make myself use one hand to pry open the other, one finger at a time. Then I would lie there with my hands open—signifying to God that I wanted him to take the burdens from me, telling him that Dave was his, and Michelle was his, too.

The second thing that helped me was envisioning the Scripture passage about Peter walking on the water. Peter focused his eyes on Jesus, stepped out of the boat, and walked toward him—on top of the water! And then, Peter looked down at the billowing waves—his circumstances—and he began to sink. I knew that my eyes were on my circumstances, and not on God. I made the choice to focus on God again.

In the previous months Sarah had fallen in love with a young man named John Skees. I was having to make decisions about their engagement and marriage. I remembered Chad and Sarah's last visit to Púcuro. Dave told them that he wanted us to meet the people they thought would be their prospective spouses. Because we loved them, he wanted us to advise them and to help them make one of the most important decisions of their lives. *How can I give my approval to Sarah and John without Dave? Shouldn't we wait a few more months? Maybe this will be over soon,* I agonized. *If Dave comes home shortly after they are married, will he wonder why we didn't wait a few more months?*

I decided to seek counsel from Tania's father. Tim said that, if he were Dave, he would want his children to get engaged and married, because having to wait indefinitely is not healthy. I took his advice. Along with that decision, I asked God to give me the strength I needed to make it a happy time and a wonderful wedding for my daughter. Many people prayed for me during the whole process. I am so thankful for the many prayers. Every step of the way, God's grace was very evident to me. I did, however, learn the true meaning of "bittersweet" as I watched Chad lead his sister down the aisle to be married.

Had we not been involved in the hostage situation, Sarah would not have been in Florida and would not have met John. This was one of the blessings God gave us in the midst of the trial we were enduring.

On the heels of John and Sarah's wedding came Chad's engagement to Janeene Johnson. Because of the hostage situation, Chad sat out one semester of his schooling, returning the following term. It was during that following term that he and Janeene met and fell in love—another blessing in the midst of our suffering. The next year, Chad and Janeene were married. Another of life's milestones was passing before our eyes—the last of Dave's children was getting married, the last opportunity for him to be present at one of their weddings. Again, in direct answer to many faithful prayers, God's grace was sufficient to allow me to enjoy the happiness of the occasion.

Our CMC continued to follow every lead that came their way. They knocked on every door that they thought might provide us with some help or some answers: human rights groups, the International Red Cross, religious groups in the region where our husbands were being held, and the media, to name a few. They sought help from our government and they built relationships with officials in Colombia. We continued to hope, and pray, and work toward the release of Dave, Mark, and Rick. The expenses were tremendous, but God provided through many people and churches who gave so generously to the Crisis Fund, through New Tribes Mission. Tania, Patti, and I are very thankful for everyone who has been a part of the effort in this way.

During these months my life was one of curious contrasts. I was either experiencing the awesome grace of God to walk above my circumstances with a peace and joy I could not describe, or I was totally miserable and felt I couldn't go on for one more day. There was no in-between. I was discovering that I couldn't walk through this trial in my own strength—not even for a little while. As the months passed on, I began to stay in the valleys for shorter periods of time, but the intensity of those times did not lessen.

Patti, Tania, and I went to Colombia three times. The first trip was to elicit media attention. We had television, newspaper, and radio interviews. We not only hoped that raising the awareness of our case would somehow precipitate action, but we also hoped that our husbands would hear our voices on a radio or read about us in a newspaper. We wanted them to know that we were still working diligently on their behalf. We wanted them to be encouraged.

We took every opportunity to speak on radio stations, such as HCJB and VOA, which could be heard in areas where we believed our husbands were being held. Hoping that Dave, Mark, and Rick could hear our words, we told them how much we and their families loved them and that thousands of people were praying for them. We also tried to let them know that we had not been harmed after they left the village that night.

On our second trip to Colombia, we ventured farther north to Medellín and then to Apartadó. Throughout that trip, the Scripture verse that I repeated to myself was Isaiah 41:10: "Fear thou not; for I am with thee: be not dismayed; for I am thy God: I will strengthen thee; yea, I will help thee; yea, I will uphold thee with the right hand of my righteousness."

Apartadó is located in the northwestern area of Colombia, the region where we believed our husbands were being held. We desperately hoped that the International Red Cross would at least deliver some messages for us. They regularly delivered messages between imprisoned guerrillas and their families. But, through the years, our letters managed to get lost. Whenever new Red Cross replacements arrived, we would have to start all over again. Our letters never were delivered.

We also met with politicians in the area and were interviewed on a local radio station. During that interview Dave was informed that his children had both married, to people he had never met. Again my heart broke at the thought of informing him of his children's marriages in such a cold way, in Spanish, and over a public radio. The tears flowed. Yet, relief filled my heart, because, at last, Dave at least had an opportunity to know. Whether or not he heard the broadcast, we don't know.

We were fearful in Apartadó—a small town that was filled with guerrilla sympathizers and, most likely, many guerrillas themselves. I constantly had the creepy feeling that someone would take me by the arm and lead me into an alley, to tell me they were holding my husband. The three of us stood out wherever we went—the whole town knew who we were. Whenever my stomach turned into a knot, I repeated the words of Isaiah 41:10 in my mind, *"Fear thou not, for I am with thee . . ."*

When we checked into the local hotel, we were given three room keys. One of the men from our contingency team was with us, and of course, he had one room. But, we were curious why they had given us two other keys. Tania's Spanish was the best of the three of us ladies, so she tried to straighten it out.

"Sir," she said in Spanish, "the three of us can stay in one room. We prefer one room."

"No, no, señora," he said. "There are only two beds in each room. You have to have two rooms."

"Okay," Tania said.

We climbed the stairs toward our rooms.

"I'll sleep in the room by myself," Tania said. "My Spanish is better."

"No, I'll stay by myself," I said. "I'm older."

Before the dialogue could continue, the doors to our rooms were opened.

"Our room has a double and a single bed," Patti said.

"That'll work!" I said, quickly bringing my suitcase into their room.

"No, no!" the shocked hotel worker exclaimed.

Apparently we were crossing a line in their culture. But none of us wanted to be alone in a room in this town where we were so afraid.

We left our suitcases in the one room and went across the street to eat. Most of the restaurants were sidewalk cafés. We sat at a table close to the street and ordered a meal. Every backfire from a passing car sent chills down our spines. Gunfire would not have seemed unusual here! Again, I felt as though I were playing a part in a spy movie.

After the meal we went back to our hotel. We unlocked the door to our room and discovered that a third bed had been moved in. Now everyone was happy!

We were fearful being in Colombia, and we felt especially vulnerable in Apartadó. That night in our room, Patti, Tania, and I read Scripture to each other and prayed together before going to bed for the night.

In the morning, we were supposed to meet at the café for breakfast with Dan Germann, the CMC member who had accompanied us. A few minutes before we had planned to go, however, we heard a knock at our door. When we answered it, Dan was standing there, obviously shaken. We asked him what had happened. In the split second that it took for him to answer, all three of us felt sure the end had come—that he had bad news about our husbands. That wasn't the news that he had, however.

"This morning at dawn," Dan said, "the FARC came into town, about three blocks from here. They captured a busload of plantation workers, massacring all twenty-three of them. There were nineteen men, three women, and a teenager. The FARC then torched the bus and pushed it into a ravine."

"Why those people?" Tania asked.

"They say it was a revenge killing," Dan answered. "The paramilitary killed twenty-some FARC members, so FARC took revenge by killing twenty-three peasants."

"That just doesn't make any sense to me," I said.

"Well, you three need to decide what you want to do now. We can cancel the rest of our meetings and just go back, or you three can go back and I'll continue on with the meetings we—"

"No!" we all interrupted.

"We don't want to go anywhere alone," I said for the three of us.

"What if we just go see the one official we still need to meet and then all of us go back to the airport and leave?" Dan suggested.

"That sounds fine to us," we all agreed.

We all left the room and went to eat breakfast at the café across the street. The local news was being aired on the television set at the restaurant. A list of names appeared on the screen—names of the victims of the massacre. Before our eyes, various patrons at nearby tables burst into tears as the names of friends or relatives appeared on the screen. The reality of the horror they lived with daily touched us deeply. My heart went out to these people—my thoughts turned to their eternity. *How many of them had trusted Christ as their Savior?* I wondered.

We checked out of the hotel and went quickly to meet the official—but he had fled the area. So we had the taxi take us directly to the airport. Along the way, we saw trucks with tarps pulled down around the sides. I wondered whether men in camouflage uniforms sat behind the tarps with machine guns in their hands. None of us spoke as we rode along in the taxicab.

We finally arrived at the small airport. We each bought a soda and sat together at one of the tables. This café was like the ones in town, with all the tables outside. A man from the Red Cross, whom we had met our first day in town, came over to talk with us. He was escorting his ex-wife to Medellín. She had just received word that her current husband had been shot and killed. She was going to identify him and bring his body home for burial.

During our two short days in Apartadó, we had already been made aware of twenty-three massacred people, a man shot and killed in Medellín, and funeral processions (which we witnessed) of two people who also had been murdered. It was not comforting to know that our husbands were most likely in this region, somewhere in the surrounding jungles.

Our small airplane was ready to board. We walked out on the tarmac to the plane and stood in the line that had formed. Patti was in front of me. She turned around and grabbed my arms.

"Nancy," she said, "do you see what's happening up there?"

"No," I replied, "what's going on?"

"That man had a gun!" she whispered urgently. "They took the gun from him and now they're leading him away. He was getting on our airplane!"

"They found the gun," I said with a lot more reassurance than I felt. "I'm sure it's okay now. He won't be on our flight."

Our plane arrived safely in Medellín. The next day we flew back to Bogotá and then home to the States. We were all very thankful to be back home. However, I learned a valuable lesson on that trip: It is easier to go through a situation in person than to be far away from it and have only your imagination to deal with. As fearful as those days were, we knew what was happening to us all of the time. We prayed together and read Scripture, we leaned on one another, and we walked through each day by God's grace. That was exactly what Dave, Mark, and Rick were doing. That realization helped me tremendously in the months and years ahead.

That trip also affirmed to my heart, again, the importance of missions. I saw the needs of suffering people, and I could not imagine living in their circumstances at all, much less without the Lord's grace and strength. Nor could I imagine living that life and not having anything better to look forward to after death and for eternity.

Reports of our husbands continued to trickle in with frustrating irregularity. One report would say that they had been killed, and the next would say that they had been sighted, alive! Not one report, however, could be traced to a first-person account. Not one could be considered a proof of life, nor even a proof of death. Yet, Guy Sier and the other members of the CMC continued to work with excruciating diligence on our behalf.

Tania, Patti, and I were invited to speak on *Larry King Live*. We flew to California and attempted to prepare ourselves for our very first live television appearance in the United States.

Larry King Live, we were told, is seen in more than two hundred countries. Colombian President Samper would be interviewed during the program via satellite. Patti, Tania, and I had no idea what to expect. We were very nervous, and we wondered how we would ever make it through the hour. Per instructions, as the cameras rolled, we stared at "blank screen number one" in front of us. At first, we must have appeared to our audience like three deer who had been caught in someone's headlights. We did, however, recover—once Larry King began to fire questions at us. Many people don't realize that interviewers rarely give their guests a list of the questions they plan to ask.

On the contrary, the interviewer seems to think that the more in the dark his guests are about what will be asked, the fresher and more candid the answers will be.

We survived our first major television broadcast. Then we were taken back to our hotel in Larry King's limousine, driven by his chauffeur.

That television broadcast precipitated U.S. government interest in our case. Soon we were making trips to Washington, D.C. We met with senators and congressmen, often with television cameras in our faces. We were definitely out of our comfort zones. But we were willing to do whatever we could—anything that might help to bring our husbands home to us. And so we persevered.

On one television interview I was asked what a certain political figure had done for us.

"I don't know; I just don't know," was my answer.

As the cameraman disassembled his equipment, I walked over to one of our CMC members and in a hushed tone asked what government position that political figure held, anyway. He burst into laughter! My answer had been perfect, and if we had been helped in any way by that office, I would have known the answer to that question.

• • •

At every birthday party, when the candles are blown out, all of us in the room know the wish that has been made. Several times I've listened as one of the younger children was asked the simple question, "What do you want for your birthday?" Often the answer has been, "I don't care if I get any presents. I'd much rather have my daddy back."

Patti, Tania, and I usually spend our wedding anniversaries trying to stay busy and trying not to think of the occasion the day stands for.

On my twenty-fifth wedding anniversary, however, I decided to rent sad movies and buy myself twenty-five pink roses. I wanted to suffer through it alone, but Sarah and Tania spent the evening trying to find the twenty-five roses—that had to be pink—and they insisted on watching the movies with me. We all had headaches from crying, but Tania fared the worst. Every time that anniversary is mentioned, Tania says, "Oh, my goodness!"

Lee and Jessica entered kindergarten. This new stage of their lives brought along with it their ever-growing awareness of other children with their fathers. They began to realize more fully what they had been missing. All of the children earnestly prayed for, cried for, and missed their fathers.

A flurry of information and activity, including more trips and more interviews for us three wives, would inevitably be followed by long periods of silence and inactivity, with no new leads and no new routes to pursue. The months and years continued to march by. New Tribes Mission's CMC labored on in our behalf, searching unceasingly for any scrap of information that might lead to knowledge about our husbands.

Dave, Mark, and Rick's families suffered through the long periods with little or no information. Then came the times of holding their breath, hoping the leads would produce answers. Never knowing for sure whether their sons, their grandsons, their brothers, their nephews were still alive, not knowing whether they would ever have answers—it is a nightmare that I wish no one else would ever have to experience.

In 1997, Patti, Tania, and I went to England to speak at a Persecuted Christian Day Conference. We also spoke in several churches and had a radio interview at BBC World Service Radio. We were home for two days and then flew to Venezuela.

The heads of state from many South American countries, and Spain, were meeting together. They were considering an alliance with Colombia to help them with their ongoing peace problems. All of our children, and my children's spouses, had joined us. Along with our CMC members, our group numbered seventeen. At times, it was a logistical nightmare. The Lord, however, arranged for the three of us wives to meet with the Colombian president, Ernesto Samper. We also had private interviews with several heads of state of the countries represented there. We were very encouraged with the contacts we were able to make.

One night we received a phone call at our hotel informing us that the queen of Spain would give us a private audience at her hotel. We drove across the island to meet with her that evening.

All of the children were disappointed that they couldn't meet the queen. I, however, was very nervous. In two taxicabs, the CMC, Tania, Patti, and I rode to the designated luxury hotel. At the gates that guarded the resort, the guard stopped our cabs.

When told that we were to have an audience with the queen, the guard looked at our cab, looked at us, and said the equivalent of, "I don't think so."

One of our CMC members gave the guard the name of the queen's aide and the phone number that we had been given. The guard made the call, then he came back and opened the gate for us. We drove up to the front door of the plush hotel.

I stepped out of the taxi and was greeted by the queen's aide. He bowed slightly and picked up my hand to kiss it. My hand was nearly at his lips when he dropped it suddenly. I wondered whether I should have somehow said or done something different.

Next he took Patti's hand, which he raised halfway to his face and then dropped it. He came to Tania and barely raised her hand, holding only her little finger.

We were ushered into a very beautiful sitting room. As we sat, I nervously wondered about the protocol of meeting a queen. *Do you lower your eyes? Do you curtsy? Do you bow your head? How should I address her in Spanish?*

After a few minutes, the aide entered the room, and in his very rapid Spanish, he informed us that the queen would arrive soon. She had only a few minutes, and we should stand at the doorway to greet her. We were not to take any photographs.

We stood at the doorway and waited nervously. Ten minutes later the door opened and the aide came in, informing us of a change of plans. Strangely enough, it seemed to him, the queen had asked that we be shown to her sitting room. He hurriedly escorted us out, walking swiftly down the polished marble hallway and into an elevator. We exited the elevator and walked toward her suite.

Suddenly everyone stood back against the wall. The king was passing by.

"Nancy, did you see him?" Tania whispered to me.

"No," I said. "I kept my head down. I think I saw his shoes, though. How do you know whether you are supposed to look at him?"

There was no time for further conversation, however. We were briskly walking toward the queen's quarters. As we stopped at her room, I realized I was first in line! She stood at the door with a regal air to greet us.

"It is an honor to meet you," I mumbled quietly in Spanish, with my head lowered—still very unsure of how to address her.

She looked down at me and said in very clear English, "What language do you speak?"

Relieved, I looked up at her and said, "English is wonderful." *Did I say that? That was a stupid thing to say,* I thought.

Graciously, she turned to Tania, who greeted her in English, and then Patti, and the rest of our CMC members.

We sat on couches around her coffee table and told her the story of our husbands' abductions. We asked her if she might remember us any time the Colombian government might approach the government of Spain. Would she ask them about our husbands?

The queen was very touched by our story. She said that she didn't hold any political power herself, but that she would speak to her husband about us.

We thanked her. We were genuinely honored that she would meet with us and that she would try to do whatever she could to help.

The interview was over, and we walked back out into the hallway and down to the front lobby. Waiting for us there was the queen's aide. He said good-bye to each of us. He held my hand, nearly to his lips, and Patti's hand halfway, and Tania he just gave a slight bow to, before taking his leave.

By the time we took our seats again in the taxicab, Tania was exploding with laughter.

"Tania," I said, "what on earth was that all about?"

"Oh, Nancy," she said, trying to control her laughter, "when we got out of the cab and the aide took your hand, I unexpectedly sneezed! I didn't have a tissue, so my hand automatically caught the sneeze. You should have seen the look on his face!"

We all laughed until our sides ached. We truly were out of our class—and out of our comfort zone. I'm sure the queen of Spain's aide will never forget the three missionary women he met in Venezuela.

The years continued to pass, with no direct word of our husbands. Patti, Tania, and I were caught in the cycle of mourning. The cycle could not end, however, because of the uncertainties and unknowns, the lack of closure. We periodically found ourselves in what we called our "numb" stage. Our hearts would seem to "check out," almost as if a safety valve had been released. We couldn't feel the pain anymore. We also couldn't pray very effectively—for the situation or for our husbands. It all felt like a distant blur. Yet people continued to pray for us. Often the numb stage ended for me when anger or frustration moved in to take its place. That misery quickly caused me to focus again on the Lord and his Word.

Through the years, however, the times we spent in the valleys became very short compared to the times we spent experiencing God's amazing grace. What helped me most was some advice by Dr. Ralph Ricco, a Christian therapist who helped Tania, Patti, and me through a particularly rough period. He told us to look for a signal that we were getting stressed out, in order to catch it before we became truly depressed. Patti and Tania seemed to know right away what they always did when they were getting weighed down by life. I, however, didn't. But Patti and Tania came to my rescue. They both said that, when I am getting stressed out, I begin to sigh. Sighing, for me, has become a signal that I am trying to carry burdens that I need to give over to God. Learning that has helped me tremendously not to fall into the pit of depression.

The Lord has opened up many opportunities for the three of us to share in churches, at conferences, banquets, and ladies' retreats. Everywhere we have spoken, either separately or together, the Lord seems to use our suffering to encourage many others who are hurting.

God has blessed us in the midst of our trials by encouraging others through our testimonies.

Several times during the years we felt sure that the end of the hostage situation was near. One of those times I bought clothes and shoes for Dave's return. They are still in the closet.

The birth of John and Sarah's daughter, Elizabeth Anne Skees (Ellie), was another milestone—our first grandchild. *But does Dave even know that both of his children are married?* was the question that haunted my mind.

Ellie is a very special bright spot in my life. Some days she goes into my closet and asks for "the other grandpa's" beads. I hand her Dave's navy dog tags and she wears them around her little neck.

We began to believe, from the information we had received, that our husbands were no longer alive. Most of the reports came from FARC defectors who were interrogated concerning Dave, Mark, and Rick. The evidence seemed overwhelming, and yet we were still seeking positive proof—their remains—before establishing final closure.

One day, when Ellie was two and a half years old, she asked her mom, "Mommy, where is your daddy?"

Sarah was shocked at first and simply said, "He's not here." Then she went to get a photograph of Dave and me. She explained that I was her mommy, and Dave was her daddy.

"Where's your daddy?" Ellie asked again.

"He's in heaven with Jesus," Sarah said and began to cry. "I'm crying because I miss my daddy."

"What happened to him?" Ellie asked.

"Some mean men took him away from Grandma," Sarah answered, surprised at the depth of Ellie's questioning.

"But where is he?" Ellie persisted.

"He died," Sarah explained. "Do you remember watching *The Lion King*? Simba's daddy died and went away. Simba couldn't see him anymore, just like I can't see my daddy. But Grandpa is in heaven with Jesus, and he's happy there. Sometimes Grandma and Mommy get sad because we miss him, but he's happy in heaven with Jesus."

What do the FARC guerrillas expect us to tell little Ellie about why they kidnapped her grandfather? The man who would love to see her face and hold her in his arms, the man who once looked at small pastel-colored Swiss Army knives, wanting to buy them for the grandchildren he already hoped for in the future—what do FARC guerrillas expect us to tell her about him?

"But, Mommy, where is your daddy?"
Photograph by Cece Husbands

I wish those men could look into the eyes of the children of Dave, Mark, and Rick and see their pain, their longing to have their father's love and input in their lives.

When Tania tried to explain to her girls the reports we had been receiving, Tamra, who was then ten years old, came up with an analogy that explained our situation quite well.

"Mom," she said, "it's like a puzzle, isn't it. We keep getting pieces to the puzzle but we don't quite have all of the pieces yet. But, even though we don't have all of the pieces, we can see enough of the picture to know what's happened."

Yes, that is exactly where we are. We have been praying for the last piece to the puzzle. We have been tracing the last lead as far as we can.

When Ellie was at my house, several months after her conversation with her mom about Dave, the subject came up again. I explained to her once more that bad men took her grandfather away from us.

At nearly three years old, her amazing statement was, "Just like *King of Dreams*, Grandma." She had seen the animated video about Joseph, and the mean things his brothers did to him, his captivity, and the unjust treatment he received.

"You're right, Ellie," I said in amazement. "It is a lot like what happened in *King of Dreams*."

Dora Tenenoff is now seventeen years old and learning to drive a car. She is looking into colleges and planning for her future. Connie, an avid reader, is twelve years old, loves horses, and is in the sixth grade. Lee, who is still all boy, is ten, and he loves sports. Patti has prayed her way through these years, and she has done a wonderful job with her children. All three have accepted the Lord as their Savior and desire to walk with God.

Eleven-year-old Tamra Rich, who is in the sixth grade, loves soccer—just like her dad,—and she is learning to play the guitar. Jessica, in fifth grade, plays the piano and loves to sing. Tamra and Jessica accepted the Lord as their Savior at early ages, too. Tania has continued to pass on the wonderful Christian heritage that was passed on to her.

Chad and Janeene Mankins are missionaries with New Tribes Mission. They have moved to Papua New Guinea, where they plan to live with a remote group of people who do not yet have a written language. Chad graduated with a master's degree in linguistics. He and Janeene are looking forward to learning an unwritten language, producing its alphabet, and eventually translating the Bible into that language. Their desire is to be part of a team that will see a church established in that village. What a blessing they are to me, and I am very proud of them.

John and Sarah Skees, along with Ellie, live near me. They continue to walk with the Lord and are a blessing in my life. I am very proud of them, too.

God has been a father of the fatherless, as stated in Psalm 68:5. He has blessed our children, even in the midst of our trials.

Parents, siblings, grandparents, and other relatives of Dave, Mark, and Rick have suffered through this horrendous separation of over eight and a half years. They have had to somehow piece their lives together again. Some relatives have passed away, and many new nieces and nephews have been born. Life has continued on despite the loss.

Over the course of many months, more pieces of the puzzle surfaced. Every piece sharpened the picture. Our husbands were dead.

Early in 1996, a FARC defector led Colombian troops to the camp where Dave, Mark, and Rick were being held. A battle ensued, and a guerrilla commander handed down the order. The fatal shots were fired. Dave, Mark, and Rick were ushered into the arms of their loving heavenly Father. More than half a dozen credible reports from different sources corroborated this picture.

In our minds, however, the last piece to the puzzle was still missing. For ten long and agonizing months, we prayed, we hoped, and we waited for the recovery of the remains of our beloved husbands. In the end, however, the facts remained the same—a triple murder. The FBI promised to pursue the murder investigation, even though it may take many years. In the dense, guerrilla-infested jungles, remains may never be recovered.

Even though we didn't have their remains, God gave us peace that we had the answer. On October 6, 2001, we held a memorial service for Dave, Mark, and Rick. More than one thousand people joined us in person, and messages poured in from all over the world.

The waiting is over.

For Patti, Tania, and me, these have been the hardest years of our lives. We would never choose to walk through them again. And yet, somehow, we would not trade the wonderful spiritual truths that we have been learning through these years. We look at our children and our lives, and we are thankful that our husbands loved us. We are thankful that they didn't choose, as some husbands choose, to walk away from us. We are thankful that they loved their children and desired more than anything to raise them and spend time with them—we know that they would have, if they could have. That is a tremendous blessing to our hearts.

And what about God in all of this? God could have ended this hostage situation for us at any time. He could have brought our husbands home. But he chose not to. Not only did he choose not to bring them home, he chose not to allow us closure, even after more than eight and a half years of waiting.

I believe that we have learned lessons about faith—faith in God and his Word—through circumstances that seem to cry out in opposition to all that seems right or fair or good. And yet, we've found victory in our faith. We've seen God for who he really is, and we have envisioned life from an eternal perspective.

The prayers that have been prayed on our behalf have not been wasted. God has taught us how to walk above our circumstances, in joy and peace. We've learned that we can and will fail, that we can question—and that God still loves us and waits patiently for us to desire his will and way for our lives again. God has not given us the answers we've wanted, but we have seen him work mightily in our hearts and lives. That is no less of a miracle. Tania, Patti, and I have, by God's grace, persevered through this race that was set before us. We are "looking unto Jesus the author and finisher of our faith . . ." (Hebrews 12:2).

Epilogue

Approximately one year after Dave, Mark, and Rick were kidnapped, Tania, Patti, and I sent an announcement to the village of Púcuro, telling them that we would not be returning. We gave our houses and most everything in them to the village. We hoped that, somehow, the FARC would receive knowledge of this action and realize that we would not be returning to the area. We prayed that the FARC would then release our husbands. However, Dave, Mark, and Rick were not set free from their captivity.

The church in Púcuro continues to meet, and though they have gone through struggles, they are currently experiencing a revival. In the midst of adversity, God is building his church.

Since his term ended as representative for the Púcuro and Paya district, Darío Pizzaro, who translated songs for the Kuna church, has been living in Panama City. He is currently translating Bible study materials for the church in Púcuro. Those materials are a tremendous blessing and help to the believers in Púcuro. As they grow in their faith and understanding of God and his Word, they will inevitably reach out to others.

A Christian Kuna couple from the San Blas Islands is moving to Púcuro, to serve there as missionaries. We praise the Lord for his wonderful provision of this couple.

Christians from the Kuna village of Mortí have also made trips to Púcuro to encourage and teach the Christians.

The Kuna people in Mortí and in the San Blas Islands speak a dialect of the language that is different from the Kuna spoken in Púcuro. Even so, speakers of the two dialects can communicate with one another. The Bible and other study materials for the people of Púcuro, however, must be translated specifically for their dialect, so they can clearly understand the written words as their own heart language.

Sandra still lives in Púcuro. She has married Luís and Mika's son, Daniel. He is a teacher at the school in Púcuro. Daniel and Sandra have a three-month-old baby boy.

Estánislau continues to walk faithfully with God. He is a strong leader in the church. His wife, Mambo, is also attending, and she is once again walking with the Lord.

Bedridden, very ill, with her eyesight almost gone, Nanzhel perhaps very soon will be in heaven, greeting her Lord face to face.

Sandra and Nancy in 1999.

Ellie, John, and Sarah Skees in 2001.
Photograph by Cece Husbands

Chad and Janeene Mankins in 2000.
Photograph by Cece Husbands

Nancy Mankins in 2001.
Photograph by Cece Husbands

Lee, Dora, Connie, and Patti Tenenoff in 2001.

Tania, Jessica, and Tamra Rich in 2001.